Programming Interviews Exposed

Programming Interviews Exposed

Secrets to Landing Your Next Job

John Mongan
Noah Suojanen

Wiley Computer Publishing

John Wiley & Sons, Inc.

NEW YORK · CHICHESTER · WEINHEIM · BRISBANE · SINGAPORE · TORONTO

Publisher: Robert Ipsen
Editor: Marjorie Spencer
Assistant Editor: Margaret Hendrey
Managing Editor: John Atkins
Text Design & Composition: Publishers' Design and Production Services, Inc.

Designations used by companies to distinguish their products are often claimed as trademarks. In all instances where John Wiley & Sons, Inc., is aware of a claim, the product names appear in initial capital or ALL CAPITAL LETTERS. Readers, however, should contact the appropriate companies for more complete information regarding trademarks and registration.

This book is printed on acid-free paper. ☺

Published by John Wiley & Sons, Inc.

Published simultaneously in Canada.

This publication is designed to provide accurate and authoritative information in regard to the subject matter covered. It is sold with the understanding that the publisher is not engaged in professional services. If professional advice or other expert assistance is required, the services of a competent professional person should be sought.

Library of Congress Cataloging-in-Publication Data:

Mongan, John, 1976–
    Programming interviews exposed : secrets to landing your next job / John Mongan,
Noah Suojanen.
        p.   cm.
    "Wiley computer publishing."
    ISBN 0-471-38356-2 (pbk. : alk. paper)
    1. Employment interviewing.   2. Computer programming—Vocational guidance.
I. Suojanen, Noah, 1978–   II. Title.
HF5549.5.I6 M664   2000
650.14—dc21   00-028304

Printed in the United States of America.

10 9 8 7 6 5 4 3 2

To my family

—Noah Suojanen

*To those who encouraged me,
living and dead*

—John Mongan

Contents

Preface

If you're like us, you don't usually read prefaces. This one has some useful information in it, though, so we hope you'll make an exception. If you're still going to skip the preface, here's what you really need to know: You'll get as much out of this book as you put into it. If you read this book cover to cover, you'll learn something, but not nearly as much as you would if you take some time trying to work through the problems on your own before you read the answers.

This book will help prepare you for the interviews you will face when seeking a job in programming, development, technical consulting, or any other field that warrants a programming interview. Programming interviews bear little resemblance to those described in traditional job-hunting and interview books. They consist almost entirely of programming problems, puzzles, and technical questions about computers. We will discuss each of the kinds of problems you are likely to encounter and illustrate how they are best approached using questions from real interviews as examples.

At this point you may be wondering who we are and what gives us the authority to write this book. We're both recent graduates who've been through a lot of interviews in the past few years. We've interviewed for jobs ranging from technical consulting with large established companies to writing device drivers for start-ups. This book is based on the experiences and observations we've taken from those interviews—what yielded offers and what didn't. We believe that this is the best possible basis for a book like this. Rather than give you some HR exec's idea of how interviewing should be done[1] or a headhunter's impression of how it might

[1] For the record, we don't think that the way interviewing is done today is necessarily the way it should be done. The current mode puts too much emphasis on ability to solve puzzles and

be done, we will tell you what interviews are really like at America's top software and computer companies and what you need to do to get the job you want.

To that end, we haven't made up any of the questions in this book. Every last one of them has come from a recent interview. The distributions of problem type and difficulty are similar to what you should expect to encounter in your interviews. We must emphasize that the problems presented in this book are a *representative* sample of the questions asked in interviews, not a comprehensive compilation. Reading this book straight through and memorizing the answers would completely miss the point. You may be asked some of the questions that appear in this book, but you should not expect that. A large and constantly changing body of questions is asked, and any intelligent interviewer who has seen this book will never again use any of the questions that appear here. On the other hand, interview questions encompass relatively few topic areas and types of questions, and these rarely change. If you work on learning to solve not just the specific problems we present, but the types of problems we present, you'll be able to handle anything they throw at you in an interview.

We've taken a couple of steps to facilitate the objective of improving your problem-solving skills. First, where appropriate, we provide reviews of important topics before we present questions on those topics. Second, instead of merely giving answers to the problems, we illustrate the problem-solving process from beginning to solution. We've found that most textbooks and nearly all puzzle books take a different approach to examples: They begin with a problem, go immediately to the answer, and then explain why the answer is correct. In our experience, the result is that the reader may understand the particular answer and why it's right, but is left with no clue as to how the author came up with that solution or how a similar problem might be solved. We hope that our step-by-step approach to solutions will address this problem, helping you to understand not only the answers but how you get the answers.

Learning by watching is never as effective as learning by doing. If you want to get the most out of this book, you will have to work out the problems yourself. We suggest the following method. After you read a problem, put the book down and try to work out the solution. If you get stuck, start reading the solution. We never blurt out the answer at the beginning, so you don't have to worry that we're going to give away the solution. Read just far enough to get the hint you need, then put down the book

---

familiarity with a relatively limited body of knowledge, and it generally fails to measure a lot of the skills that are critical to success in industry.

and keep working. Repeat this as necessary. The more of the solution you work out yourself, the better your understanding will be. In addition, this method closely resembles the actual interview experience, where you will have to solve the problems yourself, but the interviewer will give you hints when you get stuck.

Programming is a difficult and technical art. It would be impossible to teach everything you need to know about computers and programming in one book. Therefore, we've had to make some assumptions about who you are. We assume that you have a background in computers equivalent to at least the first year or two of a computer science degree. Specifically, we expect that you are comfortable with programming in C, that you've had some experience with object-oriented programming in C++ or perhaps Java, and that you know the fundamentals of computer architecture and computer science theory. These are effectively the minimum requirements for a general development job, so most interviewers will have similar expectations. If you find yourself lacking in any of these areas, you should seriously consider seeking more education before starting your job search and interviews.

It's also possible that you have a great deal more computer knowledge and experience than what we've described as the minimum requirements. If so, you may be particularly interested in some of the more advanced topics we include, such as databases, graphics, concurrency, and Perl. However, don't ignore the basic topics and questions, no matter how much experience you have. Interviewers tend to start with the fundamentals regardless of what's on your resume.

We have made every effort to ensure that all of the information in this book is correct. All of the code has been compiled and tested. Nevertheless, as you probably know all too well from your own programs, a few bugs and errors are inevitable. As we become aware of such problems, we will post corrections at http://www.wiley.com/compbooks/programminginterview/.

We're confident that you'll find this book useful in getting the job you want. We hope that you may also find it an entertaining exploration of some clever puzzles in your chosen profession. If you'd like to tell us about your reaction to our book, your thoughts on any particular problem or topic, or a problem from one of your recent interviews, we'd love to hear from you. Please e-mail us at programminginterview@wiley.com.

Go find a killer job!
John and Noah

Acknowledgments

We thank our editors, Margaret Hendrey and Marjorie Spencer, for their patience and helpfulness. We are also grateful to our reviewers and advisors, Dan Hill, Elise Lipkowitz, Charity Lu, Joe Luk, Rob Maguire, and Tom Mongan. Dan's contributions in particular have been tremendous. The quality of this work has been vastly improved by his careful and meticulous reviews.

Programming Interviews
Exposed

The Job Application Process

Interviewing and recruiting procedures are similar at most tech companies. The more prepared you are for what you will encounter, the more successful you will be. This chapter will familiarize you with the entire job search process, from contacting companies to starting your new job, so you won't have to write your first few application attempts off as learning experiences. Hiring procedures at technical companies are often substantially different from those followed by more traditional firms, so you may find this information useful even if you've spent some time in the working world.

Contacting Companies

The first step in getting a job is making contact with companies you're interested in working for. Networking (the social kind) is the best way to find jobs. Tell all your friends about what kind of job you're looking for. Even if they don't work for the kinds of companies that might hire you, they probably know people who do. Your resume, coming from "Susan's friend" or "Bill's neighbor," is sure to get more careful consideration than the hundreds of anonymous resumes that come flooding in from strangers. Once you have a contact at a company, it's up to you to make the most of it.

It's tempting to call up a contact and say, "Hi, I'd like to speak with you about getting a job." Presumably, your contact already knows that this is the ultimate reason that you're calling, so cutting to the chase may seem reasonable. This approach, though, is tactless and likely to be unsuccessful. Your contact may find it arrogant or presumptive that you would assume his company needs you before you've even heard about the company or its current needs. For best results, you need to be more circumspect. Start by setting up a time to speak. You don't want to annoy your contact by trying to talk with him at an inconvenient time. When you do speak to your contact, begin by asking about the company and finding out what it does. If it sounds like a good place to work, ask about openings. If an opening sounds ideal for you, explain why you believe that you would be a good match. Finally, thank the person for his time and ask if you can send a resume or if there's another person you can speak with about the openings.

Although networking through a contact with a company provides the highest probability of success, there are a number of other possibilities. Especially when labor markets are tight, many firms use outside recruiters known as *headhunters*[1] to help them find candidates. If you list yourself with a headhunter, he will assist you with your job search and call you when he learns of an opening that matches your skill set. Some headhunters are more helpful than others, so ask around to see if anyone you know has recommendations. If you can't locate a headhunter this way, you can search the Web for headhunters, recruiters, or staffing services. You can check out a prospective headhunter by asking for references, but be aware that headhunters deal with so many people that even those who frequently do a poor job will have 5 or 10 satisfied clients who serve as references. Avoid headhunters who want to act as your sole agent or want you to pay them fees. Reputable headhunters understand that they are only a part of your job search and that their compensation comes from employers, not applicants.

When you work with a headhunter, it's important to understand his motivation. Headhunters get paid only when an applicant they've

---

[1]The term "headhunter" is used universally by applicants and employers, but many of those to whom the term is applied find it insulting. Therefore, it's probably best not to use the word "headhunter" when talking to one.

referred is hired. It is therefore in a headhunter's best interests to get as many people as possible into as many jobs as possible as quickly as possible. A headhunter has no financial incentive to find you the best possible job—or to find a company the best possible applicant, for that matter. If you recognize that a headhunter is in business for the purpose of making a living, not for the purpose of helping you, you are less likely to be surprised or disappointed by your experiences. This is not to suggest that headhunters are bad people or that as a rule they take advantage of applicants or companies. Headhunters can be very helpful and useful, but you must not expect them to look out for your interests above their own.

You can also try contacting companies directly. The Internet is the best medium for this approach. You may know of some companies you'd like to work for, or you can search the Web to find companies in your area. Most companies' Web pages have instructions for submitting resumes. If the Web site lists specific openings, read through them and submit your resume specifically for the openings you're interested in. In many companies, resumes targeted at a specific job opportunity are forwarded to the hiring manager, while those that don't mention a specific opening languish in the human resources database. If there aren't any directions for submitting your resume, look for an e-mail address to which you can send it. Send your resume as both plain text in the body of the e-mail (so the recipient can read it without having to do any work) and as an attached Microsoft Word file (so the recipient can print a pretty copy). Not everyone upgrades to the newest version of Word, so convert your resume file so that it can be read by older versions of Word, and be *absolutely certain* that your resume isn't carrying any macro viruses. Approaching a company directly like this is a bit of a long shot, but it takes so little time and effort that you have nothing to lose.

Job fairs are an easy way to learn about and make contact with a lot of companies without much effort. Your chances of success with any one particular company at a job fair are low because each company sees so many applicants, but given the number of companies at a job fair, your overall odds may still be favorable. If you collect business cards at the job fair and follow up with people afterward, you can distinguish yourself from the rest of the job fair crowd.

You can also try more traditional job search methods, like newspaper classified ads or their electronic equivalents, the Internet job databases. If they are available to you, college career centers, alumni organizations, and professional associations can also be helpful in finding jobs.

Screening Interviews

If someone is sufficiently impressed by your resume that he wants to talk to you, the next step is a screening interview. This interview is usually conducted by phone and lasts about 30 minutes. Screening interviews may also take place on the spot at a job fair or on campus as part of a college recruiting process.

The screening interview has two major objectives. First, the interviewer wants to make sure that you're interested in doing the job he is hiring for, that you have the skills needed for the position, and that you're willing to accept any logistical requirements of the position, like relocation or travel. If these problems can be ruled out, the interviewer will usually ask you a few knowledge-based questions. These are designed to eliminate applicants who have inflated their resumes or are weak in skills that are key to the position. If you successfully answer these questions, the interviewer will get back to you, usually within a week, to invite you to schedule an interview day on site at the company's office.

On-site Interviews

Your performance in on-site interviews is the biggest factor in determining whether you get an offer. These interviews consist mostly of a variety of technical questions: problems requiring you to implement a simple program or function; questions that test your knowledge of computers, languages, and programming; and mathematics and logic puzzles. The majority of this book focuses on helping you answer these questions and succeed in your interviews.

Your on-site interviews usually last either a half day or a full day, and they typically consist of 3 to 5 interviews of 30 to 60 minutes each. Your interviewers are often the members of the team you would be working with if you were hired. Most companies have a rule that any interviewer can block an applicant from being hired, so all of your interviews are important. Sometimes you may interview with two separate teams on the same day. Usually each group you interview with will make a separate decision about giving you an offer.

The company will usually take you out for lunch midway through your interview day. A free lunch at a nice restaurant is certainly something to be enjoyed, but don't let your guard down completely. If you make a negative impression at lunch, you may lose your offer. Be polite, and avoid alcohol and messy foods like ribs. These general guidelines apply to all company outings, including evening recruiting activities. Moderate drinking is acceptable during evening outings, but show restraint. Getting drunk isn't likely to improve your chances of getting an offer.

At the end of the day, you will usually meet with the boss; if he spends a lot of time trying to sell you on working for the company, it's a pretty strong indication that you've done well in your interviews and an offer will follow.

Dress

Traditionally, people have worn suits to interviews. Most tech companies, though, are strictly business casual these days. The running joke at some of these companies is that the only people who wear suits are interview candidates and salespeople. It's probably not to your advantage to wear a suit if nobody else at the company is wearing one. On the other hand, if you wear jeans and a T-shirt, interviewers may feel you're not showing sufficient respect or seriousness, even though they may be wearing jeans themselves. A standard technical interviewing outfit consists of non-denim cotton pants, a collared shirt, and loafers (no sneakers or sandals). Unless the job you're interviewing for has a significant business or consulting aspect where formal dress will be required, you generally don't need to wear a jacket or a tie.

Recruiters

Your interviews and offer may be coordinated by a company recruiter or human resources representative. If so, the recruiter will be responsible for the scheduling and logistical aspects of your interview, including reimbursing you for travel or lodging expenses. Recruiters aren't usually involved in the hiring decision, but they may pass information about you on to those who are. They are also usually the ones who will call you back about your offer and handle negotiations.

As with headhunters, it's important to understand the position recruiters are in so you can understand how they behave. Once the decision is made to give you an offer, the recruiter's job is to do anything necessary to get you to accept the offer at the lowest possible salary. A recruiter's pay is often tied to how many candidates he signs.

Recruiters are often very good at what they do. They may focus on a job's benefits or perks to draw attention away from negative aspects of a job offer. Recruiters sometimes try to play career counselor or advisor. The recruiter asks you about each of your offers and leads you through a supposedly objective analysis to determine which is the best offer. Not surprisingly, this exercise always leads to the conclusion that the offer from the recruiter's company is clearly the best choice.

A recruiter will generally tell you that you should come to him with any questions about your offer. This is fine for questions about benefits or salary but ill-advised when you have questions about the job itself. The recruiter usually doesn't know very much about the job you're being hired to do. When you ask him a specific question about the job, the recruiter has little incentive to do the work to find the answer, especially if that answer might cause you to turn down the offer. Instead, the recruiter is likely to give you a vague response along the lines of what he thinks you want to hear. When you want straight answers to your questions, it's best to go directly to the people you'll be working for. You can also try going directly to your potential manager if you feel the recruiter is being unreasonable with you. This is a somewhat risky strategy—it certainly won't win you the recruiter's love—but often the hiring manager has the authority to overrule decisions or restrictions made by the recruiter. Hiring managers are often more willing to be flexible than recruiters. You're just another applicant to the recruiter, but to the hiring manager, you're the person he chose to work with.

Some recruiters are territorial enough about their candidates that they won't give you your prospective team's contact information. To protect against this possibility, collect business cards from your interviewers during your interviews, particularly from your prospective managers. Then you'll have the necessary information without having to go through the recruiter.

The vast majority of recruiters are honorable people deserving of your respect and courtesy. Nevertheless, don't let their friendliness fool you into thinking that their job is to help you; their job is to get you to sign with their company as quickly as possible for as little money as possible.

Offers and Negotiation

When you get an offer, you've made it through the hardest part: You now have a job, if you want it. However, the game isn't over yet. You're looking for a job because you need to make money; how you play the end game largely determines how much you get.

When your recruiter or hiring manager makes you an offer, he may also tell you how much the company is planning to pay you. Perhaps a more common practice, though, is for the recruiter or hiring manager to tell you that he would like to hire you and ask you how much you want to make. Answering this question is covered in detail in Chapter 11, "Non-Technical Questions."

Once you've been given a specific offer that includes details about salary, signing bonus, and stock options, you need to decide whether you're satisfied with it. This shouldn't be a snap decision; never accept an offer on the spot. Always spend at least a day thinking about important decisions like this; it's surprising how much can change in a day.

Recruiters often employ a variety of high-pressure tactics to get you to accept offers quickly. They may tell you that you must accept the offer within a few days if you want the job, or they may offer you an exploding signing bonus, a signing bonus that decreases by a fixed amount each day. Don't let this bullying rush your decision. If the company really wants you (and it probably does if it made you an offer) these limits and terms are negotiable, even when a recruiter claims they aren't. You may have to go over the recruiter's head and talk to your hiring manager if the recruiter refuses to be flexible. If these conditions really are non-negotiable, you probably don't want to work for a rigid company full of bullies anyway.

If, after careful consideration, your offer meets or exceeds your expectations, you're all set. On the other hand, if you're not completely happy with your offer, you should try to negotiate. All too often, applicants assume that offers are non-negotiable and reject offers without negotiation or accept offers they're not pleased with. In fact, almost every offer is negotiable to some extent.

You should never reject an offer for monetary reasons without trying to negotiate. When you're negotiating an offer that you would otherwise reject, you hold the ultimate high card. You're ready to walk, so you have nothing to lose.

Even when an offer is in the range you were expecting, it's often worthwhile to try negotiating. As long as you are respectful and truthful in your negotiations and your requests are reasonable,[2] you'll never lose an offer just because you tried to negotiate it. In the worst case, the company

---

[2]In determining what is reasonable, the authors frequently apply the maxim "Pigs get fat, but hogs get slaughtered."

refuses to change the offer and you're no worse off than before you tried to negotiate.

If you decide to negotiate your compensation package, here's how you do it. First, figure out exactly what you want. You may want a signing bonus, better pay, or more stock options. Once you know what you want, arrange a phone call with the appropriate negotiator; your negotiator is usually the same person who gave you the terms of your offer. Don't call the negotiator blind because you may catch him at an inconvenient time.

Next, say you appreciate receiving the offer and explain why you're not completely happy with it. For example, you could say, "I'm very pleased to have received the offer, but I'm having a hard time accepting it because it's not competitive with my other offers." Or you could say, "Thank you again for the offer, but I'm having trouble accepting it because I know from discussions with my peers and from talking with other companies that this offer is below market rates." If the negotiator asks you to go into greater detail about which other companies have offered you more money and how much, or where your peers work, you're under no obligation to do so. You can easily say, "I keep all my offers confidential, including yours, and feel that it's unprofessional to give out that sort of information."

The company's negotiator may ask you what you had in mind or, conversely, tell you that the offer is non-negotiable. Claiming that the offer is non-negotiable is often merely a hardball negotiation tactic, so in either case you should respond by politely and respectfully spelling out exactly what you expect in an offer. Negotiators rarely change an offer on the spot, so thank the negotiator for his time and help and say that you're looking forward to hearing from him again.

Many people find negotiation uncomfortable, especially when dealing with professional recruiters who do it every day. It's not uncommon for someone to accept an offer as close enough just to avoid having to negotiate. If you feel this way about negotiation, try looking at it this way: You rarely have anything to lose, and even modest success in negotiation can be very rewarding. If it takes you a 30-minute phone call to get your offer increased by $3,000, you've made $6,000 per hour. Even lawyers don't get paid that much.

Accepting and Rejecting Offers

At some point, your negotiations will be complete, and you will be ready to accept an offer. After you inform a company you're accepting its offer, be sure to keep in touch to coordinate start dates and paperwork.

It's also important to be professional about declining your other offers. Contacts are very important, especially in the computer business where people change jobs frequently. You've no doubt built contacts at all the companies that made you offers. It's foolish to squander your contacts at other companies by failing to inform them of your decision. If you had a recruiter at the company, you should e-mail him about your decision. You should also personally call every hiring manager who gave you an offer to thank him and state your decision. For example, you can say, "I want to thank you again for extending me the offer. I was very impressed with your company, but I've decided it's not the best choice for me right now. Thank you again, and I appreciate your confidence in me." Besides simply being classy, this approach will often get a response such as "I was pleased to meet you, and I'm sad that you won't be joining us. If things don't work out at that company, give me a call and maybe we can work something out. Best of luck."

This gives you a great place to start the next time you need to play the game.

Approaches to Programming Problems

Coding questions are generally the meat of an interview. They are your chance to demonstrate that you can do the job. These questions are a large component of the process that most computer and software companies use to decide who to hire and who not to hire. Many companies make offers to less than 10 percent of the people who interview with them. The questions are generally rather difficult. If everyone (or even most people) were able to answer a particular question quickly, the company would stop asking it because it wouldn't tell anything about the applicants. Many of the questions are designed to take up to an hour, so don't get frustrated if you don't see the answer right away. Almost no one does.

LESSON: These problems are hard! Some of the questions are designed to see how you handle a problem when you don't immediately see the solution.

The Process

In these questions, you will usually be working one on one with your interviewer. He will give you a marker and a whiteboard (or pen and paper) and ask you to write some code. The interviewer will probably want you to talk through the question before you start writing. Generally, you will be asked to code a function, but sometimes you will need to write a class definition or a series of functions. In any case, you will be writing code.

If you are applying for a job as a programmer in a specific language, you should know that language and expect to use it to solve any problems you are given. If you are applying for a general programming or development position, a thorough knowledge of C and some familiarity with C++ will be enough to get by. Your interviewer may permit you to use other mainstream languages, such as Java or Perl. If you are given a choice, select the language you know best, but expect that you will be required to solve some problems in C or C++. Interviewers are less likely to be amenable to you using less mainstream languages like Lisp, Python, Tcl, Prolog, Cobol, or Fortran, but if you are particularly expert in one of these, there's no harm in asking. Before you go to your interview, you should make sure you are completely comfortable with the use and syntax of any language you plan to use. One final note about language selection: Whether rightly or wrongly, many people consider Visual Basic and JavaScript to be lesser languages. Unless you are applying for a job where you will be using these languages it's probably best to avoid them in your interviews. The solutions in this book are all in C, C++, Perl, or Java with an emphasis on C because it's still the most common language in interviews.

The code you write in the interview is probably the only example of your code that your interviewer will see. If you write ugly code, your interviewer will assume you always write ugly code. This is your chance to shine and show your best code. Take the time to make your code solid and pretty.

LESSON: Brush up on the languages you expect to use, and write your best code.

Programming questions are designed to see both how well you can code and how you solve problems. If all the interviewer wanted to do was measure your coding ability, he could give you a piece of paper with problems and come back an hour later to evaluate how you did. However, the interviewer wants to see your thought process throughout the interview. The problem-solving process is interactive, and if you're having difficulty, the interviewer will generally guide you to the correct answer via a series of hints. Of course, the less help you need to solve the problem, the better you look, but showing an intelligent thought process and responding well to the hints you are given is also very important. If you know any additional information that pertains to the problem you may want to mention it to show your general knowledge of computers, even if it's not directly applicable to the problem at hand. In answering these problems, show that you're not just a propeller-head coder. Demonstrate that you have a logical thought process, are generally knowledgeable about computers, and can communicate well.

LESSON: Keep talking! Always explain what you are doing.

Questions are generally asked in ascending order of difficulty. This is not a hard and fast rule, but you can expect the questions to get more difficult as you answer more of them correctly. Often, different interviewers will communicate with each other about what they asked you, what you could answer, and what you couldn't answer. If you answer all the questions in your early interviews but find yourself stumped by harder questions later on, this may indicate that earlier interviewers were impressed with your responses.

About the Questions

These questions have very specific requirements. They have to be short enough that they can be explained and solved reasonably quickly, yet complex enough that not everyone can solve them. Therefore, it's unlikely that you'll be asked any real-world problems. Almost any worthy real-world problem would take at least three hours to explain, a day to examine the existing code, and a week to solve. That isn't an option in an interview. Instead, many of these problems require using tricks or uncommonly used features of a language.

The problems often prohibit you from using the most common way to do something or from using the ideal data structure. For example, you might be given a problem like this: "Write a function that determines if two integers are equal without using any comparative operators."[1] This is an outright silly and contrived problem. Almost every language that ever existed has some way to compare two integers. However, you're not off

[1] If you're wondering how you might do this, try using bit operators.

the hook if you respond, "This is a stupid question; I'd always use the equality operator. I'd never have this problem." In fact, you flunked if you answer this way. Sometimes, it may be worthwhile to comment on a better way to solve the problem, even if it has been disallowed, but you need to solve the questions as they're asked. For example, if you were asked to solve a certain problem with a hashtable, you might say, "This would be easy with a binary search tree because it's much easier to extract the largest element. But let's see how I can solve this with a hashtable . . ."

LESSON: Many questions involve ridiculous restrictions, use obscure features of languages, and seem silly and contrived. Play within the rules.

Solving the Questions

You can't solve the problem correctly if you don't understand it. Often, there are hidden assumptions in the problem, or the interviewer's explanation may be very brief or difficult to follow. You can't demonstrate your skills if you don't understand the problem. Don't hesitate to ask your interviewer questions about the problem, and don't start solving it until you understand it.

Once you understand the question, you should almost always try an example. This example may lead to insights on how to solve the problem or bring to light any remaining misunderstandings that you have. Starting with an example also demonstrates a methodical, logical thought process. Examples are especially useful if you don't see the solution right away.

LESSON: Make sure you understand the problem before you start solving it, then start with an example to solidify your understanding.

After your example, focus on the algorithm you will use to solve the problem. Often, this will take a long time and require additional examples. This is to be expected. If you stand quietly staring at the whiteboard, the interviewer has no way of knowing whether you're making productive headway or simply clueless. Therefore, talk to your interviewer and tell him what you are doing. For example, you might say something like "I'm wondering if I can store the values in an array and then sort them, but I don't think that this will work because I can't quickly look up elements in an array by value..." This demonstrates your skill, which is the point of the interview, and may also lead to hints from the interviewer. He might respond, "You're very close to the solution. Do you really need to look up elements by value, or could you . . ."

It may take you a long time to solve the problem. You may be tempted to begin coding before you figure out exactly how to solve the problem. Resist this temptation. Consider who you would rather work with: someone who thinks about a problem for a long time and then codes it correctly the first time or someone who hastily jumps into a problem, makes several errors while coding, and doesn't have any idea where he is going. Not a difficult decision, is it?

After you've figured out your algorithm and how you will implement it, explain your solution to your interviewer. This gives him an opportunity to evaluate your solution before you begin coding. Your interviewer may say, "Sounds great, go ahead and code it," or he may say something like "That's not quite right because you can't look up elements in a hashtable that way . . ." In either case, you gain valuable information.

While you code, it's important that you explain what you're doing. For example, you might say, "Here, I'm initializing the array to all 0's . . ." This narrative allows the interviewer to follow your code more easily.

LESSON: Explain what you are doing to your interviewer before and while coding the solution. Keep talking!

You generally won't be penalized for asking factual questions that you might otherwise look up in a reference. You obviously can't ask a question like "How do I solve this problem?" but it is acceptable to ask a question like "I can't remember—what format string do I use to get printf to print out octal numbers?" While it's better to know how to do this without asking, it's OK to ask this sort of question.

After you've written the code for a problem, immediately verify that the code is correct by tracing through it with an example. This step demonstrates very clearly that your code works in at least one case. It also illustrates a logical thought process and your desire to check your work and search for bugs. The example may also help you flush out minor bugs in your solution.

Finally, you should make sure you check your code for *all* error and special cases. Many error and special cases go overlooked in programming; forgetting these cases in an interview indicates you may forget them in a job. For example, if you allocate dynamic memory, make sure you check that the allocation did not fail. Also, check that you won't dereference any NULL pointers and that you can handle empty data structures. It's important to cover these cases to truly impress your interviewer and correctly solve the problem.

LESSON: Try an example, and check all error and special cases.

Once you try an example and feel comfortable that your code is correct, the interviewer may ask you questions about what you wrote. Commonly, these questions focus on running time, alternative implementations, and complexity. If your interviewer does not ask you these questions, you should volunteer the information to show that you are cognizant of these issues. For example, you could say, "This implementation has linear running time, which is the best possible because I have to check all the input values. The dynamic memory allocation will slow it down a little, as will the overhead of using recursion…"

When You Get Stuck

Often, you will get stuck on a problem. This is expected and is an important part of the interviewing process. Interviewers want to see how you respond when you don't recognize the answer to a question immediately. The worst thing to do is give up or get frustrated. Instead, show interest in the problem and keep trying to solve it. When all else fails, go back to an example. Try performing the task and analyzing what you are doing. Try extending from your specific example to the general case. You may have to use very detailed examples. This is OK.

LESSON: When all else fails, return to a specific example. Try to move from the specific example to the general case and from there to the solution.

Another fallback option is to try a different data structure. Perhaps a linked list, array, hashtable, or binary search tree will help solve the problem. If you're given an unusual data structure, look for similarities between it and more familiar data structures. Using the right data structure often makes a problem much easier.

You should also consider the less commonly used or more advanced aspects of a language when you have trouble with a problem. These can include bit operators, union types, complex pointer casting, and advanced keywords. Sometimes, the key to a problem involves one of these features.

LESSON: Sometimes a different data structure or advanced language feature is key to the solution.

Even when you don't feel stuck, you may be having problems. You may be missing an elegant or obvious way to implement something and writing too much code. One of the shared traits of almost all interview coding questions is that the correct solutions are short. You rarely need to write more than 15 lines of code and almost never more than 30. If you start writing lots of code, it should be a warning that you may be heading in the wrong direction.

One final note on writing code: You often need to compare a value to NULL or 0. In this case (at least in C or C++), you could write either:

```
if (elem != NULL) {
```

or:

```
if (elem) {
```

These two statements are equivalent to the compiler. There's something of an argument between programmers as to which alternative is visually cleaner. Some programmers argue the former implementation is easier to read and worth writing out. Other programmers argue that this is such a common situation that the latter implementation is perfectly acceptable. From an interviewer's standpoint, both implementations are technically correct. In the former definition, however, the interviewer may wonder if you know that comparing to NULL is unnecessary; in the latter case, the interviewer wonders nothing and sees you as a coding veteran. Thus, it is probably preferable to choose the latter implementation in an interview and mention that it's the same as comparing to NULL or 0.

Analysis of the Solution

The interviewer will usually ask about the efficiency of your implementation. Often, you will have to compare trade-offs between your implementation and another possibility and identify the conditions that make each choice more favorable. Common questions focus on the use of dynamic memory and recursion.

The most important part of measuring efficiency is run-time analysis. The most commonly used form of this is called *big-O analysis*. This method provides a concrete means of comparing two algorithms. The formal definition of big-O analysis is quite mathematical; this explanation deals with it on a more practical and intuitive level. If you're familiar with big-O analysis, this explanation will serve as a review. Otherwise, it should bring you up to speed on basic run-time analysis.

Big-O analysis deals specifically with the time an algorithm takes to run as a function of the size of the input. Let's start with an example of big-O analysis in action. Consider a simple function that returns the maximum value in an array of numbers. The size of the array is n. There are at least two easy ways to implement the function. First, you can keep track of the current largest number as the function iterates through the array and return that value when you are done iterating. This implementation, called CompareToMax, looks like this:

```
/* Returns the largest integer in the array */
int CompareToMax(unsigned int array[], int n)
{
    unsigned int curMax, i;

    /* Make sure that there is at least one element in the array. */
    if (n <= 0)
        return -1;

    /* Set the largest number so far to the first array value. */
    curMax = array[0];

    /* Compare every number with the largest number so far. */
    for (i = 1; i < n; i++) {
        if (array[i] > curMax) {
            curMax = array[i];
        }
    }
    return curMax;
}
```

Alternatively, you could implement this function by comparing each value to all the other values. If all other values are less than or equal to a certain value, that value must be the maximum value. This implementation, called CompareToAll, looks like this:

```
/* Returns the largest integer in the array */
int CompareToAll(unsigned int array[], int n)
{
    int i, j, isMax;
    /* Make sure that there is at least one element in the array. */
    if (n <= 0)
        return -1;

    for (i = 0; i < n; i++) {
        for (j = 0; j < n; j++) {
```

```
        isMax = 1;
        /* See if any value is greater. */
        if (array[j] > array[i])
            isMax = 0; /* array[i] is not the largest value. */
    }
    /* If isMax == 1, no larger value exists; array[i] is max. */
    if (isMax)
        return array[i];
    }
}
```

Both of these functions correctly return the maximum value. Which one is more efficient? The most accurate way to compare CompareToMax and CompareToAll is to benchmark them. In most development efforts, though, it's impractical to implement and benchmark every possible alternative. You need to be able to predict an algorithm's performance without having to implement it. Big-O analysis allows you to do exactly that: compare the predicted relative performance of different algorithms.

In Big-O analysis, input size is assumed to be n. In this case, n simply represents the number of elements in an array. In other analyses, n may represent the number of nodes in a linked list, the number of bits in a data-type, or the number of entries in a hashtable. After figuring out what n means in terms of the input, you have to determine how many times the n input items are examined in terms of n. "Examined" is a fuzzy word because algorithms differ greatly. Commonly, an examination might be something like adding an input value to a constant, creating a new input item, or deleting an input value. In big-O analysis, these operations are all considered equivalent. In both CompareToMax and CompareToAll, "examine" means comparing an array value to another value.

In CompareToMax, each array element was compared once to a maximum value. Thus, the n input items are each examined once, resulting in n examinations. This is considered O(n). O(n) is often called linear time. You may notice that in addition to examining each element once, there is a check to make sure that the array is not empty and a step that initializes the curMax variable. Thus, it may seem more accurate to call this an O(n + 2) function. Big-O analysis, however, yields the *asymptotic* running time, the limit of the running time as n gets very large. As n approaches infinity, the difference between n and n + 2 is insignificant, so the constant term can be ignored. Similarly, for an algorithm running in $n + n^2$ time, the difference between n^2 and $n + n^2$ is negligible for very large n. Thus, in big-O analysis, you eliminate all but the highest-order term, the term that is largest as n gets very large. In this case, n is the highest-order term. Therefore, the CompareToMax function is O(n).

The analysis of `CompareToAll` is a little more difficult. First, you have to make an assumption about where the largest number occurs in the array. For now, assume that the maximum element is at the end of the array. In this case, this function may compare each of n elements to n other elements. Thus, there are $n \cdot n$ examinations, and this is an $O(n^2)$ algorithm.

The analysis so far has shown that `CompareToMax` is $O(n)$ and `CompareToAll` is $O(n^2)$. This means that as the array grows, the number of comparisons in `CompareToAll` will become much larger than in `CompareToMax`. Consider an array with 30,000 elements. `CompareToMax` will compare on the order of 30,000 elements while `CompareToAll` will compare on the order of 900,000,000 elements. You would expect `CompareToMax` to be much faster because it examines 30,000 times fewer elements. In fact, one benchmark timed `CompareToMax` at less than .01 seconds while `CompareToAll` took 23.99 seconds.

You may think this comparison was stacked against `CompareToAll` because the maximum value was at the end. This is true, and it raises the important issues of best-case, average-case, and worst-case running times. The analysis of `CompareToAll` was a worst-case scenario, where the maximum value was at the end of the array. Consider the average case, where the largest value is in the middle. You have to check only half the values n times because the maximum value is in the middle. This results in checking $n(^1\!/_2) = {^{n^2}}\!/_2$ times. This would appear to be an $O({^{n^2}}\!/_2)$ running time. Consider, though, what the $\frac{1}{2}$ factor means. The actual time to check each value is highly dependent on the machine instructions that the code translates to and then on the speed in which the CPU can execute the instructions. Therefore, the $\frac{1}{2}$ doesn't mean very much. You could even come up with an $O(n^2)$ algorithm that was faster than an $O({^{n^2}}\!/_2)$ algorithm. In big-O analysis, you drop all constant factors, so the average case for `CompareToAll` is no better than the worst case. It is still $O(n^2)$.

The best case running time for `CompareToAll` is better than $O(n^2)$. In this case, the maximum value is at the beginning of the array. The maximum value is compared to all other values only once, so the result is an $O(n)$ running time.

Note that in `CompareToMax`, the best-case, average-case, and worst-case running times are identical. Regardless of the arrangement of the values in the array, the algorithm is always $O(n)$.

The general procedure for big-O run-time analysis is as follows:

1. Figure out what the input is and what n represents.
2. Express the number of operations the algorithm performs in terms of n.

3. Eliminate all but the highest-order terms.

4. Remove all constant factors.

Here's a common case to be aware of. You could make the following optimization to CompareToAll. Instead of comparing each number to every other number, compare each number to only the numbers occurring after it. In essence, every number before the current number has already been compared to the current number. Thus, the algorithm is still correct if you compare only to numbers occurring after the current number. What's the worst-case running time for this implementation? The first number is compared to n numbers, the second number to $n - 1$ numbers, the third number to $n - 2$, resulting in a number of comparisons equal to $n + (n - 1) + (n - 2) + (n - 3) + \ldots + 1$. This is a very common result; the sum of this series is

$$\frac{n^2}{2} + \frac{n}{2}.$$

n^2 is the highest-order term, so this is still an $O(n^2)$ running time.

The fastest possible running time is $O(1)$. This is commonly referred to as constant running time. This means the function always takes the same amount of time to execute, regardless of the input size. There may even be no input to the function.

Most coding problem solutions in this book include a run-time analysis. You may find these examples helpful in solidifying your understanding.

Linked Lists

Why do we devote an entire chapter to linked lists—arguably the least useful creature in the dynamic data structure menagerie? We treat them in depth here because they are the favorite dynamic data structure of interviewers. Remember that most interviewers want to ask at least two or three questions over the course of an hour-long interview. This means that they have to ask questions that you can be reasonably expected to answer in 20 to 30 minutes. Linked lists are simple enough that with a little practice you can write a relatively complete implementation in less than 10 minutes on half a sheet of paper, leaving plenty of time to answer the question. In contrast, it might take you most of the interview period to implement a more complex data structure like a hashtable. Furthermore, there is not much room for variation in implementation of linked lists. This means that an interviewer can simply say "linked list" and not waste time discussing and clarifying implementation details. On the other hand, linked lists are complex enough that an interviewer can construct challenging questions.

Because they are used less often than other dynamic data structures in real-world programming, you may not be completely conversant with linked lists. Because it's difficult for an interviewer to tell the difference between someone who's rusty and someone who doesn't know, we suggest you use the following overview to refamiliarize yourself with linked lists. If you know linked lists like the back of your hand, you can skip to the problems and get some practice.

Singly Linked Lists

When an interviewer says "linked list" he generally means a canonical singly linked list. This list consists of a number of data elements in which each data element has a *next* pointer or *next* reference (the link) to the following element (see Figure 3.1). The link of the last element in the list is marked to indicate that this element is the end of the list. In C, you mark the end by setting the next pointer equal to NULL. An element's next pointer and data are bound together, usually by either a struct (C) or a class (C++ and Java). Following is a C element type declaration for a linked list of integers:

```
typedef struct elementT {
    int data;
    struct elementT *next;
} element;
```

Solutions to linked list questions are generally coded in C, or occasionally C++. C is used because most other languages have more powerful dynamic data structures, either as fundamental types (Perl) or as part of the standard libraries (Java). Although you may be unlikely to use a linked list in a C program, you're even less likely to use one when better options are built in to the language.

Whatever language they are implemented in, singly linked lists have a host of special cases and potential programming traps. Because the links in a singly linked list consist only of next pointers, the list can be traversed only in the forward direction, so a complete traversal of the list must begin with the first element. In other words, you need a pointer to the first element of a list in order to locate all the elements in the list. Consequently, the term *linked list* is often used as a shorthand to mean a

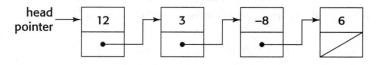

Figure 3.1   A singly linked list.

pointer to the first element of a linked list. For instance, if someone says that a function takes a linked list as an argument, he probably means that it takes a pointer to the first element of a linked list as an argument.

Modifying the Head Pointer

This concept leads to the first important caveat of linked list implementation. Because a head pointer (pointer to the first element) is used to track an entire list, the head pointer must be updated whenever a new first element is added to the list or the old first element is removed. Updating the head pointer becomes a problem when you make the alteration inside a function (which is the usual case) because you must update the first element pointer in the calling function, not just the local copy of it. For example, the following code is incorrect because it fails to update the head pointer in the calling function:

```
int BadInsert(element *head)
{
    element *newElem;
    newElem = (element *) malloc(sizeof(element));
    if (!newElem)
        return 0;

    newElem->next = head;

    /* Incorrectly updates local copy of head.
     * Calling code retains the old value for the first element
     * pointer, so it now points at the second element of the list.
     */
    head = newElem;
    return 1;
}
```

The correct way to update the head pointer in C is to pass a pointer to the head pointer, allowing you to modify the calling function's pointer to the first element, as shown here:

```
int Insert(element **head)
{
    element *newElem;
    newElem = (element *) malloc(sizeof(element));
    if (!newElem)
        return 0;

    newElem->next = *head;

    /* *head gives the calling function's head pointer, so
     * the change is not lost when this function returns
```

```
    */
    *head = newElem;
    return 1;
}
```

LESSON Any function that can change the first element of a linked list must be passed a pointer to the head pointer.

Traversing

Often you need to work with list elements other than the head element. Operations on any but the first element of a linked list require traversal of some elements of the list. If you don't check for the end of the list as you traverse, you risk dereferencing a NULL pointer. For instance, suppose you were to search for the first 6 in a linked list of integers in the following manner:

```
element *FindSix(element *elem)
{
    while (elem->data != 6) {
        elem = elem->next;
    }
    /* Found elem->data == 6 */
    return elem;
}
```

This search method works fine, as long as the list actually has a 6 in it. If it doesn't, then elem is eventually set to NULL when you try to traverse past the last element, causing the conditional of the while loop to dereference a NULL pointer and crash the program. Instead, you could use the conditional of the while loop to test the traversal pointer, ensuring that traversal will halt at the end of the list, as follows:

```
element *FindSix(element *elem)
{
    while (elem) {
        if (elem->data == 6) {
            /* Found elem->data == 6 */
            return elem;
        }
        elem = elem->next;
    }
    /* No elem->data == 6 exists */
    return NULL;
}
```

You may need to adapt this general form to meet the needs of a particular function.

Always test for the end of a linked list as you traverse it.

Insertion and Deletion

Because links in a singly linked list are maintained exclusively with next pointers, any insertion or deletion of elements in the middle of a list requires modification of the previous element's next pointer. This means that to insert an element, you need pointers to the elements immediately before and after the insertion point; to delete an element you need pointers to both the element to be deleted and the immediately preceding element. In fact, because the preceding element's next pointer provides a pointer to the following element, a pointer to the preceding element is sufficient. However, if you're given a pointer to the latter element (the element to delete or the element immediately after the insertion point) there's no easy way to find the preceding element. You must traverse the list. Following is an example of how you might find the element immediately preceding the one you need to delete:

```
int DeleteElement(element **head, element *deleteMe)
{
    element *elem = *head;

    if (deleteMe == *head) { /* special case for head */
        *head = elem->next;
        free(deleteMe);
        return 1;
    }

    while (elem) {
        if (elem->next == deleteMe) {
            /* elem is element preceding deleteMe */
            elem->next = deleteMe->next;
            free(deleteMe);
            return 1;
        }
        elem = elem->next;
    }
    /* deleteMe not found */
    return 0;
}
```

Deletion and insertion require a pointer to the element immediately preceding the deletion or insertion location.

Performing deletions raises another issue. Suppose you want to free all the elements of a linked list. The natural inclination is to use a single pointer to traverse the list, freeing elements as you go. A problem arises, however, when this is implemented. Do you advance the pointer or free the element first? If you advance the pointer first, then the free is impossible because you overwrote the pointer to the element to be freed. If you free the element first, advancing the pointer is impossible because it involves reading the next pointer in the element that was just freed. The solution is to use two pointers, as in the following example:

```
void DeleteList(element *head)
{
    element *next, *deleteMe;
    deleteMe = head;
    while (deleteMe) {
        next = deleteMe->next;
        free(deleteMe);
        deleteMe = next;
    }
}
```

LESSON   Deletion of an element always requires at least two pointer variables.[1]

Doubly Linked Lists

Doubly linked lists eliminate many difficulties inherent in singly linked lists (see Figure 3.2). A doubly linked list differs from a singly linked list in that each element has a previous pointer as well as a next pointer (the previous pointer of the first element is usually set to NULL). This additional pointer makes it possible to traverse the list in either direction. Enabling traversal in both directions allows complete traversal of the list starting from any element. Insertion and deletion become much easier because finding the next and previous elements is trivial when next and previous pointers are available. It's even possible to delete elements with a single pointer variable because you can use the previous pointers to delete elements behind your traversal position. Doubly linked lists are encountered infrequently in interview questions. Many questions that are difficult for singly linked lists are trivial when doubly linked lists are used. On the other hand, if a question is not made easier by using a doubly linked list, there is no point increasing the list's complexity.

---

[1]In fact, insertion requires two pointer variables as well, but because one of them is used for an element in the list and the other for the pointer returned by the memory allocation call, there's little danger of forgetting this in the insertion case.

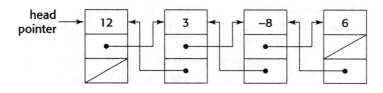

Figure 3.2   A doubly linked list.

Circular Linked Lists

The final variation on the linked list theme is the circular linked list, which comes in singly and doubly linked varieties. Circular lists have no ends, so the primary problem in traversal changes from detecting the end of the list to avoiding traversing infinitely. Though circular linked lists have some interesting properties, they rarely appear in interview questions.

More complex topologies of linked elements, generally categorized as trees, graphs, or networks, are discussed in Chapter 4, "Trees and Graphs."

Problem: Stack Implementation

- Discuss the stack data structure. Implement a stack in C using either a linked list or a dynamic array, and justify your decision. Design the interface to your stack to be complete, consistent, and easy to use.

This question is aimed at determining three things: your knowledge of basic abstract (stack) and fundamental (linked list and dynamic array) data structures, your ability to write routines to manipulate these structures, and your ability to design consistent interfaces to a group of routines.

A stack is a last-in-first-out (LIFO) data structure. This means that when you remove an element you get the last element that was added. Stacks are useful data structures for tasks completed by performing multiple levels of subtasks. Some examples of stack use are tracking return addresses, parameters, and local variables for subroutines and tracking tokens when parsing a grammar in a compiler. The add element and remove element operations are conventionally called *push* and *pop*, respectively.

Linked lists are discussed in the introduction to this chapter. A dynamic array is an array that changes size as needed when elements are added. See the introduction to Chapter 5, "Arrays and Strings," for a more complete discussion of dynamic arrays. The principal advantage of dynamic arrays over linked lists is random access (you can immediately access any element). Operations on a stack always work on the end of the data structure (the top of the stack), however, so the random accessibility of a dynamic array gains little. As a dynamic array grows, it must occasionally be resized. This is a time-consuming operation. On the other hand, if resizing is planned intelligently, a dynamic array may grow more efficiently than a linked list because a linked list must dynamically allocate memory for each element. A linked list also has a memory overhead of one pointer for each element. If you store small pieces of data on the stack, like single integers, this overhead is significant. For these reasons, a stack based on a dynamic array will usually have superior performance to one based on a linked list. In the context of an interview, though, the primary concern is ease and speed of implementation. Implementing a linked list is far less complicated than implementing a dynamic array, so a linked list is probably the best choice for your solution.

Having explained your linked list decision to the interviewer, you can design the routines and their interfaces. If you take a moment to design your code before writing it you can avoid mistakes and inconsistencies in implementation. More importantly, this shows you won't skip right to coding on a larger project where good planning is essential to success.

Your stack will need `Push` and `Pop` routines. What will the prototype for these functions be? Each function must be passed the stack it operates on. `Push` will be passed the data it is to push, and `Pop` will return a piece of data from the stack. The simplest way to pass the stack is to pass a pointer to the stack. Because the stack will be implemented as a linked list, the pointer to the stack will be a pointer to the first element of the linked list. In addition to the pointer to the stack, you could pass the data as a second parameter to `Push`. `Pop` could take only the pointer to the stack as an argument and return the value of the data it popped from the stack. To write the prototypes, you need to know the type of the data that will be stored on the stack. You should declare a struct for a linked list element with the appropriate data type. If the interviewer doesn't make any suggestion, storing void pointers is a good general-purpose solution. Void pointer storage yields a struct and prototypes that look like the following:

```
typedef struct elementT {
    struct elementT *next;
    void *data;
} element;

void Push(element *stack, void *data);
void* Pop(element *stack);
```

Let's consider what will happen in these routines in terms of proper functionality and error handling.

Push and Pop both change the first element of the list. The calling routine's stack pointer must be modified to reflect this change, but any change you make to the pointer that is passed to these functions won't be propagated back to the calling routine. You can solve this problem by having both routines take a pointer to a pointer to the stack. This way you can change the calling routine's pointer so that it continues to point at the first element of the list. Implementing this change gives the following:

```
void Push(element **stack, void *data);
void* Pop(element **stack);
```

Next you need to consider error handling. Push will have to dynamically allocate memory for a new element. Allocation is an operation that can fail. Remember to check that allocation succeeded when you write this routine. You also need some way to indicate to the calling routine whether the push succeeded or failed. In C it's generally most convenient to have a routine indicate success or failure by its return value. This way, the routine can be called from the conditional of an if statement with error handling in the body. So, pass Push a pointer to a pointer to the stack and the data to store, and it will return true for success and false for failure.

Can Pop fail? It doesn't have to allocate memory, but what if it is asked to pop an empty stack? It ought to indicate that the operation was unsuccessful, but it still has to be able to return data when it is successful. A C function has a single return value, but Pop really needs to return two values: the data it popped and an error code.

There are a number of possible solutions to this problem, none of which are entirely satisfactory. One approach is to use the single return value for both purposes. If Pop is successful, have it return the data; if it is unsuccessful, return NULL. As long as your data is a pointer type and you never need to store NULL pointers on the stack, this works fine. If you have to store NULL pointers, however, there's no easy way to determine whether a NULL pointer returned by Pop represents a legitimate element that you stored or an empty stack. Although restricting the stack to storing non-NULL pointers might be acceptable in some cases, we will assume that for this problem it is not.

If you cannot use the return value for both the data and error code, you must return two distinct values. Besides its return value, how else can a function return data? As with the stack parameter, if you pass the function a pointer to a variable, the function can return data by using the pointer to change the value of the variable.

Using this method of returning two values, there are two possibilities for the interface to Pop. You can either have Pop take a pointer to an error code variable as an argument and return data, or you can have it take a pointer to a data variable and return an error code. Intuitively, most programmers would expect Pop to return data. However, using Pop is awkward if the error code is not its return value. Instead of simply calling Pop in the conditional of an if or while statement, you have to explicitly declare a variable for the error code and check its value in a separate statement after you call Pop. Furthermore, if you choose this option, Push takes a data argument and returns an error code while Pop takes an error code argument and returns data. This may offend your sense of symmetry (it does ours). On the other hand, as we mentioned, most programmers intuitively expect Pop to return data. Neither alternative is clearly correct; there are serious problems with both. In an interview, it wouldn't matter so much which alternative you chose, as it would that you were able to identify the pros and cons of each and justify your choice. We think error code arguments are particularly irksome, so we continue this discussion assuming you chose to have Pop return an error code. This gives the following prototypes:

```
int Push(element **stack, void *data);
int Pop(element **stack, void **data);
```

You will also want to write CreateStack and DeleteStack functions. Neither of these is absolutely necessary in a linked list implementation. You could delete the stack by calling Pop until the stack is empty, and you could create a stack by passing Push a pointer to NULL as the stack argument. Writing these functions provides a complete, implementation-independent interface to the stack. A stack implemented as a dynamic array would probably need CreateStack and DeleteStack functions. By including these functions in your implementation you leave open the possibility that someone could change the underlying implementation of the stack without having to change the programs that use the stack.

With the goals of implementation independence and consistency in mind, it's a good idea to have these functions return error codes, too. Even though in a linked list implementation neither CreateStack nor DeleteStack can fail, under a different implementation it could be possible for them to fail (if, for instance, CreateStack couldn't allocate memory for a dynamic array). If you design the interface with no way for these functions to indicate failure, you severely handicap anyone who might want to change your implementation. Again, you face the same problem as with Pop.

CreateStack must return both the empty stack and an error code. You can't use a NULL pointer to indicate failure because a NULL pointer is the empty stack for a linked list implementation. In keeping with our previous decision, we show an implementation with an error code as the return value. Because CreateStack won't be able to return the stack as its value, it will have to take a pointer to a pointer to the stack. Because all the other functions take a pointer to the stack pointer, it makes sense to have DeleteStack take its stack parameter in the same way. This way, if you declare the stack pointer as element *stack; you can always pass the stack argument as &stack—you don't have to remember which functions take stack and which take &stack. This reasoning gives you the following prototypes.

```
int CreateStack(element **stack);
int DeleteStack(element **stack);
```

Once you have everything designed properly, coding becomes clear. CreateStack sets the stack pointer to NULL and returns success, as follows:

```
int CreateStack(element **stack)
{
    *stack = NULL;
    return 1;
}
```

Push allocates the new element, checks for failure, sets the data of the new element, places it at the top of the stack, and adjusts the stack pointer, as follows:

```
int Push(element **stack, void *data)
{
    element *elem;
    elem = (element *) malloc(sizeof(element));
    if (!elem)
        return 0;
    elem->data = data;
    elem->next = *stack;
    *stack = elem;
    return 1;
}
```

Pop checks that the stack isn't empty, fetches the data from the top element, adjusts the stack pointer, and frees the element that is no longer on the stack, as follows:

```
int Pop(element **stack, void **data)
{
```

```
    element *elem;
    if (!(elem = *stack))
        return 0;
    *data = elem->data;
    *stack = elem->next;
    free(elem);
    return 1;
}
```

DeleteStack could call Pop repeatedly, but it is more efficient to simply traverse the data structure, freeing as you go. Don't forget that you need a temporary pointer to hold the address of the next element while you free the current one.

```
int DeleteStack(element **stack)
{
    element *next;
    while (*stack) {
        next = (*stack)->next;
        free(*stack);
        *stack = next;
    }
    return 1;
}
```

Before we complete our discussion of this problem, it is worth noting (and probably worth mentioning to the interviewer) that the interface design would be much more straightforward in an object-oriented language like C++. CreateStack and DeleteStack become the constructor and destructor, respectively. The Push and Pop routines are bound to the stack object, so they don't need to have the stack explicitly passed to them, and the bother with pointers to pointers evaporates. Most notably, you can configure the memory manager so that an exception is thrown if an allocation fails. This allows you to use the return value of Pop for data because you no longer need it for an error code. A C++ version looks like the following:

```
class Stack
{
public:
    Stack();
    ~Stack();
    void Push(void *data);
    void *Pop();
protected:
    // Element struct needed only internally
    typedef struct elementT {
        struct elementT *next;
```

```
        void *data;
    } element;

    element *firstEl;
};

Stack::Stack() {
    firstEl = NULL;
    return;
}

Stack::~Stack() {
    element *next;
    while (firstEl) {
        next = firstEl->next;
        delete firstEl;
        firstEl = next;
    }
    return;
}

void Stack::Push(void *data) {
    //Allocation error will throw exception
    element *element = new element;
    element->data = data;
    element->next = firstEl;
    firstEl = element;
    return;
}

void *Stack::Pop() {
    element *popElement = firstEl;
    void *data;

    /* Assume StackError exception class is defined elsewhere */
    if (firstEl == NULL)
        throw StackError(E_EMPTY);

    data = firstEl->data;
    firstEl = firstEl->next;
    delete popElement;
    return data;
}
```

This implementation assumes that the application that uses it employs exceptions for error handling. Because exceptions are a relatively recent addition to C++, this might not be the case. You could eliminate this implementation's reliance on exceptions by adding explicit C-style error handling along the lines of that used in your C implementation.

Problem: Maintain Linked List Tail Pointer

- **head** and **tail** are global pointers to the first and last element, respectively, of a singly linked list of integers. Implement C functions for the following prototypes:

```
int Delete(element *elem);
int InsertAfter(element *elem, int data);
```

> The argument to **Delete** is the element to be deleted. The two arguments to **InsertAfter** give the data for the new element and the element after which the new element is to be inserted. It should be possible to insert at the beginning of the list by calling **InsertAfter** with NULL as the element argument. These functions should return 1 if successful and 0 if unsuccessful.
>
> Your functions must keep the head and tail pointers current.

This problem seems relatively straightforward. Deletion and insertion are common operations for a linked list, and you should be accustomed to using a head pointer to locate a linked list. The requirement of maintaining a tail pointer is the only unusual aspect of this problem. This requirement doesn't seem to fundamentally change anything about the list or the way you operate on it, so it doesn't look as if you need to design any new algorithms. Just make sure to update the head and tail pointers when necessary.

When will you need to update these pointers? Obviously, operations in the middle of a long list will not affect either the head or tail. You need to update the pointers only when you change the list such that a different element appears at the beginning or end. More specifically, when you insert a new element at either end of the list, that element becomes the new beginning or end of the list. When you delete an element at the beginning or end of the list, the next-to-first or next-to-last element becomes the new first or last element.

For each operation you will have a general case for operations in the middle of the list and special cases for operations at either end. When you are dealing with many special cases, it can be easy to miss some of them, especially if some of the special cases have more specific special cases of their own. One technique for identifying special cases is to consider what circumstances are likely to lead to special cases being invoked. Then, you can check to see whether your proposed implementation works in each of these circumstances. If you discover a circumstance that creates a problem, you have discovered a new special case.

We already discussed the circumstances where you are instructed to operate on the ends of the list. Another problem-prone circumstance is a NULL pointer argument. The only other thing that can change is the list on which you are operating—specifically its length. What lengths of lists might create problematic circumstances? You can expect somewhat different cases for the beginning, middle, and end of the list. Any list that doesn't have these three distinct classes of elements could lead to additional special cases. An empty list has no elements, so it obviously has no beginning, middle, or end elements. A one-element list has no middle elements and one element that is both the beginning and end element. A two-element list has distinct beginning and end elements, but no middle element. Any list longer than this has all three classes of elements and is effectively the general case of lists—unlikely to lead to additional special cases. Based on this reasoning, you should explicitly check that your implementation works correctly for lists of length 0, 1, and 2.

At this point in the problem, you can begin writing `Delete`. As we said, you need a special case for deleting the first element of the list. You can compare the element to be deleted to `head` to determine if you need to invoke this case.

```
int Delete(element *elem)
{
    if (elem == head) {
        head = elem->next;
        free(elem);
        return 1;
    }
    ...
```

Now write the general middle case. You'll need an element pointer to keep track of your position in the list (we'll call the pointer `curPos`). Recall that to delete an element from a linked list, you need a pointer to the preceding element so you can change its next pointer. The easiest way to find the preceding element is to compare `curPos->next` to `elem`, so `curPos` points to the preceding element when you find `elem`. You also need to construct your loop so as not to miss any elements. If you initialize `curPos` to head, then `curPos->next` starts as the second element of the list. Starting at the second item is fine because you treat the first element as a special case, but make your first check before advancing `curPos` or you'll miss the second element. If `curPos` becomes NULL, you have reached the end of the list without finding the element you were supposed to delete, so you should return failure. The middle case yields the following (added code is bold):

```
int Delete(element *elem)
{
    element *curPos = head;

    if (elem == head) {
        head = elem->next;
        free(elem);
        return 1;
    }

    while (curPos) {
        if (curPos->next == elem) {
            curPos->next = elem->next;
            free(elem);
            return 1;
        }
        curPos = curPos->next;
    }

    return 0;
    ...
```

Next, consider the last element case. The last element's next pointer is NULL. To remove it from the list, you need to make the next-to-last element's next pointer NULL and free the last element. If you examine the loop constructed for middle elements, you will see that it can delete the last element as well as middle elements. The only difference is that you need to update the tail pointer when you delete the last element. If you set `curPos->next` to NULL, you know you changed the end of the list and must update the tail pointer. Adding this to complete the function, you get the following:

```
int Delete(element *elem)
{
    element *curPos = head;

    if (elem == head) {
        head = elem->next;
        free(elem);
    }

    while (curPos) {
        if (curPos->next == elem) {
            curPos->next = elem->next;
            free(elem);
            if (curPos->next == NULL)
                tail = curPos;
            return 1;
        }
```

```
        curPos = curPos->next;
    }

    return 0;
}
```

This solution covers the three argument-determined special cases we discussed. Before you present the interviewer with this solution, you should check behavior for NULL pointer arguments and the three potentially problematic list length circumstances. What happens if elem is NULL? The while loop traverses the list until curPos->next is NULL (when curPos is the last element). Then on the next line, evaluating elem->next dereferences a NULL pointer. Because it's never possible to delete NULL from the list, the easiest way to fix this problem is to return 0 if elem is NULL.

If the list has zero elements, then head and tail are both NULL. Because you'll be checking that elem isn't NULL, elem == head will always be false. Further, because head is NULL, curPos will be NULL, and the body of the while loop won't be executed. There doesn't seem to be any problem with zero element lists. The function simply returns 0 because nothing can be deleted from an empty list.

Now try a one-element list. In this case, head and tail both point to the one element, which is the only element you can delete. Again, elem == head is true. elem->next is NULL, so you correctly set head to NULL and free the element; however, tail still points to the element you just freed. As you can see, you need another special case to set tail to NULL for one-element lists. What about two-element lists? Deleting the first element causes head to point to the remaining element, as it should. Similarly, deleting the last element causes tail to be correctly updated. The lack of middle elements doesn't seem to be a problem. You can add the two additional special cases and then move on to InsertAfter:

```
int Delete(element *elem)
{
    element *curPos = head;

    if (!elem)
        return 0;

    if (elem == head) {
        head = elem->next;
        free(elem);
        /* special case for 1 element list */
        if (!head)
            tail = NULL;
```

```
            return 1;
        }

    while (curPos) {
        if (curPos->next == elem) {
            curPos->next = elem->next;
            free(elem);
            if (curPos->next == NULL)
                tail = curPos;
            return 1;
        }
        curPos = curPos->next;
    }

    return 0;
}
```

You can apply similar reasoning to writing `InsertAfter`. Because you are allocating a new element in this function, you must take care to check that the allocation was successful and that you don't leak any memory. Many of the special cases encountered in `Delete` are relevant in `InsertAfter`, however, and the code is structurally very similar.

```
int InsertAfter (element *elem, int data)
{
    element *newElem, *curPos = head;

    newElem = (element *) malloc(sizeof(element));
    if (!newElem)
        return 0;
    newElem->data = data;

    /* Insert at beginning of list */
    if (!elem) {
        newElem->next = head;
        head = newElem;

        /* Special case for empty list */
        if (!tail)
            tail = newElem;
        return 1;
    }

    while (curPos) {
        if (curPos == elem) {
            newElem->next = curPos->next;
            curPos->next = newElem;

            /* Special case for inserting at end of list */
```

```
            if (!(newElem->next))
                tail = newElem;
            return 1;
        }
        curPos = curPos->next;
    }

    /* Insert position not found; free element and return failure */
    free(newElem);
    return 0;
}
```

This problem turns out to be an exercise in special cases. It's not particularly interesting or satisfying to solve, but it's very good practice. Many interview problems have special cases, so you should expect to encounter them frequently. In the real world of programming, unhandled special cases represent bugs that may be difficult to find, reproduce, and fix. A programmer who identifies special cases as he is coding is likely to be more productive than one who finds special cases through debugging. Intelligent interviewers recognize this and pay attention to whether a candidate identifies special cases as part of the coding process or needs to be prompted to recognize special cases.

Problem: Bugs in RemoveHead

■ **Find and fix the bugs in the following function that is supposed to remove the head element from a singly linked list:**

```
void RemoveHead(node *head)
{
    free(head);          /* Line 1 */
    head = head->next;   /* Line 2 */
}
```

These bug-finding problems occur with some frequency, so it's worthwhile to discuss a generic strategy that you can apply to this and other problems.

Because you will generally be given only a small amount of code to analyze, your bug-finding strategy will be a little different than in real-world programming. You don't need to worry about interactions with other modules or other parts of the program. Instead, you must do a systematic analysis of every line of the function without the help of a debugger. There are four common problems areas to consider for any function you are given:

1. **Check that the data comes into the function properly.** Make sure you aren't accessing a variable that you don't have, you aren't reading something as an int that should be a long, and you have all the values you need to perform the task.

2. **Check that each line of the function works correctly.** The function is undoubtedly performing a task. Verify that the task is executed correctly at each line and that the desired result is produced at the end.

3. **Check that the data comes out of the function correctly.** The return value should be what you expect. Also, if the function is expected to update any caller variables, make sure this occurs.

4. **Check the common error conditions.** Error conditions vary depending on the specifics of a problem. They tend to involve unusual argument values. For instance, functions that operate on data structures may have trouble with empty or nearly empty data structures; functions that take a pointer as an argument may fail if passed a NULL pointer.

Starting with the first step, verify that data comes into the function properly. In a linked list, you can access every node given only the head. Because you are passed the list head, you have access to all the data you require—no bugs so far.

Now do a line-by-line analysis of the function. The first line frees head—OK so far. Line 2 then assigns a new value to head but uses the old value of head to do this. That's a problem. You have already freed head, and you are now dereferencing freed memory. You could try reversing the lines, but this would cause the element after head to be freed. You need to free head, but you also need its next value after it has been freed. You can solve this problem by using a temporary variable to store head's next value. Then you can free head and use the temporary variable to update head. These steps make the function look like the following:

```
void RemoveHead(node *head)
{
    node *temp = head->next;   /* Line 1 */
    free(head);                /* Line 2 */
    head = temp;               /* Line 3 */
}
```

Now, move to step 3 of the strategy and make sure the function returns values properly. Though there is no explicit return value, there is an implicit one. This function is supposed to update the caller's head value. In C all function parameters are passed by value, so functions get a local copy of each argument, and any changes made to that local copy are not reflected outside the function. Any new value you assign to head on line 3 has no effect—another bug. To correct this, you need a way to change the value of head in the calling code. Variables cannot be passed by reference in C, so the solution is to pass a pointer to the variable you wish to change—in this case, a pointer to the head pointer. After the change, the function should look like this:

```
void RemoveHead(node **head)
{
    node *temp = (*head)->next;  /* Line 1 */
    free(*head);                 /* Line 2 */
    *head = temp;                /* Line 3 */
}
```

Now you can move on to the fourth case and check error conditions. Check a one-element and a zero-element list. In a one-element list, this function works properly. It removes the one element and sets the head to NULL, indicating that the head was removed. Now take a look at the zero-element case. A zero-element list is simply a NULL pointer. If head is a NULL pointer, you would dereference a NULL pointer on line 1. To correct this, check whether head is a NULL pointer and make sure not to dereference it in this case. This check makes the function look like the following:

```
void RemoveHead(node **head)
{
    node *temp;
    if (!(*head)) {
        temp = (*head)->next;
        free(*head);
        *head = temp;
    }
}
```

You have checked that the body of the function works properly, that the function is called correctly and returns values correctly, and that you have dealt with the error cases. You can declare your debugging effort complete and present this version of RemoveHead to the interviewer as your solution.

Problem: Mth-to-Last Element of a Linked List

- Given a singly linked list, devise a time- and space-efficient algorithm to find the *m*th-to-last element of the list. Implement your algorithm, taking care to handle relevant error conditions. Define mth to last such that when $m = 0$, the last element of the list is returned.

Why is this a difficult problem? Finding the mth element from the beginning of a linked list would be an extremely trivial task. Singly linked lists are data structures that can be traversed only in the forward direction. For this problem you are asked to find a given element based on its position relative to the end of the list. While you traverse the list, however, you don't know where the end is, and when you find the end there is no easy way to back-track the required number of elements.

You may want to tell your interviewer that a singly linked list is a particularly poor choice for a data structure when you frequently need to find the mth-to-last element. If you were to encounter such a problem while implementing a real program, the correct and most efficient solution would probably be to substitute a more suitable data structure (such as a doubly linked list) for the singly linked list. Although this comment shows that you understand good design, the interviewer will still want you to solve the problem as it was originally phrased.

How then can you get around the problem that there is no way to traverse backward through this data structure? You know that the element you want is m elements from the end of the list. So, if you traverse m elements forward from an element and that places you exactly at the end of the list, you have found the element you were searching for. One approach is to simply test each element in this manner until you find the one you're searching for. Intuitively, this feels like an inefficient solution because you will be traversing over the same elements many times. If you analyze this potential solution more closely, you will see that you would be traversing m elements for most of the elements in the list. If the length of the list is n, the algorithm would be approximately $O(mn)$. You need to find a solution more efficient than $O(mn)$.

What if you stored some of the elements (or, more likely, pointers to the elements) as you traversed the list? Then when you hit the end of the list, you could look back m elements in your storage data structure to find the appropriate element. If you use an appropriate temporary storage data structure, this algorithm would be $O(n)$ because it requires only one traversal through the list. Yet this approach is far from perfect. As m becomes large the temporary data structure would become large as well. In the worst-case scenario, this approach might require almost as much storage space as the list itself—not a particularly space-efficient algorithm.

Perhaps working back from the end of the list is not the best approach. Since counting from the beginning of the list is trivial, is there any way to count from the beginning to find the desired element? The desired element is m from the end of the list, and you know the value of m. It must also be l elements from the beginning of the list, although you don't know l. However, $l + m = n$, the length of the list. It's easy to count all the elements in the list. Then you can calculate $l = n - m$, and traverse l elements from the beginning of the list. Although this process involves two passes through the list, it's still O(n). It requires only a few variables' worth of storage, so this method is a significant improvement over the previous attempt. If you could change the functions that modify the list such that they would increment a count variable for every element added and decrement it for every element removed, you could eliminate the count pass, making this a relatively efficient algorithm. Again, though this point is worth mentioning to the interviewer, he is probably looking for a solution that doesn't modify the data structure or place any restrictions on the methods used to access it.

Assuming you must explicitly count the elements in the current algorithm, you will have to make almost two complete traversals of the linked list. A very large list on a memory-constrained system might exist mostly in paged-out virtual memory (on disk). In such a case, each complete traversal of the list would require a large amount of disk access to swap the relevant portions of the list in and out of memory. Under these conditions an algorithm that made only one complete traversal of the list might be significantly faster than an algorithm that made two traversals, even though they would both be O(n). Is there a way to find the target element with a single traversal?

The counting-from-the-beginning algorithm obviously demands that you know the length of the list. If you can't track the length so that you know it ahead of time, you can determine the length only by a full-list traversal. There doesn't seem to be much hope for getting this algorithm down to a single traversal. Try reconsidering the previous linear time algorithm, which required only one traversal but was rejected for requiring too much storage. Is it possible to reduce the storage requirements of this approach?

When you reach the end of the list, you are really interested in only one of the m elements you've been tracking—the element that is m elements behind your current position. You are tracking the rest of the m elements merely because the element m behind your current position changes every time your position advances. Keeping a queue m elements long where you add the current element to the head and remove an element from the end every time you advance your current position ensures that the last element in the queue is always m elements behind your current position.

In effect, you are using this m element data structure to make it easy to implicitly advance an m-behind pointer in lock step with your current position pointer. But this data structure is unnecessary—you can explicitly advance the m-behind pointer by following each element's next pointer just as you do for your current position pointer. This is as easy as (or perhaps easier than) implicitly advancing by shifting through a queue, and it eliminates the need to track all the elements between your current position pointer and your m-behind pointer. This algorithm seems to be the one you've been looking for: linear time, a single traversal, and negligible storage requirements. Now you just need to work out the details.

You'll use two pointers: a current position pointer and an m-behind pointer. You will have to ensure that the two pointers are actually spaced m elements apart; then you can advance them at the same rate. When your current position is the end of the list, m-behind will point to the mth-to-last element. How can you get the pointers spaced properly? If you count elements as you traverse the list, you can move the current position pointer to the mth element of the list. If you then start the m-behind pointer at the beginning of the list, they will be spaced m elements apart. Are there any error conditions you need to watch for? If the list is less than m elements long, then there is no mth-to-last element. In such a case, you would run off the end of the list as you tried to advance the current position pointer to the mth element, possibly dereferencing a NULL pointer in the process. So, check that you don't hit the end of the list while doing this initial advance.

With this caveat in mind, you can implement the algorithm. Note that it's easy to introduce off-by-one errors in any code that spaces any two things m items apart or counts m items from a given point. You may want to refer to the exact definition of "mth to last" given in the problem and try a little example on paper to make sure you get your counts right, particularly in the initial advancement of the current pointer.

```
element *FindMToLastElement(element *head, int m)
{
    element *current, *mBehind;
    int i;

    /* Advance current m elements from beginning,
     * checking for the end of the list
     */
```

```
    current = head;
    for (i = 0; i < m; i++) {
        if (current->next) {
            current = current->next;
        } else {
            return NULL;
        }
    }

    /* Start mBehind at beginning and advance pointers
     * together until current hits last element
     */
    mBehind = head;
    while (current->next) {
        current = current->next;
        mBehind = mBehind->next;
    }

    /* mBehind now points to the element we were
     * searching for, so return it
     */
    return mBehind;
}
```

Problem: List Flattening

- Start with a standard doubly linked list. Now imagine that in addition to next and previous pointers, each element has a child pointer, which may or may not point to a separate doubly linked list. These child lists may have one or more children of their own, and so on, to produce a multilevel data structure, as shown in Figure 3.3.

  Flatten the list so that all the nodes appear in a single-level, doubly linked list. You are given the head and tail of the first level of the list. Each node is a C struct with the following definition:

```
typedef struct nodeT {
    struct nodeT *next;
    struct nodeT *prev;
    struct nodeT *child;
    int value;
} node;
```

This list-flattening question gives you plenty of freedom. You have simply been asked to flatten the list. There are many ways to accomplish this task. Each way results in a one-level list with a different node ordering.

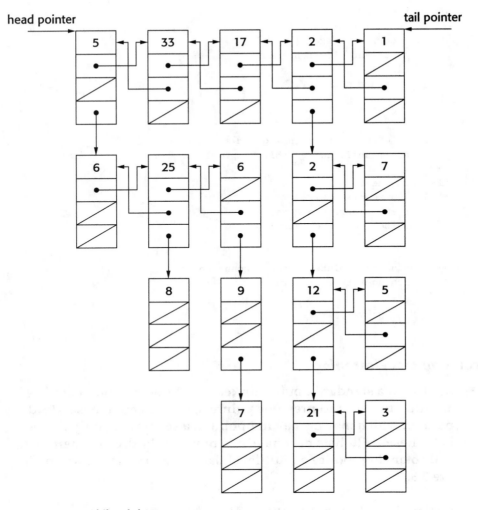

Figure 3.3 Multilevel data structure.

Start by considering several choices for algorithms and the node orders they would yield. Then implement the algorithm that looks easiest and most efficient.

Begin by looking at the data structure itself. This data structure is a little unusual for a list. It has levels and children—somewhat like a tree. A tree also has levels and children, but in a tree, no nodes on the same level are connected. You might try to use a common tree traversal algorithm and copy each node into a new list as you visit it as a simple way to flatten the structure.

The data structure is not exactly a normal tree, so any traversal algorithm you use will have to be modified. From the perspective of a tree, each separate child list in the data structure forms a single extended tree-node. This may not seem too bad: Where a standard traversal algorithm checks the child pointers of each tree-node directly, you just need to do a linked list traversal to check all the child pointers. Every time you check a node, you can copy it to a duplicate list. This duplicate list will be your flattened list. Before you work out the details of this solution, consider its efficiency.

Every node is examined once, so this is an O(*n*) solution. There is likely to be some overhead for the recursion or data structure required for the traversal. Also, you are making a duplicate copy of each node to create the new list. This copying is inefficient, especially if the structure is very large. Therefore, you should search for a more efficient solution that doesn't require so much copying.

So far, the proposed solution has concentrated on an algorithm and let the ordering follow. Instead, try focusing on an ordering and then try to deduce an algorithm. You can focus on the data structure's levels as a source of ordering. It helps to define the parts of a level as *child lists*. Just as rooms in a hotel are ordered by level, you can order nodes by the level in which they occur. Every node is in a level and appears in an ordering within that level (arranging the child lists from left to right). Therefore, you have a logical ordering just like hotel rooms. You can order by starting with all the first-level nodes, followed by all the second-level nodes, followed by all the third-level nodes, and so on. Applying these rules to the example data structure, you should get the ordering shown in Figure 3.4.

Now try to discover an algorithm that yields this ordering. One property of this ordering is that you never rearrange the order of the nodes in their respective levels. So, you could connect all the nodes on each level into a list and then join all the connected levels. But to find all the nodes on a given level so that you can join them, you would have to do a breadth-first search of that level. Breadth-first searching is inefficient, so you should continue to look for a better solution.

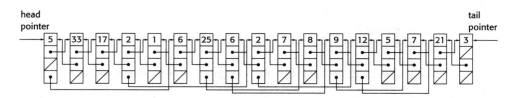

Figure 3.4   Ordering of nodes.

In Figure 3.3, the second level is composed of two child lists. Each child list starts with a different child of a first-level node. You could try to append the child lists one at a time to the end of the first level instead of combining the child lists.

To append the child lists one at a time, traverse the first level from the start, following the next pointers. Every time you encounter a node with a child, append the child (and thus the child list) to the end of the first level and update the tail pointer. Eventually, you will append the entire second level to the end of the first level. You can continue traversing the first level and arrive at the start of the old second level. If you continue this process of appending children to the end of the first level, you will eventually append every child list to the end and have a flattened list in the required order. More formally, this algorithm is as follows:

Start at the beginning of the first level

While you are not at the end of the first level

    If the current node has a child

        Append the child to the end of the first level

        Update the tail pointer

    Advance to next node

This algorithm is easy to implement because it's so simple. In terms of efficiency, every node after the first level is examined twice. Each node is examined once when you update the tail pointer for each child list and once when you examine the node to see if it has a child. The nodes in the first level get examined only once when you examine them for children because you had a first-level tail pointer when you began. So, there are no more than $2n$ comparisons in this algorithm, and it is an $O(n)$ solution. This is the best time order you can achieve because every node must be examined.[2]

The code for this algorithm is as follows:

```
void FlattenList(node *head, node **tail)3
{
    node *curNode =  head;
    while (curNode){
        /* The current node has a child */
```

[2]There are other, equally efficient solutions to this problem. One such solution involves inserting child lists after their parents rather than at the end of the list.
[3]You need a pointer to the tail pointer so that changes to the tail pointer are retained when the function returns.

```
        if (curNode->child) {
            Append(curNode->child, tail);
        }
        curNode = curNode->next;
    }
}


/* Appends the child list to the end of the tail and updates
 * the tail.
 */
void Append(node *child, node **tail)
{
    node *curNode;

    /* Append the child child list to the end */
    (*tail)->next = child;
    child->prev = *tail;

    /*Find the new tail, which is the end of the child child
     *list.
     */
    for (curNode = child; curNode->next;
        curNode = curNode->next)
        ; /* Body intentionally empty */

    /* Update the tail pointer now that curNode is the new
     * tail.
     */
    *tail = curNode;
}
```

- **Unflatten the list. Restore the data structure to its original condition before it was passed to FlattenList.**

You already know a lot about this data structure. One important insight is that you can create the flattened list by combining all of the child lists into one long level. Now, to get back the original list, you must separate the long flattened list back into its original child lists. First, try doing the exact opposite of what you did to create the list. When flattening the list, you traversed down the list from the start and added child lists to the end. To reverse this, you go backward from the tail and break off parts of the first level. You could break off a part when you encounter a node that was the beginning of a child list in the unflattened list. Unfortunately, this is more difficult than it might seem because you can't easily determine whether a particular node is a child (indicating that it started a child list) in the original data structure. The only way to determine whether a node is a child is to scan through the child pointers of all the previous nodes.

All this scanning would be inefficient, so you should examine some additional possibilities to find an efficient solution.

One way to get around the child node problem is to go through the list from start to end, storing pointers to all the child nodes in a separate data structure. Then you could go backward through the list and separate every child node. Looking up nodes in this way frees you from repeated scans to determine whether a node is a child or not. This is a good solution, but it still requires an extra data structure. Now try looking for a solution without an extra data structure.

It seems you have exhausted all the possibilities for going backward through the list, so try an algorithm that traverses the list from the start to the end. You still can't immediately determine whether a node is a child. One advantage of going forward, however, is that you can find all the child nodes in the same order that you appended them to the first level. You would also know that every child began a child list in the original list. If you separate each child node from the node before it, you get the unflattened list back.

You can't simply traverse the list from the start, find each node with a child, and separate the child from its previous node. You would get to the end of the list at the break between the first and second level, leaving the rest of the data structure untraversed. This solution is not too bad, though. You can traverse every child list, starting with the first level (which is a child list itself). When you find a child, continue traversing the original child list and also traverse the newly found child list. You can't traverse both at the same time, however. You can save one of these locations in a data structure and traverse it later. But, rather than designing and implementing a data structure, you can use recursion. Specifically, every time you find a node with a child, separate the child from its previous node, start traversing the new child list, and then continue traversing the original child list.

This is an efficient algorithm because each node gets checked at most twice, resulting in an $O(n)$ running time. Again, an $O(n)$ running time is the best you can do because you must check each node at least once to see if it is a child. In the average case, the number of function calls is small in relation to the number of nodes, so the recursive overhead is not too bad. In the worst case, the number of function calls is no more than the number of nodes. This solution is approximately as efficient as the earlier proposal that required an extra data structure, but somewhat simpler and easier to code. Therefore, this recursive solution would probably be the best choice in an interview. In outline form, the algorithm looks like the following:

Explore path:

> While not at the end
>> If current node has a child
>>> Separate the child from its previous node
>>> Explore path beginning with the child
>>> Go onto the next node

The code for this algorithm is as follows:

```
/*This is a wrapper function that also updates the tail pointer.*/
void Unflatten(node *start, node **tail)
{
    node *curNode;
    ExploreAndSeparate(start);

    /* Update the tail pointer */
    for (curNode = start; curNode->next;
                curNode = curNode->next)
        ; /* Body intentionally empty */
    *tail = curNode;
}


/* This is the function that actually does the recursion and
 * the separation
 */
void ExploreAndSeparate(node *childListStart)
{
    node *curNode = childListStart;

    while (curNode) {
        if (curNode->child) {
            /* terminates the child list before the child */
            curNode->child->prev->next = NULL;
            /* starts the child list beginning with the child */
            curNode->child->prev = NULL;
            ExploreAndSeparate(curNode->child);
        }
        curNode = curNode->next;
    }
}
```

Problem: Null or Cycle

- You are given a linked list that is either NULL-terminated (acyclic), as shown in Figure 3.5, or ends in a cycle (cyclic), as shown in Figure 3.6.

head pointer

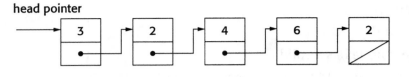

Figure 3.5   An acyclic list.

head pointer

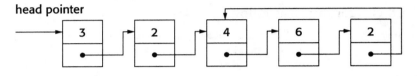

Figure 3.6   A cyclic list.

> **Write a function that takes a pointer to the head of a list and determines if the list is cyclic or acyclic. Your function should return 0 if the list is acyclic and 1 if it is cyclic. You may not modify the list in any way.**

Start by looking at the pictures to see if you can determine an intuitive way to differentiate a cyclic list and an acyclic list.

The difference between the two lists appears at their ends. In the cyclic list, there is an end node that points back to one of the earlier nodes. In the acyclic list, there is an end node that is NULL terminated. Thus, if you can find this end node, you can test whether the list is cyclic or acyclic. In the acyclic list, it is easy to find this end node. You traverse the list until you reach a NULL terminated node. In the cyclic list, though, it is more difficult. If you just traverse the list, you go in a circle and won't know if you're in a cyclic list or just a long acyclic list. You need a more sophisticated approach.

Try looking at the end node a bit more. The end node points to a node that has another node pointing at it. This means that there are two pointers pointing at the same node. This node is the only node with two elements pointing at it. You can design an algorithm around this property. You can traverse the list and check every node to see if there are two other nodes pointing at it. If you find such a node, the list must be cyclic. Otherwise, the list is acyclic, and you will eventually encounter a NULL pointer.

Unfortunately, it is difficult to check the number of nodes pointing at each element. See if you can find another special property of the end node in a cyclic list. When you traverse the list, the end node's next node is a node that you have previously encountered. Instead of checking for a node with two pointers pointing at it, you can check whether you have already encountered a node. If you find a previously encountered node, you have a cyclic list. If you encounter a NULL pointer, you have an acyclic list. This is only part of the algorithm. You still have to figure out how to determine whether or not you have previously encountered a node.

The easiest way to do this would be to mark each element as you visit it, but you've been told you're not allowed to modify the list. You could keep track of the nodes you've encountered by putting them in a separate, already-encountered list. Then you would compare the current node to all of the nodes in the already-encountered list. If the current node ever points to a node in the already-encountered list, you have a cycle. Otherwise, you'll get to the end of the list and see that it's NULL terminated and thus acyclic. This would work, but in the worst case the already-encountered list would require as much memory as the original list itself. See if you can reduce this memory requirement.

What are you storing in the already-encountered list? The already-encountered list's first node points to the original list's first node, its second node points to the original list's second node, its third node points to the original list's third node . . . You're creating a list that mirrors the original list. This is unnecessary—you can just use the original list.

Try this approach. Because you know your current node in the list and the start of the list, you can compare your current node's next pointer to all of its previous nodes directly. For the ith node, compare its next pointer to nodes 1 to $i - 1$. If any are equal, you have a cycle.

What's the time order of this algorithm? For the first node, 0 previous nodes are examined; for the second node, one previous node is examined; for the third node, two previous nodes are examined... Thus, the algorithm examines $0 + 1 + 2 + 3 + ... + n$ nodes. As discussed in Chapter 2, "Approaches to Programming Problems," such an algorithm is $O(n^2)$.

That's about as far as you can go with this approach. Although it's difficult to discover without some sort of hint, there is a better solution involving two pointers. What can you do with two pointers that you couldn't do with one? You can advance them on top of each other, but then you might as well have one pointer. You could advance them with a fixed interval between them, but this doesn't seem to gain anything. What happens if you advance the pointers at different speeds?

In the acyclic list, the faster pointer will reach the end. In the cyclic list they will both loop endlessly. The faster pointer will eventually catch up with and pass the slower pointer. If the fast pointer ever passes the slower pointer, you have a cyclic list. If it encounters a NULL pointer, you have an acyclic list. In outline form, this algorithm looks like this:

Start two pointers at the head of the list

Loop infinitely

    If the fast pointer reaches a NULL pointer

      Return that the list is NULL terminated

    If the fast pointer moves onto or over the slow pointer

      Return that there is a cycle

    Advance the slow pointer one node

    Advance the fast pointer two nodes

You can now implement this solution.

```
/* Takes a pointer to the head of a linked list and determines if
 * the list ends in a cycle or is NULL terminated
 */
int DetermineTermination(node *head)
{
    node *fast, *slow;
    fast = slow = head;
    while (1) {
        if (!fast || !fast->next)⁴
            return 0;
        else if (fast == slow || fast->next == slow)
            return 1;
        else {
            slow = slow->next;
            fast = fast->next->next;
        }
    }
}
```

Is this algorithm faster than the earlier solution? If this list is acyclic, the faster pointer comes to the end after examining n nodes while the slower pointer traverses $\frac{1}{2} n$ nodes. Thus, you examine $\frac{3}{2} n$ nodes, which is an O(n) algorithm.

---

[4]This statement uses the short circuit property of the || operator.

What about a cyclic list? The slower pointer will never go around any loop more than once. When the slower pointer has examined n nodes, the faster pointer will have examined $2n$ nodes and have "passed" the slower pointer, regardless of the loop's size. Therefore, in the worst case you examine $3n$ nodes, which is still $O(n)$. Regardless of whether the list is cyclic or acyclic, this two-pointer approach is much better than the one-pointer approach to the problem.

CHAPTER 4

Trees and Graphs

Trees and graphs are common data structures in programming, and so they are both fair game in a programming interview. Trees, in particular, come up frequently because they allow an interviewer to easily test your knowledge of recursion and run-time analysis. Trees are also simple enough that you can implement them within the time constraints of an interview. Although graph problems are interesting, they are usually very complicated and do not lend themselves to interview questions. Thus, we will put most of our emphasis on trees.

Trees

A tree is made up of nodes (data elements) with zero, one, or several child pointers or references to other elements. Each node has only one other node pointing to or referencing it.

The result is a data structure that looks like Figure 4.1.

As in a linked list, a node's pointers and data are bound together by a `struct` (C), `class` (C++ and Java), or similar construct in another language. Following is a sample C node type declaration for a tree of integers:

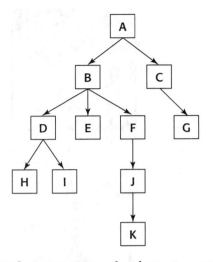

Figure 4.1 Tree of nodes.

```
typedef struct nodeT {
    /* struct nodeT** because it points to an array of struct nodeT* */
    struct nodeT **children;
    int value;
} node;
```

In this definition, `children` points to an array that keeps track of all the nodes that this node points to.

Solutions to tree problems can be implemented in any language that includes pointers or references. C is still the most common interview language, so our examples will be in C.

Looking at the tree shown in Figure 4.1, you will see that there is only one top-level node. From this node, it is possible to follow pointers and reach every other node. This top-level node is called the *root*. The root is the only node from which you are guaranteed to have a path to every other node. The root node is inherently the start of any tree. Therefore, people will often say tree when talking about the root node of the tree.

Following is some additional tree-related vocabulary:

Parent. A node that points to other nodes is the *parent* of those nodes. Every node except the root has one parent. In Figure 4.1, B is the parent of D, E, and F.

Child. A node is the *child* of any node that points to it. So in Figure 4.1, D, E, and F are child nodes of B.

Descendant. All the nodes that can be reached by following a path of child nodes from a particular node are the *descendants* of that node. In Figure 4.1, D, E, F, H, I, J, and K are the descendants of B.

Ancestor. An *ancestor* of a node is any other node that can reach it by following a series of children. For example, A, B, and D are the ancestors of I.

Leaves. The *leaves* are the nodes that do not have any children. G, H, I, and K are leaves.

Binary Trees

So far, we have been using the most general definition of a tree. In practice, when an interviewer says "tree," he usually means a special type of tree called a *binary tree*. In a binary tree, each node has no more than two children. Often, the two children are called *right* and *left*. Figure 4.2 shows an example of a binary tree.

Adapting the previous node definition for a binary tree yields the following:

```
typedef struct nodeT {
    struct nodeT *left;
    struct nodeT *right;
    int value;
} node;
```

When an element has no left or right child, the corresponding pointer is set to NULL.

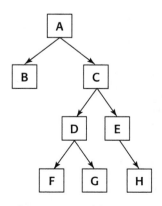

Figure 4.2   A binary tree.

Problems involving only binary trees can often be solved more quickly than equivalent problems about generic trees, but they are no less challenging. Because time is at a premium in an interview, most tree questions will be binary tree questions. If an interviewer just says "tree," it's a good idea to clarify whether he is referring to a generic tree or a binary tree.

LESSON   People often say "tree" when they mean "binary tree."

Binary Search Trees

Trees are often used to store sorted or ordered data. By far, the most common way to store data in a tree is using a special tree called a *binary search tree* (BST). In a BST, the value of each node's left child is less than or equal to its value, and the value of each node's right child is greater than or equal to its value. Figure 4.3 is an example of a BST.

BSTs are so common, in fact, that many people mean a BST when they say "tree."

LESSON   People often say "tree" when they mean "binary search tree."

Lookup

One advantage of a binary search tree is that the lookup operation (locating a particular node in the tree) is fast and simple. This is particularly useful for data storage. In outline form, the algorithm to perform a lookup in a BST is as follows:

Start at the root node

Loop while current node isn't NULL

    If the current node's value is equal to your value

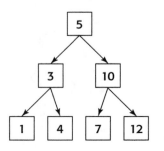

Figure 4.3   A binary search tree.

Return the current node

If the current node's value is less than your value

Make the left node your current node

If the current node's value is greater than your value

Make the right node your current node

End loop

If you fall out of the loop, the node wasn't in the tree.

For example, to look up the value 6, do the following:

```
node *FindSixNode(node *root)
{
    node *curNode = root;
    while (curNode) {
        /* You've found the curNode */
        if (curNode->value == 6) return curNode;
        else if (curNode->value < 6) curNode = curNode->right;
        else if (curNode->value > 6) curNode = curNode->left;
    }
    return NULL;   /*No appropriate node exists */
}
```

This lookup is a fast operation because you eliminate half the nodes from your search on each iteration by choosing either the left child or the right child. In the worst case, you will know whether the lookup was successful by the time there is only one node left to search. So, the running time of the lookup is equal to the number of times that you can halve n nodes before you get to 1. This number, x, is the same as the number of times you can double 1 before reaching n, and it can be expressed as $2^x = n$. You can find x using a logarithm. For example, $\log_2 8 = 3$ because $2^3 = 8$, and so the running time of the lookup operation is $O(\log_2(n))$. It is common to leave off the base 2^1 and call this $O(\log(n))$. $\log(n)$ is very fast. Consider that $\log_2 1{,}000{,}000{,}000 \approx 30$.

LESSON   Lookup is an $O(\log(n))$ operation in a binary search tree.

There is one caveat to saying that lookup is $O(\log(n))$ in a BST. Lookup is only $O(\log(n))$ if you can guarantee that the number of nodes remaining to be searched will be halved or nearly halved on each iteration. In the worst case, each node has only one child. In such a case, you have a

---

[1]Logarithms with different bases differ by a constant factor, so the base is ignored in big-O notation.

linked list because each node points to only one other node. Lookup then becomes an O(n) operation just as in a linked list. The good news is that there are ways to guarantee that every node has approximately the same number of nodes on its left side as its right.[2] A tree with approximately the same number of nodes on each side is called a balanced tree.

Without going into too much detail (as the special cases get very nasty), it is also possible to delete and insert into a balanced BST in O($\log(n)$) time.

LESSON   Deletion and insertion are O($\log(n)$) operations in binary search trees.

Binary search trees have other important properties. For example, it is possible to obtain the smallest element by following all the left child pointers and to obtain the largest element by following all of the right child pointers. The nodes can be printed out in order in O(n) time. It is even possible, given a node, to find the next highest node in O($\log(n)$) time.

Tree problems are often designed to test your ability to think recursively. Each node in a tree is the root of a subtree beginning at that node. This subtree property is conducive to recursion because recursion generally involves solving a problem in terms of similar subproblems and a base case. In tree recursion you start with a root, perform an action, and then move to the left or right subtree (or both, one after the other). This process continues until you reach a NULL pointer, which is the end of a tree (and a good base case). For example, the lookup operation can be implemented recursively as follows:

```
node *FindSixNode(node *root)
{
    if (!root) return NULL;
    else if (root->value == 6) return root;
    else if (root->value < 6) return LookupSix(root->right);
    else if (root->value > 6) return LookupSix(root->left);
}
```

Most problems with trees have this recursive form. A good way to start thinking about any problem involving a tree is to start thinking recursively.

LESSON   Many tree operations can be implemented recursively.

[2]The most common of these methods is called a red-black tree.

Heaps

Another common tree is a *heap*. All heaps are binary trees.[3] Heaps have the property that each node's value is less than its parent node's value, so the root node has the greatest value. The biggest advantage of a heap is that it is possible to find the maximum value in constant time by simply returning the root value. Insertion and deletion are still O(log(n)), but lookup becomes O(n). It is not possible to find the next-higher node to a given node in O(log(n)) time or to print out the nodes in sorted order in O(n) time as in a BST.

You could model the patients waiting in a hospital emergency room with a heap. As each patient enters, he is assigned a priority and put into the heap. A heart attack patient would get a higher priority than a patient with a stubbed toe. When a doctor becomes available, the doctor would want to examine the patient with the highest priority. The doctor can determine the patient with the highest priority by extracting the max value from the heap, which is a constant time operation.

LESSON   If extracting the max value needs to be fast, use a heap.

Common Searches

It's nice when you have a tree with ordering properties such as a BST or a heap. Often you're given a tree that isn't a BST or a heap. For example, you may have a tree that is a representation of a family tree or a company job hierarchy. You have to use different techniques to retrieve data from this kind of tree. One common class of problems involves searching for a particular node. There are two very common search algorithms for accomplishing this task.

Breadth-First Search

One way to search a tree is to do a *breadth-first search* (BFS). In a BFS you start with the root, move left to right across the second level, then move left to right across the third level, and so forth. You continue the search until you have examined all of the nodes or you find the node you are searching for. The time to find a node is O(n), so this type of search is best avoided for large trees. A BFS also uses a large amount of memory

---

[3]The data implementation of a heap can be different from the structures we discussed previously.

because it is necessary to store pointers to a level's child nodes while searching that level.

Depth-First Search

Another common way to search for a node is by using a *depth-first search* (DFS). A depth-first search follows one branch of the tree down as many levels as possible until the target node is found or the end is reached. When the search can't go down any farther, it is continued at the nearest ancestor with unexplored children. DFS has much lower memory requirements than BFS because it is not necessary to store all of the child pointers at each level. Also, DFS has the advantage that it doesn't examine any single level last (BFS examines the lowest level last). This is useful if you suspect that the node you are searching for will be in the lower levels. For example, if you were searching a job hierarchy tree looking for an employee who started less than three months ago, you would suspect that lower-level employees are more likely to have started recently. In this case, if the assumption were true, a DFS would usually find the target node more quickly than a BFS. There are other types of searches, but these are the two most common that you will encounter in an interview.

Traversals

One other common class of tree problems in an unordered tree is called a *traversal*. As opposed to searching for a particular node and stopping when you find it as in a search, a traversal visits every node and performs some operation on it. Again, there are many common types of traversals, each of which visits nodes in a different order. The three most common types of traversals are *preorder*, *in-order*, and *postorder*. Though you should be familiar with the term *traversal* and you may be asked to implement one, you won't be expected to memorize details about the various types, and any interviewer would happily define them for you. If you are asked to implement a traversal, you should strongly consider using recursion.

> **LESSON**   If you're asked to implement a traversal, recursion is a good way to start thinking about the problem.

Graphs

Graphs are more complicated than trees. They consist of nodes that have zero, one, or several pointers to other nodes. Unlike in a tree, many ele-

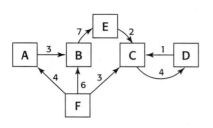

Figure 4.4 A directed graph.

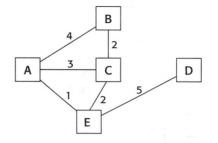

Figure 4.5 An undirected graph.

ments may point to the same node, possibly creating a loop. Also, the links themselves may have values or weights. These links are called *edges* because they may have more information than just a pointer. In a graph, edges can be one-way or two-way. A graph with one-way edges is called a *directed graph*. A graph with only two-way pointers is called an *undirected graph*. A directed graph is shown in Figure 4.4, and an undirected graph is shown in Figure 4.5.

Graphs are commonly used to model real-world problems that are difficult to model with other data structures. For example, a directed graph could represent aqueducts connecting cities. You might use such a graph to help you find the fastest way to get water from city A to city D. An undirected graph could also represent something complicated, like a series of relays in signal transmission.

Unlike trees, there are many ways to represent graph data structures in code. The choice of representation is often determined by the algorithm being implemented. Graphs are often used in real-world programming, but graph problems are difficult to solve in the time allotted for an interview. As such, they are very uncommon in interviews; the preceding overview of graph definitions should be sufficient.

Problem: Preorder Traversal

- Informally, a preorder traversal involves walking around the tree in a counter-clockwise manner starting at the root, sticking close to the edges, and printing out the nodes as you encounter them. For the tree shown in Figure 4.6, the result is 100, 50, 25, 75, 150, 125, 110, 175. Perform a preorder traversal of a binary search tree, printing the value of each node. Use the following function prototype:

```
void PreorderTraversal(node *root);
```

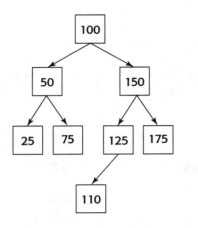

Figure 4.6 A binary search tree.

To discover an algorithm for printing out the nodes in the correct order, you should examine what happens as you print out the nodes. You go to the left as far as possible, come up the tree, go one node to the right, and then go to the left as far as possible, come up the tree again, and so on. You can think of this process in terms of subtrees.

The two largest subtrees are rooted at 50 and 150. You should note one very important thing about the nodes in these two subtrees. All of the nodes in the subtree rooted at 50 are printed out before any of the nodes in the subtree rooted at 150. Also, the root nodes are printed out before the rest of the respective subtree. Generally, for any node in a preorder traversal, you would print the node itself, then the left subtree, then the right subtree. If you begin the printing process at the root node, you would have a recursive definition as follows:

Print out the root (or subtree's root) value.

Do a preorder traversal on the left subtree.

Do a preorder traversal on the right subtree.

If you translate the steps to C code you get the following:

```
void PreorderTraversal(node *root)
{
    if (root)
        printf("%d\n", root->value);
    else
        return;
```

```
        PreorderTraversal(root->left);
        PreorderTraversal(root->right);
}
```

What's the running time on this algorithm? Every node gets examined once, so it's O(n).

Problem: Preorder Traversal, No Recursion

- Perform a preorder traversal of a binary search tree, printing the value of each node. This time you may not use recursion. Use the same function prototype:

```
void PreorderTraversal(node *root);
```

Without recursion, how do you solve the problem? Sometimes, recursive algorithms can be replaced with iterative algorithms that operate in a fundamentally different manner using different data structures, but can accomplish the same task. Consider the data structures you know and think about how they could be helpful. For instance, you might try using a list, an array, or another binary tree. Unfortunately, because recursion is so intrinsic to the definition of a preorder traversal, you may have trouble finding an entirely different iterative algorithm to use in place of the recursive algorithm. In such a case, the best course of action is to understand what is happening in recursion and try to emulate the process iteratively. Recursion implicitly uses a stack data structure by placing data on the call stack. That means there should be an equivalent solution that avoids recursion by explicitly using a stack. Assume you have a stack that can store node pointers (writing a stack is a separate problem). It has the following functions:[4]

```
    int Push(element **stack, void *data);
    int Pop(element **stack, void **data);
    int CreateStack(element **stack);
    int DeleteStack(element **stack);
```

Reexamine your recursive solution to plot exactly what is occurring. If you understand exactly how the recursive implementation implicitly stored data on the stack, you can write an iterative implementation that explicitly stores data on a stack in the same fashion.

The recursive algorithm, again, is as follows:

[4]If you're not sure what each of these functions does, look at "Stack Implementation" in Chapter 3.

Print out the root (or subtree's root) value.

Do a preorder traversal on the left subtree.

Do a preorder traversal on the right subtree.

When you first enter the procedure, you print the root node's value. Next you recursively call the procedure to traverse the left subtree. When you make this recursive call, the calling procedure's state is saved on the stack so that when the recursive call returns, the calling procedure can pick up where it left off. In this algorithm, the calling procedure picks up where it left off by doing a traversal of the right subtree. Effectively, the recursive call serves to implicitly store the address of the right tree on the stack so it can be traversed after the traversal of the left tree is complete. Each time you print a node and move to its left child, you store the right child on an implicit stack. Whenever there is no child, you return from a recursive call, effectively popping a right child node off the implicit stack so you can continue traversing. In summary, this algorithm prints the value of the current node, pushes the right child onto an implicit stack, and moves onto the left child. The algorithm pops the stack to obtain a new current node when there are no more children (when it reaches a leaf). This continues until you have traversed the entire tree and the implicit stack is empty.

You could try to implement this algorithm directly, but first you should try to remove any unnecessary special cases that would make the algorithm more difficult to implement. Instead of coding separate cases for the left and right children, you should be able to push pointers to both nodes onto the stack. Find an order that allows you to push both nodes onto the stack so that the left node is always popped first.

Because a stack is a last-in-first-out data structure, you can push the right node onto the stack and then the left node. Then, rather than examining the left child explicitly, simply pop the first node from the stack, print its value, and push both of its children onto the stack in the order described. If you start the procedure by pushing the root node onto the stack and then pop, print, and push as described, you should be able to exactly emulate the recursive preorder traversal. To summarize:

Create the stack

Push the root node on the stack

While the stack is not empty

    Pop a node

    If the node is not NULL

Print its value

Push the node's right child on the stack

Push the node's left child on the stack

The code for this algorithm is (ignoring error conditions like the stack being unable to allocate memory):

```
void PreorderTraversal(node *root)
{
    element *theStack;
    void *data;
    node   *curNode;

    CreateStack(&theStack);
    Push(&theStack, root);

    while (Pop(&theStack, &data)) {
        curNode = (node *) data;
        if (curNode) {
            printf("%d\n", curNode->value);
            Push(&theStack, curNode->right);
            Push(&theStack, curNode->left);
        }
    }
    DeleteStack(&theStack);
}
```

What is the running time for this algorithm? Each node is examined only once and pushed on the stack only once. Therefore, this is an $O(n)$ algorithm. You don't have the overhead of many function calls in this implementation. On the other hand, the stack used in this implementation will probably require dynamic memory allocation. So, it is unclear whether the iterative implementation would be more or less efficient than the recursive solution.

Problem: Lowest Common Ancestor

- **Given the value of two nodes in a binary search tree, find the lowest common ancestor. You may assume that both values already exist in the tree. The function prototype is as follows:**

```
int FindLowestCommonAncestor(node *root, int value1,
                             int value2);
```

For example, assume 4 and 14 are given as `value1` and `value2`, respectively, for the tree in Figure 4.7. The lowest common ancestor would be 8 because it's an ancestor to both 4 and 14 and there is no node lower on the tree that is an ancestor to both 4 and 14.

Figure 4.7 suggests an intuitive algorithm: Follow the lines up from each of the nodes until they converge. To implement this algorithm make lists of all the ancestors of both nodes and then search through these two lists to find the first node where they differ. The node right above this divergence will be the lowest common ancestor. This is a good solution, but there is a more efficient one.

The first algorithm doesn't use any of the special properties of a binary search tree. The tree could be any type of tree, and the method would work. You should try to use some of the special properties of a binary search tree to help you find the lowest common ancestor more efficiently.

Binary search trees have two special properties. First, every node has zero, one, or two children. This fact doesn't seem to help find a new algorithm. Second, the left child's value is less than or equal to the value of the current node, and the right child's value is greater than or equal to the value of the current node. This property looks more promising.

Looking at the example tree, the lowest common ancestor to 4 and 14, the node with value 8, is different from the other ancestors to 4 and 14 in an important way. All the other ancestors are either greater than both 4 and 14 or less than both 4 and 14. Only 8 is between 4 and 14. You can use this insight to design a better algorithm.

The root node is an ancestor to all nodes because there is a path from it to all other nodes. Therefore, you can start at the root node and follow a path through the common ancestors of both nodes. When your target values are both less than the current node, you go left. When they are both

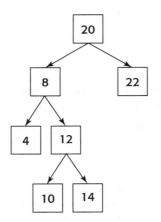

Figure 4.7   Lowest common ancestor.

greater, you go right. The first node you encounter that is between your target values is the lowest common ancestor.

Based on this description, you can derive the following algorithm:

Examine the current node

If `value1` and `value2` are less than the current node's value

Examine the left child

If `value1` and `value2` are greater than the current node's value

Examine the right child

Otherwise

The current node is the lowest common ancestor

This solution may seem to suggest using recursion because it is a tree and the algorithm has a recursive structure to it, but recursion is not necessary here. Recursion is most useful when moving through multiple branches of a tree or examining some special pattern of nodes. Here you are only traveling down the tree. It's easy to implement this kind of traversal iteratively.

```
int FindLowestCommonAncestor(node *root, int value1,
                             int value2)
{
    node *curNode  = root;

    while (1) {
        /* Go to the left child */
        if (curNode->value > value1 && curNode->value > value2)
            curNode = curNode->left;

        /* Go to the right child */
        else if (curNode->value < value1 &&
                curNode->value < value2)
            curNode = curNode->right;

        /* Else, you've found the correct node */
        else
            return curNode->value;
    }
}
```

What's the running time of this algorithm? You are traveling down a path to the lowest common ancestor. Recall that traveling a path to any one node takes $O(\log(n))$. Therefore, this is an $O(\log(n))$ algorithm. Also, this is slightly more efficient than a similar recursive solution because you don't have the overhead of repeated function calls.

Arrays and Strings

Arrays and strings occupy an intermediate space in the world of computer data. They are more complex than simple, single-value types like integers and floating-point numbers, but less complex than classes or dynamic data structures. Arrays have some fundamental properties that are constant across all languages and some implementation details that are language specific. Strings tend to be more language dependent than arrays, but they have a very close relationship to arrays, especially in C and C++.

Arrays

An array consists of a number of variables of the same type arranged contiguously in a block of memory. Because arrays play an important role in every major language used in commercial development, we assume you're at least somewhat familiar with their syntax and usage. With that in mind, we focus on the theory and application of arrays with particular attention to strings, an important array-related application.

Like a linked list, an array provides an essentially linear form of storage,[1] but its properties are significantly different. In a linked list, lookup is always an O(n) operation, but array lookup is O(1) as long as you know the index of the element you want. The provision regarding the index is important—if you know only the value, lookup is still O(n) in the worst case. For example, suppose you have an array of characters. Locating the sixth character is O(1), but locating the character with value 'w' is O(n).

The price for this improved lookup is paid in decreased efficiency for insertion and deletion of data in the middle of the array. Because an array is accessed in terms of physical memory locations, it's not possible to create or eliminate storage between any two elements as it is with a linked list. Instead, you must move data within the array to make room for an insertion or close the gap left by a deletion.

Arrays are not dynamic data structures: They have a finite, fixed number of elements. Memory must be allocated for every element in an array, even if only part of the array is used. Arrays are best used when you know how many elements you need to store before the program executes. When the program needs a variable amount of storage, the size of the array imposes an arbitrary limit on the amount of data that can be stored. If you make the array large enough that the program always operates below the limit, you will probably be wasting a lot of memory in the unused portion of the array.

Dynamic arrays (sometimes called D-arrays) are dynamic data structures that have the properties of arrays but can change size to efficiently store as much or as little data as necessary. We won't go into the details of implementing a dynamic array, but it is important to know that most dynamic array implementations use static arrays internally. A static array cannot be resized, so dynamic arrays are resized by allocating a new array of the appropriate size, copying every element from the old array into the new array and freeing the old array. This is an expensive operation, so you should try to resize as infrequently as possible when programming with dynamic arrays.

Each language handles arrays somewhat differently, giving each language a different set of array programming pitfalls. We'll take a look at arrays in three languages, C/C++, Java, and Perl, to get a feel for the problems that can arise.

---

[1]Of course, multidimensional arrays are not exactly linear, but they are implemented as linear arrays of linear arrays (of linear arrays… repeated as needed), so even multidimensional arrays are linear in each dimension.

C/C++

Despite the differences between C and C++, they are very similar in their treatment of arrays. In most cases, an array name is equivalent to a pointer constant[2] to the first element of the array.[3] This means that you can't initialize the elements of one array with another array using a simple assignment.

For example, if you say

```
arrayA = arrayB;   /* Compile error: arrayA is not an lvalue */
```

it is interpreted as an attempt to make `arrayA` refer to the same area of memory as `arrayB`. If `arrayA` has been declared as an array, this causes a compile error because you can't change the memory location to which `arrayA` refers. To copy `arrayB` into `arrayA`, you have to write a loop that does an element-by-element assignment or use a library function like `memcpy`.

In C and C++, the compiler tracks only the location of arrays, not their size. This means the programmer is completely responsible for keeping track of array sizes. There is no bounds checking on array accesses. The language won't complain if you store something in the twentieth element of a ten-element array. Unfortunately, you will probably overwrite some other data structure, leading to all manner of curious and difficult-to-find bugs. A variety of development tools is available to help programmers identify out-of-bounds array accesses and other memory-related problems in their C programs.

Java

Unlike a C array, a Java array is a unique reference type that is not interchangeable with a reference to an element of the array. As in C, arrays cannot be copied with a simple assignment. If two array references have the same type, assignment of one to the other is allowed, but it results in both symbols referring to the same array.

---

[2]Pointers and constants can be confusing concepts separately; they are often nearly incomprehensible in combination. When we say *pointer constant* we mean a pointer declared like `char *const chrPtr` that cannot be altered to point at a different place in memory, but that can be used to change the contents of the memory it points to. This is not the same as the more commonly seen *constant pointer*, declared like `const char *chrPtr`, which can be changed to point at a different memory location but cannot be used to change the contents of a memory location. If you find this confusing, you're certainly not the only one.

[3]For an excellent discussion of when this analogy breaks down, see *Expert C Programming: Deep C Secrets* by Peter Van Der Linden (Prentice-Hall, 1994).

```
byte arrayA[] = new byte[10], arrayB = new byte[10];
arrayA = arrayB; // arrayA now refers to the same array as arrayB
```

Java tracks the size of arrays, and throws an `ArrayIndexOutOfBounds-Exception` if you try to access an array out of bounds.

Perhaps the most peculiar feature of the Java array is that allocating an array of objects does not actually construct the objects. You must construct the objects yourself and assign them to the elements of the array.

```
Button myButtons[] = new Button[5]; // Buttons not yet constructed
for (int i = 0; i < 5; i++) {
    myButtons[i] = new Button();  // Constructing Buttons
}
// All Buttons constructed
```

Perl

Perl arrays are very powerful data structures. We won't try to cover them comprehensively here. Instead, we'll just hit the high points for comparison with other languages.

Perl is unique in that it has no static arrays: Its array type is a dynamic array. If an array is accessed out of bounds, it simply resizes so the access is within the new bounds. Because scalar is the only simple type in Perl, there is only one array type. This is unlike most other languages where, for instance, an array of floats would be a different type than an array of integers.

In further contrast to most C-derived languages, you *can* initialize one array with another:

```
@arrayA = @arrayB; # still two separate arrays, now with same contents
```

Perhaps the most common Perl array mistake is inadvertently evaluating an array in scalar context, in which case the array's value is its size, not the values of its elements. For instance:

```
@a = (1, 2, 3);
print @a;  # prints 123
print @a + 2; # + creates scalar context, prints 5 instead of 345
```

Strings

Strings are simply sequences of characters. Most languages store strings internally as arrays, although languages differ in how similarly they treat arrays and strings. As before, we'll look at each language separately.

C

A C string is nothing more than a char array. Just as C doesn't track the size of arrays, it doesn't track the size of strings. Instead, the end of the string is marked with a NUL character, represented in the language as '\0'. The character array must have room for the NUL terminator. For instance, if you want to store a 10-character string, you need at least an 11-character array. This scheme makes finding the length of the string an $O(n)$ operation instead of $O(1)$ as you might expect: strlen() (the library function that returns the length of a string) must scan through the string until it finds the end.

For the same reason that you can't assign one C array to another, you cannot copy C strings using the = operator. Instead, you generally use the strcpy() function.

It is often convenient to read or alter a string by addressing individual characters of the array. If you change the length of a string in this manner, you must make sure you write a NUL character ('\0') after the new last character in the string, and that the character array you are working in is large enough to accommodate the new string and terminator. It's easy to truncate a C string by setting the character after the new end of the string to NUL.

C++

In general, C++ uses the same NUL terminated strings that C does. Using the object-oriented facilities provided by C++, however, it is possible to write a string class providing more extensive string functionality, such as easy concatenation and dynamic string growth. Many class libraries supply such a class, for instance, the string class provided as a specialization of the basic_string template class by the Standard C++ Library.

Java

Java strings are objects of the java.lang.String class. Although Strings can be readily converted to and created from character arrays, they are a distinct type. Because methods of the String class allow you to read individual characters from the strings, this affects syntax more than function as far as reading is concerned.

Writing to strings is significantly different. Unlike a C string, which can be written to at random, a Java String object is *immutable*: Once it is constructed, its contents can't be changed. If you need to manipulate the contents of a `String`, you must construct a `StringBuffer` from the `String`. This restriction is not as onerous as it sounds. For instance, the concatenation operator (+) creates a new string based on the contents of the strings it is concatenating. A `StringBuffer` is really necessary only when you need to alter a string character by character.

Perl

While C makes strings and arrays roughly synonymous, Perl takes the opposite tack and treats strings as one of the kinds of data the scalar type can hold. Although it is easy to transform a Perl string into an array of characters using the `split()` function, it is rarely necessary, given the rich set of operators and functions Perl provides for string manipulation. In fact, many argue that Perl's string and text manipulation facilities are the best reason for using the language. Most notable among these is a complete set of regular expression-based search and replace operators. For example, suppose we wanted to make a string refer to the authors a little more respectfully:

```
$Complaint = "On occasion, John and Noah rant incoherently.";
$Complaint =~ s/John and Noah/Mr. Mongan and Mr. Suojanen/;
print $Complaint;
# Prints:
# On occasion, Mr. Mongan and Mr. Suojanen rant incoherently.
```

Problem: First Non-repeated Character

- Write an efficient function to find the first non-repeated character in a string. For instance, the first non-repeated character in "total" is 'o' and the first non-repeated character in "teeter" is 'r'. Discuss the efficiency of your algorithm.

At first, this task seems almost trivial. If a character is repeated, it must appear in at least two places in the string. Therefore, you can determine whether a particular character is repeated by comparing it with all other characters in the string. It's a simple matter to perform this search for each character in the string, starting with the first. When you find a character that has no match elsewhere in the string you've found the first non-repeated character.

What's the time order of this solution? If the string is n characters long, then in the worst case you'll make almost n comparisons for each of the n

characters. That gives worst case $O(n^2)$ for this algorithm. You are unlikely to encounter the worst case for single-word strings, but for longer strings, such as a paragraph of text, it's likely that most characters would be repeated, and the most common case might be close to the worst case. The ease with which you arrived at this solution suggests that there are better alternatives—if the answer were truly this trivial, the interviewer wouldn't bother you with the question. There must be an algorithm with a worst case better than $O(n^2)$.[4]

Why was the previous algorithm $O(n^2)$? One factor of n came from checking each character in the string to see if it was non-repeated. Because the non-repeated character could be anywhere in the string, it seems unlikely that you'll be able to improve efficiency here. The other factor of n was due to searching the entire string when trying to look up matches for each character. If you improve the efficiency of this search, you'll improve the efficiency of the overall algorithm. The easiest way to improve search efficiency on a set of data is to put it in a data structure that allows more efficient searching. What data structures can be searched more efficiently than $O(n)$? Binary trees can be searched in $O(\log(n))$. Arrays and hashtables both have constant time element lookup. Begin by trying to take advantage of an array or hashtable because these data structures offer the greatest potential for improvement.

You'll want to be able to quickly determine whether a character is repeated, so you'll need to be able to search the data structure by character. This means you'll have to use the character as the index[5] (in an array) or key (in a hashtable). What values would you store in these data structures? A non-repeated character appears only once in the string, so if you stored the number of times each character appeared, it would help you identify non-repeating characters. You'll have to scan the entire string before you have the final counts for each character.

Once you've completed this, you could scan through all the count values in the array or hashtable looking for a 1. That would find a non-repeated character, but it wouldn't necessarily be the first one in the original string.

Therefore, you need to search your count values in the order of the characters in the original string. This isn't difficult—you just look up the

---

[4]The algorithm described can be improved somewhat by comparing each character with only the characters following it because it has already been compared with the characters preceding it. This would give you a total of $(n - 1) + (n - 2) + ...+ 1$ comparisons. As discussed in Chapter 2, this is still $O(n^2)$.

[5]You can cast a character to an integer in order to use it as an index.

count value for each character until you find a 1. When you find a 1, you've located the first non-repeated character.

Consider whether this new algorithm is actually an improvement. You will always have to go through the entire string to build the count data structure. In the worst case, you might have to look up the count value for each character in the string to find the first non-repeated character. Because the operations on the array or hash you're using to hold the counts are constant time, the worst case would be two operations for each character in the string, giving $2n$, which is $O(n)$—a major improvement over the previous attempt.

Both hashtables and arrays provide constant-time lookup; you need to decide which one you will use. Hashtables have a higher lookup overhead than arrays. On the other hand, an array would initially contain random values that you would have to take time to set to zero, whereas a hashtable initially has no values. Perhaps the greatest difference is in memory requirements. An array would need an element for every possible value of a character. This would amount to a relatively reasonable 256 elements if you were processing ASCII strings, but if you had to process Unicode strings you would need more than 65,000 elements (Unicode uses 16-bit characters). In contrast, a hashtable would require storage for only the characters that actually exist in the input string. So, arrays are a better choice for long strings with a limited set of possible character values; hashtables are more efficient for shorter strings or when there are many possible character values.

You could implement the solution either way. We'll assume the code may need to process Unicode strings and choose the hashtable implementation. You might choose to write the function in Java, which has built-in support for both hashtables and Unicode. In outline form, the function you'll be writing looks like this:

First, build the character count hashtable:

For each character

If no value is stored for the character, store 1

Otherwise, increment the value

Second, scan the string:

For each character

Return character if count in hashtable is 1

If no characters have count 1, return null

Now implement the function. Because you don't know what class your function would be part of, implement it as a public static function (this is equivalent to a normal C function). You'll also need to remember that the Java Hashtable stores Objects, which means you can store the reference type Integer, but not the fundamental type int.

```
public static Character FirstNonRepeated(String str)
{
    Hashtable charHash = new Hashtable();
    int i, length;
    Character c;
    Integer intgr;

    length = str.length();

    // Scan str, building hashtable
    for (i = 0; i < length; i++) {
        c = new Character(str.charAt(i));
        intgr = (Integer) charHash.get(c);
        if (intgr == null) {
            charHash.put(c, new Integer(1));
        } else {
            // Increment count corresponding to c
            charHash.put(c, new Integer(intgr.intValue() + 1));
        }
    }

    // Search hashtable in order of str
    for (i = 0; i < length; i++) {
        c = new Character(str.charAt(i));
        if (((Integer)charHash.get(c)).intValue() == 1)
            return c;
    }
    return null;
}
```

Problem: Remove Specified Characters

■ Write an efficient function in C that deletes characters from a string. Use the prototype

```
void RemoveChars(char str[], char remove[]);
```

where any character existing in `remove` must be deleted from `str`. For example, given a `str` of "Battle of the Vowels: Hawaii vs. Grozny" and a `remove` of "aeiou", the function should transform `str` to "Bttl f th Vwls: Hw vs. Grzny". Justify any design decisions you make and discuss the efficiency of your solution.

This problem breaks down into two separate tasks. For each character in str, you must determine whether it should be deleted. Then, if appropriate, you must delete the character. We'll discuss the second task, deletion, first.

Strings are stored in arrays, so your task is to delete an element from an array. An array is a contiguous block of memory, so you can't simply remove an element from the middle as you might with a linked list. Instead, you'll have to rearrange the data in the array so it remains a contiguous sequence of characters after the deletion. For example, if you wish to delete 'c' from the string "abcd" you could either shift 'a' and 'b' forward one position (toward the end) or shift 'd' back one position (toward the beginning). Either approach would leave you with the characters "abd" in contiguous elements of the array. In addition to shifting the data, you need to decrease the size of the string by one character. If you shift characters before the deletion forward, you need to eliminate the first element; if you shift the characters after the deletion backward you need to eliminate the last element. In C, you can easily eliminate the last element of a string by writing a NUL character ('\0') after the new last character. On the other hand, eliminating characters from the beginning of the string would be much more problematic. Shifting characters backward seems to be the cleanest choice.

How would the proposed algorithm fare in the worst-case scenario where you need to delete all the characters in str? For each deletion, you would shift all the remaining characters back one position. If str were n characters long, you would move the last character $n - 1$ times, the next to last $n - 2$ times, and so on, giving worst case $O(n^2)$ for the deletion.[6] Moving the same characters many times seems awfully inefficient. How might you avoid this?

What if you allocated a temporary string buffer and built your modified string there instead of in place? Then you could simply copy the characters you need to keep into the temporary string, skipping the characters you want to delete. When you finish building the modified string, you can copy it from the temporary buffer back into str. This way you move each character at most twice, giving $O(n)$ deletion. However, you've incurred the memory overhead of a temporary buffer the same size as the original string and the time overhead of copying the modified string back over the original string. Is there any way you could avoid these penalties while retaining your $O(n)$ algorithm?

---

[6]If you start at the end of the string and work back toward the beginning, it's somewhat more efficient but still $O(n^2)$ in the worst case.

To implement the O(n) algorithm just described, you'll need to track a source position for the read location in the original string and a destination position for the write position in the temporary buffer. These positions both start at zero. Source will be incremented every time you read and destination every time you write. In other words, when you copy a character you'll increment both positions, but when you delete a character you'll increment only the source position. This means the source position will always be the same as or ahead of the destination position. Once you read a character from the original string (that is, the source position has advanced past it), you no longer need that character—in fact, you're just going to copy the modified string over it. Because the destination position in the original string is always a character you don't need any-more, you can write directly into the original string, eliminating the tem-porary buffer entirely. This is still an O(n) algorithm, but without the overhead of the earlier version.

Now that you know how to delete characters, consider the task of deciding whether to delete a particular character. The easiest way to do this is to compare the character to each character in `remove` and delete it if it matches any of them. How efficient is this? If `str` is *n* characters long and `remove` is *m* characters long, then in the worst case you make *m* com-parisons for each of *n* characters, so the algorithm is O(*nm*). You can't avoid checking each of the *n* characters in `str`, but perhaps you can make the lookup that determines whether a given character is in `remove` better than O(*m*).

If you've read the solution to the problem on page 80, this should sound very familiar. Just as you did in that problem, you can use `remove` to build an array[7] or hashtable that has constant time lookup, thus giving an O(n) solution. We've discussed the trade-offs between hashes and arrays. In this case, an array is most appropriate when `str` and `remove` are long and characters have relatively few possible values (for example, ASCII strings). A hashtable may be a better choice when `str` and `remove` are short or characters have many possible values (for example, Unicode strings). This time, we'll assume that we're processing long ASCII strings and use an array instead of a hashtable.

Coding in C, your function will have three parts. First, set all the ele-ments in your lookup array to false. Next, iterate through each character

---

[7]But why build an array? Isn't `remove` already an array? Yes it is, but it is an array of characters indexed by an arbitrary (that is, meaningless for this problem) position, requiring you to search through each element. The array we refer to here would be an array of boolean values indexed by all the possible values for a char. This lets you determine whether a character is in `remove` by checking a single element.

in `remove`, setting the corresponding value in the lookup array to true. Finally, iterate through `str` with a source and destination index, copying each character only if its corresponding value in the lookup array is false.

Now that you've combined both subtasks into a single algorithm, analyze the overall efficiency for `str` of length n and `remove` of length m. Because the size of a character is fixed for a given platform, zeroing the array is constant time. You perform a constant time assignment for each character in `remove`, so building the lookup array is $O(m)$. Finally, you do at most one constant time lookup and one constant time copy for each character in `str`, giving $O(n)$ for this stage. Summing these parts yields $O(n + m)$, so the algorithm has linear running time.

Having justified and analyzed your solution, you're ready to code it:

```
void RemoveChars(char str[], char remove[])
{
    int src, dst, removeArray[256];

    /* Zero all elements in array */
    for (src = 0; src < 256; src++) {
        removeArray[src] = 0;
    }

    /* Set true for chars to be removed */
    src = 0;
    while (remove[src]) {
        removeArray[remove[src]] = 1;
        src++;
    }

    /* Copy char unless it must be removed */
    src = dst = 0;
    do {          /* do..while terminates after copying NUL */
        if (!removeArray[str[src]]) {
            str[dst++] = str[src];
        }
    } while (str[src++]);
}
```

For comparison, it's interesting to note that this problem has a one-line solution in Perl:

```
$str =~ s/[$remove]//g;
```
[8]

[8]If you're a Perl aficionado, you may wonder why we didn't use `tr///` here. We chose `s///` so we could avoid the additional complication of using an `eval`, which would be necessary with `tr///` because it builds its translation table at compile time. We would need to use `tr///` for an $O(n)$ solution. Also, it would be wise to escape any metacharacters in $remove like this `$str =~ s/[\Q$remove\E]//g;`, but we didn't want to make the example look too intimidating.

The existence of simple, one-line solutions to problems like this is one of the main reasons many people use Perl, especially for text processing. On the other hand, the incomprehensibility of this line to programmers not familiar with the language is one of the main reasons many people don't use Perl. Should you fall into the latter category, don't despair—it's not as complicated as it looks. s/// is the replacement operator. It looks for whatever is between the first pair of slashes (in this case, any of the characters in $remove) and replaces them with whatever is between the second set (nothing, in this case). The g at the end means replace all occurrences, not just the first, and $str =~ tells it to perform the replacement on $str.

Problem: Reverse Words

- **Write a function that reverses the order of the words in a string. For instance, your function should transform the string "Do or do not, there is no try." to "try. no is there not, do or Do". Assume that all words are space delimited and treat punctuation the same as letters.**

You probably already have a pretty good idea how you're going to start this problem. Because you need to operate on words, you have to be able to recognize where words start and end. You can do this with a simple token scanner that iterates through each character of the string. Based on the definition given in the problem statement, your scanner will differentiate between *non-word characters*, namely space, and *word characters*, which for this problem are all characters except space. A word begins, not surprisingly, with a word character and ends at the next non-word character or the end of the string.

The most obvious approach is to use your scanner to identify words, write these words into a temporary buffer, and then copy the buffer back over the original string. To reverse the order of the words, you will either have to scan the string backward to identify the words in reverse order or write the words into the buffer in reverse order (starting at the end of the buffer). It doesn't matter which method you choose; in the following discussion we've chosen to identify the words in reverse order.

As always, you should consider the mechanics of how this will work before you begin coding. First, you'll need to allocate a temporary buffer of the appropriate size. Then you'll enter the scanning loop, starting with the last character of the string. When you find a non-word character, you can write it directly to the buffer. When you find a word character, however, you can't write it immediately to the temporary buffer. Because you're scanning the string in reverse, the first word character you encounter is the last character of the word, so if you were to copy the characters in the order you find them, you'd write the characters within each word backward. Instead, you need to keep scanning until you find the first character of the word and then copy each character of the word in the correct, non-reversed order.[9] When you're copying the characters of a word, you need to be able to identify the end of the word so that you know when to stop. You could do this by checking whether each character is a word character, but because you already know the position of the last character in the word, a better solution is to continue copying until you reach that position.

An example may help to clarify. Suppose you were given the string "piglet quantum". The first word character you encounter is 'm'. If you were to copy the characters as you found them, you would end up with the string "mutnauq telgip", which is not nearly as good a name for a techno group as the string you were supposed to produce, "quantum piglet". To get "quantum piglet" from "piglet quantum", you need to scan until you get to 'q', and then copy the letters in the word in the forward direction until you get back to 'm' at position 13. Next, copy the space character immediately because it's a non-word character. Then, just as for "quantum", you would recognize the character 't' as a word character, store position 5 as the end of the word, scan backward to 'p', and finally write the characters of "piglet" until you got to position 5.

Finally, after you scan and copy the whole string, write a NUL character to terminate the string in the temporary buffer and call `strcpy` to copy the buffer back over the original string. Then you can deallocate the temporary buffer and return from the function. This process is illustrated graphically in Figure 5.1.

It's obviously important that your scanner stop when it gets to the first character of the string. Although this sounds simple, it can be easy to forget to check that the read position is still in the string, especially when the read position is changed at more than one place in your code. In this function, you move the read position in the main token scanning loop to get to the next token and in the word scanning loop to get to the next character of the word. Make sure neither loop runs past the beginning of the string.

Programmed in C, the algorithm described so far looks like the following:

---

[9]You may think you could avoid this complication by scanning the string forward and writing the words in reverse. However, you then have to solve a similar, related problem of calculating the start position of each word when writing to the temporary buffer.

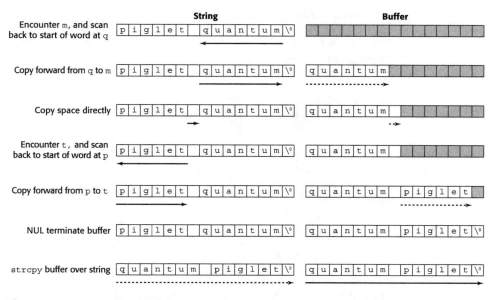

Figure 5.1: Reversing "piglet quantum".

```c
int ReverseWords (char str[])
{
    char *buffer;
    int tokenReadPos, wordReadPos, wordEnd, writePos = 0;

    /* Position of the last character is length - 1 */
    tokenReadPos = strlen(str) - 1;

    buffer = (char *) malloc(tokenReadPos + 2);
    if (!buffer)
        return 0; /* ReverseWords failed */

    while (tokenReadPos >= 0) {

        if (str[tokenReadPos] == ' ') { /* Non-word characters */

            /* Write character */
            buffer[writePos++] = str[tokenReadPos--];

        } else {   /* Word characters */

            /* Store position of end of word */
            wordEnd = tokenReadPos;

            /* Scan to next non-word character */
            while (tokenReadPos >= 0 && str[tokenReadPos] != ' ')
```

```
            tokenReadPos--;

            /* tokenReadPos went past the start of the word */
            wordReadPos = tokenReadPos + 1;

            /* Copy the characters of the word */
            while (wordReadPos <= wordEnd) {
                buffer[writePos++] = str[wordReadPos++];
            }
        }
    }
    /* NUL terminate buffer and copy over str */
    buffer[writePos] = '\0';
    strcpy(str, buffer);

    free(buffer);

    return 1; /* ReverseWords successful */
}
```

The preceding token scanner-based implementation is the general-case solution for this type of problem. It is reasonably efficient, and its functionality could easily be extended. It is important that you are able to implement this type of solution, but the solution is not perfect. All the scanning backward, storing positions, and copying forward is somewhat lacking in algorithmic elegance. The need for a temporary buffer is also less than desirable.

Often, interview problems have obvious general solutions and less obvious special-case solutions. The special-case solution may be less extensible than a general solution, but more efficient or elegant. Reversing the words of a string is such a problem. You have seen the general solution, but a special-case solution also exists. In an interview, you might have been steered away from the general solution before you got to coding it. We followed the general solution through to code because token scanning and string scanning are important techniques that we wanted to illustrate.

One way to improve an algorithm is to focus on a particular, concrete deficiency and try to remedy that. Because elegance, or lack thereof, is hard to quantify, you might try to eliminate the need for a temporary buffer from your algorithm. You can probably see that this is going to require a significantly different algorithm. You can't simply alter the preceding approach to write to the same string it reads from—by the time you get halfway through you will have overwritten the rest of the data you need to read.

Rather than focus on what you can't do without a buffer, you should turn your attention to what you can do. It is possible to reverse an entire string in place by exchanging characters. Try an example to see whether this might be helpful: "in search of algorithmic elegance" would become "ecnagele cimhtirogla fo hcraes ni". Look at that! The words are in exactly the order you need them, but the characters in the words are backward. All you have to do is reverse each word in the reversed string. You can do that by locating the beginning and end of each word using a scanner similar to the one used in the preceding implementation and calling a reverse function on each word substring.

Now you just have to design an in-place reverse string function. The only trick is to remember that there's no one-statement method of exchanging two values in C—you have to use a temporary variable and three assignments. Your reverse string function should take a string, a start index, and an end index as arguments. Begin by exchanging the character at the start index with the character at the end index, then increment the start index and decrement the end index. Continue like this until the start and end index meet in the middle (in a string with odd length) or end is less than start (in a string with even length)—put more succinctly, continue while end is greater than start.

In C, these functions would look like the following:

```
void ReverseWords(char str[])
{
    int start = 0, end = 0, length;

    length = strlen(str);

    /* Reverse entire string */
    ReverseString(str, start, length - 1);

    while (end < length) {
        if (str[end] != ' ') { /* Skip non-word characters */

            /* Save position of beginning of word */
            start = end;

            /* Scan to next non-word character */
            while (end < length && str[end] != ' ')
                end++;

            /* Back up to end of word */
            end--;

            /* Reverse word */
            ReverseString(str, start, end);
        }
        end++; /* Advance to next token */
```

```
        }
        return;
    }

    void ReverseString (char str[], int start, int end) {
        char temp;
        while (end > start) {
            /* Exchange characters */
            temp = str[start];
            str[start] = str[end];
            str[end] = temp;

            /* Move indices towards middle */
            start++; end--;
        }
        return;
    }
```

This solution does not need a temporary buffer and is considerably more elegant than the previous solution. It's also more efficient, mostly because it doesn't suffer from dynamic memory overhead and doesn't need to copy a result back from a temporary buffer.

As a final aside on this problem, this is another place where many pages of algorithm design and C code can be reduced to a single line of Perl:

```
$ReversedWords = join(" ", reverse(split(/ /, $Words)));
```

In this example, `split` separates `$Words` on space delimiters to generate a list of words, `reverse` reverses the order of the list of words, and `join` replaces the spaces and concatenates the resultant list into a single string. Though this is much easier and faster to write in Perl than C, the resultant code is significantly less efficient, providing yet another example of the trade-offs between *programmer*-efficient high-level languages and *program*-efficient low-level languages.

Problem: Integer/String Conversions

- Write functions for the following prototypes. The first function should convert an ASCII string to a signed integer, and the second function a signed integer to an ASCII string.

```
int StrToInt(char str[]);
void IntToStr(int num, char str[]);
```

Assume the buffer passed to IntToStr is large enough to accommodate any number within the range of an int. Also assume that the string passed to StrToInt contains only digits and '-', that it is a properly formatted integer number, and that the number is within the range of an `int`.

In C, you normally perform these conversions using `sscanf()` and `sprintf()`. You should mention to the interviewer that under normal circumstances, you know better than to duplicate functionality provided by standard libraries. This doesn't get you off the hook—you still have to implement the functions called for by the problem.

You can start with `StrToInt`. This function will be passed a valid string representation of an integer. Think about what that gives you to work with. Suppose you were given "137". You would have a three-character string with the ASCII value for '1' at position 0, '3' at position 1, and '7' at position 2. From grade school, you recall that the 1 represents 100 because it is in the hundreds place, the 3 represents 30 because it is in the tens place, and the 7 is just 7 because it is in the ones place. Summing these values gives the complete number: 100 + 30 + 7 = 137.

This gives you a framework for dissecting the string representation and building it back into a single integer value. You need to determine the numeric (integer) value of the digit represented by each character, multiply that value by the appropriate place value, and then sum these products.

Consider the ASCII character to numeric value conversion first. What do you know about the ASCII values of digit characters? They are all sequential: '0' has an ASCII value one less than '1', which in turn is followed by '2', '3', and so on.[10] So the ASCII value of a digit character is equal to the digit plus the ASCII value of '0'.[11] This means you subtract the ASCII value of '0' from a digit character to find the numeric value of the digit. You probably don't remember the ASCII value of '0' off the top of your head, but the compiler knows. You can just say `-'0'`, which the compiler will interpret as "subtract the ASCII value of 0."

Next you need to know what place value each digit must be multiplied by. Working through the digits left to right seems problematic because you don't know what the place value of the first digit is until you know how long the number is. For instance, the first character of "367" is identical to that of "31", although it represents 300 in the first case and 30 in the second case. The most obvious solution is to scan the digits from right to left because the rightmost position is always the ones place, the next to rightmost is always the tens, and so on. This allows you to start at the

---

[10]Of course, if you *didn't* know this, you'd have to ask the interviewer.
[11]Note that "the ASCII value of '0'" is the non-zero code number representing the character '0'.

right end of the string with a place value of 1 and work backward through the string, multiplying the place value by 10 each time you move to a new place. This method, however, requires two multiplications per iteration, one for multiplying the digit by the place value and another for increasing the place value. That seems a little inefficient.

Perhaps the alternative of working through the characters left to right was too hastily dismissed. Is there a way you could get around the problem of not knowing the place value for a digit until you've scanned the whole string? Returning to the example of "367", when you encounter the first character, '3', you register a value of 3. If the next character were the end of the string, the number's value would be 3. However, you encounter '6' as the next character of the string. Now the '3' represents 30 and the 6 represents '6'. On the next iteration, you read the last character, '7', so the '3' represents 300, the '6' 60, and the '7' 7. In summary, the value of the number you've scanned so far increases by a factor of 10 every time you encounter a new character. It really doesn't matter that you don't initially know whether the '3' represents 3, 30, or 30,000—every time you find a new digit you just multiply the value you've already read by 10 and add the value of the new digit. You're no longer tracking a place value, so this algorithm saves you a multiplication on each iteration. The optimization described in this algorithm is frequently useful in computing checksums and is considered clever enough to merit a name: *Horner's Rule*.

Up to this point, we've discussed only positive numbers. How can you expand your strategy to include negative numbers? A negative number will have a '-' character in the first position. You'll want to skip over the '-' character so you don't interpret it as a digit. After you've scanned all the digits and built the number, you'll need to change the number's sign so that it's negative. You can change the sign by multiplying by –1. You have to check for the '-' character before you scan the digits so you know whether to skip the first character, but you can't multiply by negative 1 until after you've scanned all the digits. One way around this problem is to set a flag if you find the '-' character and then multiply by –1 only if the flag is set.

In summary, the algorithm is as follows:

Start number at 0

If the first character is '-'

    Set the negative flag

    Start scanning with the next character

For each character in the string

Multiply number by 10

Add (digit character – '0') to number

Return number

Coding this in C gives:

```c
int StrToInt(char str[])
{
    int i = 0, isNeg = 0, num = 0;

    if (str[0] == '-') {
        isNeg = 1;
        i = 1;
    }

    while (str[i]) {
        num *= 10;
        num += (str[i++] - '0');
    }

    if (isNeg)
        num *= -1;

    return num;
}
```

Before you declare this function finished, you should visually check it for cases that may be problematic. At minimum, you should check –1, 0, and 1, so you've checked a positive value, a negative value, and a value that's neither positive nor negative. You should also check a multidigit value like 324 to be sure the loop has no problems. The function appears to work properly for these cases, so you can move on to IntToStr.

In IntToStr, you will be performing the inverse of the conversion you did in StrToInt. Given this, much of what you discovered in writing StrToInt should be of use to you here. For instance, just as you converted ASCII digits to integer values by subtracting '0' from each digit, you can convert integer values back to ASCII digits by adding '0' to each digit.

Before you can convert values to ASCII characters, you need to know what those values are. Consider how you might do this. Suppose you have the number 732. Looking at this number's decimal representation on paper, it seems a simple matter to identify the digit values 7, 3, and 2. However, you must remember that the computer isn't using a decimal representation, but rather the binary representation 1011011100. Because you can't select decimal digits directly from a binary number, you'll have to calculate the value of each digit. It seems logical to try to find the digit values either left to right or right to left.

Try left to right first. Integer dividing 732 by the place value (100) gives the first digit, 7. But now if you integer divide by the next place value (10) you get 73, not 3. It looks as if you need to subtract the hundreds value you found before moving on. Starting over with this new process gives you this:

$$732 \div 100 = 7 \text{ (first digit)}; 732 - 7 \times 100 = 32$$
$$32 \div 10 = 3 \text{ (second digit)}; 32 - 3 \times 10 = 2$$
$$2 \div 1 = 2 \text{ (third digit)}$$

To implement this algorithm, you're going to have to find the place value of the first digit and divide the place value by 10 for each new digit. This algorithm seems workable but complicated. What about working right to left?

Starting again with 732, what arithmetic operation can you perform to yield 2, the rightmost digit? 732 modulo 10 will give you 2.[12] Now how can you get the next digit? 732 modulo 100 gives 32. You could integer divide this by 10 to get the second digit, 3, but now you have to track two separate place values.

What if you did the integer divide before the modulo? Then you'd have 732 integer divide by 10 is 73; 73 modulo 10 is 3. Repeating this for the third digit you have 73 / 10 = 7; 7 % 10 = 7. This seems like an easier solution—you don't even have to track place values, you just divide and modulo until there's nothing left.

The major downside of this approach is that you find the digits in reverse order. Because you don't know how many there will be until you've found them all, you don't know where in the string to begin writing. You could run through the calculations twice—once to find the number of digits so you know where to start writing them and again to actually write the digits—but this seems wasteful. Perhaps a better solution is to write the digits out backward as you discover them and then reverse them into the proper order when you're done. You could do this in place in the output string, or because the largest possible value of an integer yields a relatively short string, you could write the digits into a temporary buffer and then reverse them into the final string.

---

[12]Modulo gives the remainder of an integer division. In C and C-like languages, the modulo operator is %.

Again, we've ignored negative numbers so far. This modulo-based approach doesn't work well with negative numbers. For instance, –32 % 10 is 8, not –2 or 2. You can imagine checking for the case of a negative number and then making an appropriate adjustment to each digit. This seems workable but complicated and inefficient. In StrToInt, you treated the number as if it were positive and then made an adjustment at the end if it was, in fact, negative. How might you employ this type of strategy here? You could start by multiplying the number by –1 if it were negative. Then it would be positive, so treating it as a positive number wouldn't be a problem. The only wrinkle would be that you'd need to write a '-' if the number had originally been negative. But this isn't difficult—you just have to set a flag indicating that the number is negative when you multiply by –1.

You've solved all the important subproblems in IntToStr—now assemble these solutions into an outline you can use to write your code.

If number less than zero

    Multiply number by –1

    Set negative flag

While number not equal to 0

    Add '0' to number % 10 and write this to temp buffer

    Integer divide number by 10

If negative flag is set

    Write '-' into next position in temp buffer

Write characters in temp buffer into output string in reverse order

Terminate output string with a NUL.

Rendering this in C might give the following:

```c
#define MAX_DIGITS_INT 10
void IntToStr(int num, char str[])
{
    int i = 0, j = 0, isNeg = 0;
    /* Buffer big enough for largest int, - sign and NUL */
    char temp[MAX_DIGITS_INT + 2];

    /* Check to see if the number is negative */
    if (num < 0) {
        num *= -1;
        isNeg = 1;
    }
```

```
    /* Fill buffer with digit characters in reverse order */
    while (num) {
        temp[i++] = (num % 10) + '0';
        num /= 10;
    }

    if (isNeg)
        temp[i++] = '-';

    /* Reverse the characters */
    while (i > 0)
        str[j++] = temp[--i];

    /* NUL terminate the string */
    str[j] = '\0';
}
```

Again, check the same potentially problematic cases you tried for StrToInt (multidigit, –1, 0, and 1). Multidigit numbers, –1, and 1 cause no problems, but if num is 0 you never go through the body of the while loop. This causes the function to write an empty string instead of "0". How can you fix this bug? You need to go through the body of the while loop at least once, so that you write a '0' even if num starts at 0. You can ensure that the body of the loop is executed at least once by changing it from a while loop to a do...while loop. This fix yields the following code, which can handle converting 0 as well as positive and negative values to strings.

```
#define MAX_DIGITS_INT 10
void IntToStr(int num, char str[])
{
    int i = 0, j = 0, isNeg = 0;
    /* Buffer big enough for largest int, - sign and NUL */
    char temp[MAX_DIGITS_INT + 2];

    /* Check to see if the number is negative */
    if (num < 0) {
        num *= -1;
        isNeg = 1;
    }

    /* Fill buffer with digit characters in reverse order */
    do {
        temp[i++] = (num % 10) + '0';
        num /= 10;
    } while (num);

    if (isNeg)
```

```
        temp[i++] = '-';

    /* Reverse the characters */
    while (i > 0)
        str[j++] = temp[--i];

    /* NUL terminate the string */
    str[j] = '\0';
}
```

CHAPTER
6

Recursion

Recursion is a deceptively simple concept: Any function or subroutine that calls itself is recursive. Despite this apparent simplicity, understanding and applying recursion can be surprisingly complex. One of the major barriers to understanding recursion is that general descriptions tend to become highly theoretical, abstract, and mathematical. Although there is certainly value in that approach, we will instead follow a more pragmatic course, focusing on example, application, and comparison of recursive and iterative (non-recursive) algorithms.

Recursion is most useful for tasks that can be defined in terms of similar subtasks. For example, sort, search, and traversal problems often have simple recursive solutions. A recursive function performs a task in part by calling itself to perform the subtasks. At some point, the function encounters a subtask that it can perform without calling itself. This case, where the function does not recurse, is called the *base case*; the former, where the function calls itself to perform a subtask, is referred to as the *recursive case*.

LESSON Recursive algorithms have two types of cases, recursive cases and base cases.

We can illustrate these concepts with a simple and commonly used example: the factorial operator. $n!$ (pronounced "n factorial") is essentially the product of all integers between n and 1. For instance, $4! = 4 \times 3 \times 2 \times 1 = 24$. $n!$ can be more formally defined as

$$n! = n\ (n-1)!$$
$$0! = 1! = 1$$

This definition leads easily to a recursive implementation of factorial. The task is determining the value of $n!$, and the subtask is determining the value of $(n-1)!$ In the recursive case, when n is greater than 1, the function calls itself to determine the value of $(n-1)!$ and multiplies that by n. In the base case, when n is 0 or 1, the function simply returns 1. Rendered in C, this looks like the following:

```
int Factorial(int n) {
    if (n > 1) {  /* Recursive case */
        return Factorial(n-1) * n;
    }
    else {          /* Base case */
        return 1;
    }
}
```

Figure 6.1 illustrates the operation of this function when computing $4!$. Notice that n decreases by 1 each time the function recurses. This ensures that the base case will eventually be reached. If a function is written incorrectly such that it does not always reach a base case, it will recurse infinitely. In practice, there is usually no such thing as infinite recursion:[1] eventually a stack overflow occurs and the program crashes—a similarly catastrophic event.

LESSON **Every recursive case must eventually lead to a base case.**

Our implementation of factorial represents an extremely simple example of a recursive function. In many cases, your recursive functions may need additional data structures or an argument that tracks the recursion level. Often the best solution in such cases is to move the data structure or argument initialization code into a separate function. This

---

[1]There is a form of recursion, called *tail recursion,* that can be optimized by the compiler to use the same stack frame for each recursive call. An appropriately optimized tail recursive algorithm could recurse infinitely because it wouldn't overflow the stack.

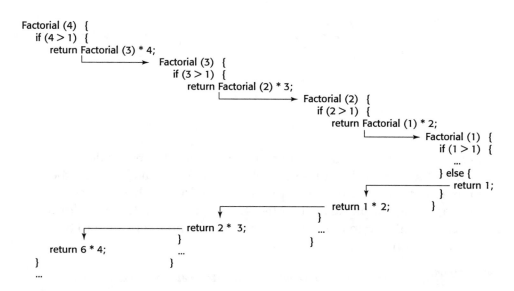

Figure 6.1   Computation of 4 factorial.

wrapper function, which performs initialization and then calls the purely recursive function, provides a clean, simple interface to the rest of the program.

For example, suppose you needed a factorial function that would return all of its intermediate results (factorials less than *n*), as well as the final result (*n!*). You would most naturally return these results as an integer array, which means the function would need to allocate an array. You would also need to know where in the array each result should be written. These tasks are most easily accomplished using a wrapper function, as follows:

```c
int *AllFactorials(int n) /* Wrapper function */
{
    int *results;
    int length = (n == 0 ? 1 : n);
    results = (int *) malloc(sizeof(int) * length);
    if (!results)
        return NULL;
    DoAllFactorials(n, results, 0);
    return results;
}

int DoAllFactorials(int n, int *results, int level)
{
```

```
if (n > 1) {  /* Recursive case */
    results[level] = n * DoAllFactorials(n - 1, results, level + 1);
    return results[level];
}
else {         /* Base case */
    results[level] = 1;
    return 1;
}
}
```

You can see that using a wrapper function hides the messy details of memory allocation and recursion level tracking without cluttering the recursive function. In this case, it probably would have been possible to determine the appropriate array index from n, avoiding the need for the level argument, but in many cases there will be no alternative to tracking the recursion level as we have shown here.

LESSON   It may be useful to write a separate wrapper function to do initialization for a complex recursive function.

Although recursion is a very powerful technique, it is not always the best and rarely the most efficient approach. This is due to the relatively large overhead for function calls on most platforms. For a simple recursive function like factorial, many computer architectures spend more time on function call overhead than the actual calculation. Iterative functions, which use looping constructs instead of recursive function calls, do not suffer from this overhead and are frequently more efficient.

LESSON   Iterative solutions are usually more efficient than recursive solutions.

Any problem that can be solved recursively can also be solved iteratively. Iterative algorithms are often quite easy to write, even for tasks that might appear to be fundamentally recursive. For instance, an iterative implementation of factorial is relatively simple. It may be helpful to expand the definition of factorial, such that we describe *n!* as the product of every integer between *n* and 1, inclusive. We can use a for loop to iterate through these values and calculate the product. In C, we would write the following:

```
int Factorial(int i) {
    int n, val = 1;
    for (n = i; n > 1; n==)   /* n of 0 or 1 fall through */
        val *= n;
    return val;
}
```

This implementation is significantly more efficient than our previous recursive implementation. In one benchmark test, it runs almost three times faster than the recursive alternative. Although it represents a different way of thinking about the problem, it's not really any more difficult to write than the recursive implementation.

For some problems, there are no obvious iterative algorithms. It is possible, though, to implement a recursive algorithm without using recursive function calls. Recursive function calls are generally used to preserve the current values of local variables so these values can be restored when the subtask performed by the recursive function call is completed. Because local variables are allocated on the program's stack, each recursive instance of the function has a separate set of the local variables. Thus, recursive function calls implicitly store variable values on the program's stack. You can eliminate the need for recursive function calls by allocating your own stack and manually storing and retrieving values of local variables from this stack. Implementing this type of function tends to be significantly more complicated than implementing an equivalent function using recursive function calls. Iterative implementations of recursive algorithms aren't much more efficient than recursive function calls unless the overhead of the stack implementation you use is small relative to the function call overhead. Given the large increase in complexity and relatively minor performance differences, you should implement recursive algorithms with recursive function calls unless instructed otherwise. An example of a recursive algorithm implemented without recursive function calls is given in the solution to the "Preorder Traversal, No Recursion" problem in Chapter 4, "Trees and Graphs."

LESSON A recursive algorithm can be implemented without recursive function calls using a stack, but it's usually more trouble than it's worth.

In an interview, a working solution is of primary importance; an efficient solution is secondary. Therefore, unless you've been told otherwise, go with whatever type of solution comes to you first. If that should happen to be a recursive solution, you might want to mention the inefficiencies inherent in recursive solutions to your interviewer, so it's clear that you know about them. In the rare instance that you see a recursive and an iterative solution of roughly equal complexity at about the same time, you should probably mention them both to the interviewer and say you're going to work out the iterative solution because it's likely to be more efficient.

Problem: Binary Search

- Implement a function to perform a binary search on a sorted array of integers to find the index of a given integer. Use the prototype:

```
int BinarySearch(int* array, int lower, int upper, int target);
```

Comment on the efficiency of this search and compare it with other search methods.

In a binary search, you compare the central element in your search space (an array, in this case) with the item you're looking for. If it's less than what you're searching for you can eliminate the first half of the search space; if it's more you can eliminate the second half of the search space. In the third case, if the central element is equal to the search item, you've found it and can stop there. Otherwise, you repeat the process on the remaining portion of the search space. If not already familiar to you from computer science courses, this algorithm may remind you of the optimum strategy in the children's number guessing game where one child guesses numbers in a given range and a second responds "higher" or "lower" to each incorrect guess.

Because a binary search can be described in terms of binary searches on successively smaller portions of the search space, it lends itself to a recursive implementation. Your function will need to be passed the array it is searching, the limits within which it should search, and the element for which it is searching. You can subtract the lower limit from the upper limit to find the size of the search space, then divide this size by two and add it to the lower limit to find the index of the central element. Next compare this element to the search element. If they're equal, return the index; if the search element is smaller, the new upper limit becomes the central index − 1; if the search element is larger, the new lower limit is the central index + 1, and you recurse until you match the element you're searching for.

Before you code, you should consider what error conditions you'll need to handle. One way to think about this is to consider what assumptions you're making about the data you are being given and then consider how these assumptions might be violated. One assumption, explicitly stated in the problem, is that only a sorted array can be binary searched; you'll want to detect unsorted lists. You can do this by checking whether the value at the upper limit is less than the value at the lower limit. If this occurs, you should return an error code. Another way to handle this case would be to call a sort routine and then restart the search, but that's more than you need to do in an interview. Another assumption implicit in a search may be a little less obvious: The element you're searching for is assumed to exist in the array. If you don't terminate the recursion until you find the element, you'll recurse infinitely when the element is missing from the array. You can avoid this by returning an error code if the upper and lower limits are equal and the element at that location is not the element you're searching for. Finally, you assume that the lower limit is less than or equal to the upper limit. For simplicity, you can just return an error code in this case, although in a real program you'd probably want to either define this as an illegal call and use an assert to check it (for more efficient programs) or silently reverse the limits when they are out of order (for easier programming).

Now you can translate these algorithms and error checks into code:

```
#define E_TARGET_NOT_IN_ARRAY -1
#define E_ARRAY_UNORDERED -2
#define E_LIMITS_REVERSED -3

int BinarySearch(int* array, int lower, int upper, int target)
{
    int center, range;

    range = upper - lower;
    if (range < 0) {
        return E_LIMITS_REVERSED;
    } else if (range == 0 && array[lower] != target) {
        return E_TARGET_NOT_IN_ARRAY;
    }

    if (array[lower] > array[upper])
        return E_ARRAY_UNORDERED;

    center = ((range)/2) + lower;

    if (target == array[center]) {
        return center;
    } else if (target < array[center]) {
        return BinarySearch(array, lower, center - 1, target);
    } else {
        return BinarySearch(array, center + 1, upper, target);
    }
}
```

Although this completes the given task, it is not as efficient as it could be. As we discussed at the beginning of this chapter, recursive implementations are generally less efficient than equivalent iterative implementations.

If you analyze the recursion in the previous solution, you can see that each recursive call serves only to change the search limits. There's no reason why you can't change the limits on each iteration of a loop and avoid the overhead of recursion. The function that follows is a more efficient, iterative analog of the recursive binary search.

```
int IterBinarySearch(int* array, int lower, int upper, int target)
{
    int center, range;

    if (lower > upper)
        return E_LIMITS_REVERSED;

    while (1) {
        range = upper - lower;
        if (range == 0 && array[lower] != target)
            return E_TARGET_NOT_IN_ARRAY;

        if (array[lower] > array[upper])
            return E_ARRAY_UNORDERED;

        center = ((range)/2) + lower;

        if (target == array[center]) {
            return center;
        } else if (target < array[center]) {
            upper = center - 1;
        } else {
            lower = center + 1;
        }
    }
}
```

A binary search is $O(\log(n))$ because half of the search is eliminated (in a sense, searched) on each iteration. This is more efficient than a simple search through all elements, which would be $O(n)$. However, in order to perform a binary search the array must be sorted, an operation that is usually $O(n \log(n))$.

Problem: Permutations of a String

- Implement a function that prints all possible orderings of the characters in a string. In other words, print all permutations that use all the characters from the original string. For instance, given the string "hat" your function should print the strings "tha", "aht", "tah", "ath", "hta", and "hat". Treat each character in the input string as a distinct character, even if it is repeated. Given the string "aaa", your function should print "aaa" six times. You may print the permutations in any order you choose.

Manually permuting a string is a relatively intuitive process, but describing an algorithm for the process can be difficult. In a sense, the question here is like being asked to describe how you tie your shoes: You know the answer, but you probably still have to go through the process a few times to figure out what steps you're taking.

Try applying that method to this problem: Manually permute a short string and try to reverse-engineer an algorithm out of the process. We'll take the string "abcd" as an example. Because you're trying to construct an algorithm from an intuitive process, you'll want to go through the permutations in a systematic order. Exactly which systematic order you use isn't terribly important—different orders are likely to lead to different algorithms, but as long as you're systematic about the process you should be able to construct an algorithm. You'll want to choose a simple order that will make it easy to identify any permutations that you might accidentally skip.

You might consider listing all the permutations in alphabetical order. This means the first group of permutations will all start with "a". Within this group, you'll first have the permutations with a second letter of "b", then "c", and finally "d". Continue in a like fashion for the other first letters.

abcd	bacd	cabd	dabc
abdc	badc	cadb	dacb
acbd	bcad	cbad	dbac
acdb	bcda	cbda	dbca
adbc	bdac	cdab	dcab
adcb	bdca	cdba	dcba

Before you continue, make sure you didn't miss any permutations. There are four possible letters that can be placed in the first position. For each of these four possibilities, there are three remaining possible letters for the second position. Thus there are $4 \times 3 = 12$ different possibilities for the first two letters of the permutations. Once you've selected the first two letters, two different letters remain available for the third position, and the last remaining letter is put in the fourth position. So if you multiply $4 \times 3 \times 2 \times 1$ you have a total of 24 different permutations; there are 24 permutations in the previous list, so nothing has been missed. This calculation can be expressed more succinctly as $4!$—you may recall that $n!$ is the number of possible arrangements of n objects.

Now examine the list of permutations for patterns. The rightmost letters vary faster than the leftmost letters. For each letter that you choose for the first (leftmost) position, you write out all the permutations beginning with that letter before you change the first letter. Likewise, once you've picked a letter for the second position, you write out all permutations beginning with this two-letter sequence before changing the letters in either the first or second position. In other words, you can define the permutation process as picking a letter for a given position and performing the permutation process starting at the next position to the right before coming back to change the letter you just picked. This sounds like the basis for a recursive definition of permutation. Try to rephrase it in explicitly recursive terms: To find all permutations starting at position n, successively place all allowable letters in position n, and for each new letter in position n find all permutations starting at position $n + 1$ (the recursive case). When n is greater than the number of characters in the input string, a permutation has been completed; print it and return to changing letters at positions less than n (the base case).

You almost have an algorithm; you just need to define "all allowable letters" a little more rigorously. Because each letter from the input string can appear only once in each permutation, "all allowable letters" can't be defined as every letter in the input string. Think about how you did the permutations manually. For the group of permutations beginning with "b", you never put a "b" anywhere but the first position because when you selected letters for later positions, "b" had already been used. For the group beginning "bc" you used only "a" and "d" in the third and fourth positions because both "b" and "c" had already been used. So "all allowable letters" means all letters in the input string that haven't already been chosen for a position to the left of our current position (a position less than n). Algorithmically, you could check each candidate letter for position n against all the letters in positions less than n to see if it had been used. You can eliminate these inefficient scans by maintaining an array of boolean values corresponding to the positions of the letters in the input string and using this array to mark letters as used or unused, as appropriate.

In outline form, this algorithm looks like:

If you're past the last position[2]

---

[2]Separating the base case from the recursive case as we have done here is considered good style and may make the code easier to understand, but it does not provide optimum performance. The code can be significantly optimized by invoking the base case directly without a recursive call if the next recursive call would invoke the base case. In this algorithm, that would involve checking whether the letter just placed was the last letter—if so, one would print the permutation and make no recursive call; otherwise a recursive call would be made. This would eliminate $n!$ function calls, reducing the function call overhead by approximately a factor of n (where n is

Print the string

Return

Otherwise

For each letter in the input string

If it's marked as used, skip to the next letter

Else place the letter in the current position

Mark the letter as used

Permute remaining letters starting at current position + 1

Mark the letter as unused

Just for a change of pace, let's try coding this in Perl:

```perl
sub Permute {
    my ($inString) = @_;
    # $in, $out and $used are references to arrays
    my ($in, $out, $used) = ([], [], []);
    @$in = split //, $inString;  # One char in each element of $in
    DoPermute($in, $out, $used, 0);
}

sub DoPermute {
    my ($in, $out, $used, $recursLev) = @_;
    my ($i);

    # Base case
    if ($recursLev == @$in) {
        print @$out, "\n";
        return;
    }

    # Recursive case
    for ($i = 0; $i < @$in; $i++) { # @$in gives array length
        next if $used->[$i];        # if used, skip to next letter
        $out->[$recursLev] = $in->[$i];# put this letter in output
        $used->[$i] = 1;            # mark this letter as used
        DoPermute($in, $out, $used, $recursLev + 1);
        $used->[$i] = 0;            # unmark this letter
    }
}
```

the length of the input string). Short-circuiting the base case in this manner is referred to as "arms length recursion" and is considered poor style, especially in academic circles. Whichever way you choose to code the solution, it is worthwhile to mention the advantages of the alternate approach to your interviewer.

Structurally, this function uses a wrapper function called `Permute` to allocate three arrays and do some processing on the input string. Then it calls the recursive portion, `DoPermute`, to actually do the permutation. If you're not completely conversant with Perl syntax, the following few reminders may be helpful. `my` is used to declare a local variable[3] here. Arguments to a subroutine are passed in the `@_` array. The second line of `Permute` says that `$in`, `$out`, and `$used` are local variables that will be references to arrays (references are like pointers). `@` is the array dereferencing operator. In scalar context, like the conditional of an `if`, an array evaluates to the number of elements in the array; in list context, like a print statement, an array evaluates to the concatenated values of the elements in the array.

Of course, this algorithm can be just as easily implemented in C. You may find it helpful to compare the C and Perl implementations:

```c
int Permute( char inString[]) {
    int length, i, *used;
    char *out;

    length = strlen(inString);
    out = (char *) malloc(length+1);
    if (!out)
        return 0; /* Failed */

    /* so printf doesn't run past the end of the buffer */
    out[length] = '\0';
    used = (int *) malloc(sizeof(int) * length);
    if (!used)
        return 0; /* Failed */

    /* start with no letters used, so zero array */
    for (i = 0; i < length; i++) {
        used[i] = 0;
    }

    DoPermute(inString, out, used, length, 0);

    free(out);
    free(used);
    return 1; /* Success! */
}
```

---

[3]Just to keep things interesting, Perl also has the keyword `local`, which makes a local copy of a global variable. To keep it simple, just remember that `my` declares a local variable and `local` shouldn't be used without good reason.

```
void DoPermute(char in[], char out[], int used[],
               int length, int recursLev)
{
    int i;

    /* Base case */
    if (recursLev == length) {
        printf("%s\n", out); /* print permutation */
        return;
    }

    /* Recursive case */
    for (i = 0; i < length; i++) {
        if (used[i])                /* if used, skip to next letter */
            continue;

        out[recursLev] = in[i]; /* put current letter in output */
        used[i] = 1;            /* mark this letter as used */
        DoPermute(in, out, used, length, recursLev + 1);
        used[i] = 0;            /* unmark this letter */
    }
}
```

Problem: Combinations of a String

- Implement a function that prints all possible combinations of the characters in a string. These combinations range in length from one to the length of the string. Two combinations that differ only in ordering of their characters are the same combination. In other words, "12" and "31" are different combinations from the input string "123", but "21" is the same as "12".

This is a companion problem to finding the permutations of the characters in a string. If you haven't yet worked through that problem, you may wish to do so before you tackle this one.

Following the model of the solution to the permutation problem, try working out an example by hand and see where that gets you. Because you'll be trying to divine an algorithm from the example, you'll again need to be systematic in your approach. You might try listing combinations in order of length. We'll use "wxyz" as our sample input string. Because the ordering of letters within each combination is arbitrary, we'll keep them in the same order as they are in the input string to minimize confusion.

w	wx	wxy	wxyz
x	wy	wxz	
y	wz	wyz	
z	xy	xyz	
	xz		
	yz		

Some interesting patterns seem to be emerging, but there's nothing clear yet, certainly nothing that seems to suggest an algorithm. Listing output in terms of the order of the input string (alphabetical order, for this input string) turned out to be helpful in the permutation problem. Try rearranging the combinations you generated and see if that's useful here.

w	x	y	z
wx	xy	yz	
wxy	xyz		
wxyz	xz		
wxz			
wy			
wyz			
wz			

This looks a little more productive. There is a column for each letter in the input string. The first combination in each column is a single letter from the input string. The remainder of each column's combinations consist of that letter prepended to each of the combinations in the columns to the right. Take, for example, the "x" column. This column has the single letter combination "x". The columns to the right of it have the combinations "y", "yz", and "z", so if you prepend "x" to each of these combinations you find the remaining combinations in the "x" column: "xy", "xyz", and "xz". You could use this rule to generate all of the combinations, starting with just "z" in the rightmost column and working your way to the left, each time writing a single letter from the input string at the top of the column and then completing the column with that letter prepended to each of the combinations in columns to the right. This is a recursive method for generating the combinations. It is space inefficient because it requires storage of all previously generated combinations, but it indicates that this problem can be solved recursively. See if you can gain some insight on a more efficient recursive algorithm by examining the combinations you've written a little more closely.

Look at which letters appear in which positions. All four letters appear in the first position, but "w" never appears in the second position. Only "y" and "z" appear in the third position, and "z" is in the fourth position in the only combination that has a fourth position ("wxyz"). So, a potential algorithm might involve iterating through all allowable letters at each position: w–z in the first position, x–z in the second position, and so on. Check this idea against the example to see if it would work: It seems to successfully generate all the combinations in the first column. However, when you select "x" for the first position this candidate algorithm would start with "x" in the second position, generating an illegal combination of "xx". Apparently the algorithm needs some refinement.

In order to generate the correct combination "xy", you really need to begin with "y", not "x" in the second position. When you select "y" for the first position (third column) you need to start with "z" because "yy" is illegal and "yx" and "yw" have already been generated as "xy" and "wy". This suggests that in each output position you need to begin iterating with the letter in the input string following the letter selected for the preceding position in the output string. We'll call this letter our input start letter.

It may be helpful to summarize this a little more formally. You need to track the output position as well as the input start position. Begin with the first position as the output position, and the first character of the input as the input start position. For a given position, sequentially select all letters from the input start position to the last letter in the input string. For each letter you select, print the combination and then generate all other combinations beginning with this sequence by recursively calling the generating function with the input start position set to the next letter after the one you've just selected and the output position set to the next position. You should check this idea against the example to make sure it works. It does—no more problems in the second column. Before you code, it may be helpful to outline the algorithm just to make sure you have it.[4]

For each letter from input start position to end of input string

Select the letter into the current position in output string

Print letters in output string

---

[4]For comparison, we've chosen the performance side of the arm's-length recursion style/performance trade-off discussed in the permutation problem. The performance and style differences between the two possible approaches are not as dramatic for the combination algorithm as they were for the permutation algorithm.

If the current letter isn't the last in the input string

Generate remaining combinations starting at next position with iteration starting at next letter beyond the letter just selected

After all that hard work, the algorithm looks pretty simple! You're ready to code it. If you choose C, you'll need a little wrapper function to allocate an appropriately sized output buffer for writing combinations. Because you'll be using this buffer to print strings of many different lengths, you'll have to remember to tack a NUL character ('\0') to the end of each string to keep printf from printing whatever garbage is in the rest of the buffer.

```c
int Combine(char inString[])
{
    int length;
    char *out;
    length = strlen(inString);
    /* allocate output buffer */
    out = (char *) malloc(length + 1);
    if (!out)
        return 0; /* failed */

    /* enter recursive portion */
    DoCombine(inString, out, length, 0, 0);
    free(out);
    return 1; /* success! */
}

void DoCombine(char in[], char out[], int length,
               int recursLev, int start)
{
    int i;
    for (i = start; i < length; i++) {
        out[recursLev] = in[i];     /* select current letter */
        out[recursLev + 1] = '\0'; /* tack on NUL for printf */
        printf("%s\n", out);
        if (i < length - 1) /* recurse if more letters in input */
            DoCombine(in, out, length, recursLev + 1, i + 1);
    }
}
```

This solution would be sufficient in most interviews. Nevertheless, you can make a rather minor optimization to DoCombine that eliminates the if statement. Given that this is a recursive function, the performance increase is probably negligible compared to the function call overhead, but you might want to see if you can figure it out just for practice.

For comparison, we'll show a Perl implementation, just as we did for permutations. Instead of the array-based approach we used for permutations, we'll do it in terms of strings. We'll also employ a somewhat more Perl-centric strategy of passing only the remaining portion of the input string to each recursive call rather than a start offset for the entire input string. Finally, we'll implement the little optimization suggested previously.

```perl
sub Combine {
    my ($in, $comb) = @_;        # Get arguments
    my ($letter, $i);            # declare local variables
    for ($i = 0; $i < length($in) - 1; $i++) {
        $letter = substr($in, $i, 1);  # Select current letter
        print $comb, $letter, "\n";
        Combine(substr($in, $i + 1), $comb . $letter);
    }
    print $comb, substr($in, length($in) - 1, 1), "\n";
}
```

Notice that the `if` statement is eliminated by removing the final iteration from the loop and moving the code that would have executed during that iteration past the end of the loop. The general case of this optimization is referred to as *loop partitioning*, and `if` statements that can be removed by loop partitioning are called *loop index dependent conditionals*. Again, this optimization doesn't make much difference here, but it can be important inside nested loops.

Problem: Telephone Words

- People often give out their telephone number as a word representing the seven-digit number. For example, if my telephone number were 866-2665, I could tell people my number was "TOOCOOL," instead of the hard-to-remember seven-digit number. Note that many other possibilities (most of which are nonsensical) can represent 866-2665. You can see how letters correspond to numbers on a telephone keypad in Figure 6.2.

  Write a function that takes a seven-digit telephone number and prints out all of the possible "words" or combinations of letters that can represent the given number. Because the 0 and 1 keys have no letters on them, you should change only the digits 2–9 to letters.

  Use the function prototype:

Figure 6.2 Telephone keypad.

```
void PrintTelephoneWords(int phoneNumber[]);
```

where phoneNumber is an array of seven integers with each element being one digit in the number. You may assume that only valid phone numbers will be passed to your function.
   You may use the function:

```
char GetCharKey(int telephoneKey, int place)
```

which takes a telephone key (0–9) and a place of either 1, 2, 3 and returns the character corresponding to the letter in that position on the specified key. For example, GetCharKey(3, 2) will return 'E' because the telephone key 3 has the letters "DEF" on it and 'E' is the second letter.

It's worthwhile to define some terms for this problem. A telephone number is made up of digits. Three letters correspond to each digit (except for 0 and 1, but when 0 and 1 are used in the context of creating a word, you can call them letters). The lowest letter, middle letter, and highest letter will be called the digit's low value, middle value, and high value, respectively. You will be creating words, or strings of letters, to represent the given number.

First, impress the interviewer with your math skills by determining how many words can correspond to a seven-digit number. This requires combinatorial mathematics, but if you don't remember this type of math, don't panic. First, try a one-digit phone number. Clearly, this would have three words. Now, try a two-digit phone number, say 56. There are three possibilities for the first letter, and for each of these there are three possibilities for the second letter. This yields a total of nine words that can correspond to this number. It appears that each additional digit increases the number of words by a factor of 3. Thus, for 7 digits, you have 3^7 words and for a phone number of length n, you have 3^n words. Because 0 and 1 have no corresponding letters, a phone number with 0s or 1s in it would have fewer words, but 3^7 is the upper bound on the number of words for a seven-digit number.

Now you need to figure out an algorithm for printing these words. Try writing out some words representing one of the author's old college phone numbers, 497-1927, as an example. The most natural manner to list the words is alphabetical order. This way, you always know which word comes next and you'll be less likely to miss words. You know that there are of the order of 3^7 words that can represent this number so you won't have time to write them all out. Try writing just the beginning and the end of the alphabetical sequence. You will probably want to start with the word that uses the low letter for each digit of the phone number. This will guarantee that your first word is the first word in alphabetical order. Thus, the first word for 497-1927 would be 'G' for 4 since 4 has "GHI" on it, 'W' for 9 which has "WXY" on it, 'P' for 7 which has "PRS" on it, and so on, resulting in "GWP1WAP".

As you continue to write down words, you'll ultimately get a list that looks like:

GWP1WAP

GWP1WAR

GWP1WAS

GWP1WBP

GWP1WBR

...

IYS1YCR

IYS1YCS

It was easy to create this list because the algorithm for generating the words is relatively intuitive. Formalizing this algorithm is more challenging. A good place to start is by examining the process of going from one word to the next word in alphabetical order.

Because you know the first word in alphabetical order, determining how to get to the next word at any point will give you an algorithm for writing all the words. One important part of the process of going from one word to the next seems to be that the last letter always changes. It continually cycles through a pattern of P-R-S. Whenever the last letter goes from S back to P, it causes the next to last letter to change. Try investigating this a little more and see if you can come up with specific rules. Again, it's probably best to try an example. You may have to write down more words than in the example list to see a pattern (a three-digit phone number should be sufficient, or the previous list will work if it's expanded a bit). It looks as if the following is always true: Whenever a letter changes, its right neighbor goes through all of its values before the original letter changes again. Conversely, whenever a letter resets to its low value, its left neighbor increases to the next value.

From these observations, there are probably two reasonable paths to follow as you search for the solution to this problem. You can start with the first letter and have a letter affect its right neighbor, or you can start with the last letter and have a letter affect its left neighbor. Both of these approaches seem reasonable, but you'll have to choose one. For now, try the former and see where that gets you.

You should examine exactly what you're trying to do at this point. You're working with the observation that whenever a letter changes, it causes its right neighbor to cycle through all of its values before it will change again. You're now using this observation to determine how to get from one word to the next word in alphabetical order. It may help to formalize this observation: Changing the letter in position i causes the letter in position $i + 1$ to cycle through its values. When an algorithm can be written in terms of how elements i and $i + 1$ interact with each other, it often indicates recursion, so try to figure out a recursive algorithm.

You have already discovered most of the algorithm. You know how each letter affects the next; you just need to figure out how to start the process and determine the base case. Looking again at the list to try to figure out the start condition, you'll see that the first letter cycles only once. So, if you start by cycling the first letter, this will cause multiple cycles of the second letter, which will cause multiple cycles of the third letter— exactly as desired. After you change the last letter, you can't cycle anything else so this is a good base case to end the recursion. When the base case occurs, you should also print out the word because you've just generated the next word in alphabetical order. The one special case you have to be aware of occurs if there is a 0 or 1 in the given telephone number. You don't want to print out any word three times, so you should check for this case and cycle immediately if you encounter it.

In list form, the steps look like this:

If the current digit is past the last digit

    Print the word because you're at the end

Else

For each of the three digits that can represent the current digit, going from low to high

Have the letter represent the current digit

Move to next digit and recurse

If the current digit is a 0 or a 1, return

The code is as follows:

```
#define PHONE_NUMBER_LENGTH 7

void PrintTelephoneWords(int phoneNum[])
{
    char result[PHONE_NUMBER_LENGTH + 1];

    /* tack on the NUL character at the end */
    result[PHONE_NUMBER_LENGTH] = '\0';

    DoPrintTelephoneWords(phoneNum, 0, result);
}

void DoPrintTelephoneWords(int phoneNum[], int curDigit,
    char result[])
{
    int i;

    if (curDigit == PHONE_NUMBER_LENGTH) {
        printf("%s\n", result);
        return;
    }

    for (i = 1; i <= 3; i++) {
        result[curDigit] = GetCharKey(phoneNum[curDigit], i);
        DoPrintTelephoneWords(phoneNum, curDigit + 1, result);
        if (phoneNum[curDigit] == 0 ||
                phoneNum[curDigit] == 1) return;

    }
}
```

What is the running time of this algorithm? It can be no less than $O(3^n)$ because there are 3^n solutions, so any correct solution must be at least $O(3^n)$. Getting each new word requires only constant time operations so the running time is indeed $O(3^n)$.

■ **Reimplement `PrintTelephoneWords` without using recursion.**

The recursive algorithm doesn't seem to be very helpful in this situation. Recursion was inherent in the way that you wrote out the steps of the algorithm. You could always try emulating recursion using a stack-based data structure, but there may be a better way involving a different algorithm. In the recursive solution, you solved the problem from left to right. You also made an observation that suggested the existence of another algorithm going from right to left. The observation was that whenever a letter changes from its high value to its low value, its left neighbor is incremented. Explore this observation and see if you can find a non-recursive solution to the problem.

Again, you're trying to figure out how to determine the next word in alphabetical order. Because you're working from right to left, you should look for something that always happens on the right side of a word as it changes to the next word in alphabetical order. Looking back at the original observations, you noticed that the last letter always changes. This seems to indicate that a good way to start would be incrementing the last letter. If the last letter is at its high value and you increment it, you will reset the last letter to its low value and increment the second-to-last letter. But suppose the second-to-last number is already at its high value. Try looking at the list to figure out what you need to do. From the list, it appears that you would then reset the second-to-last number to its low value and increment the third-to-last number. You will continue carrying your increment like this until you don't have to reset a letter to its low value.

This sounds like the algorithm you want, but you still have to work out how to start it and how to know when you're finished. You can start by manually creating the first string as you did when writing out the list. Now you need to determine how to end. Look at the last string and figure out what happens if you try to increment it. Every letter resets to its low value. You can check to see if every letter is at its low value, but this seems inefficient. The first letter resets only once, when you've printed out all of the words. You can use this to signal that you're done printing out all of the words. Again, you have to consider the cases where there is a 0 or a 1. Because 0 and 1 effectively can't be incremented (they always stay as 0 and 1), you should always treat a 0 or 1 as if it's at its highest letter value and increment its left neighbor. In outline form, the steps are as follows:

Create the first word character by character

Loop infinitely:

    Print out the word

    Increment the last letter and carry the change

    If the first letter has reset, you're done

Here is the solution based on this sort of algorithm.[5]

```
#define PHONE_NUMBER_LENGTH 7

void PrintTelephoneWords(int phoneNum[])
{
    char result[PHONE_NUMBER_LENGTH + 1];
    int i;

    /* Initialize the result (in our example,
     * put GWP1WAR in result).
     */
    for (i = 0; i < PHONE_NUMBER_LENGTH; i++)
        result[i] = GetCharKey(phoneNum[i], 1);

    /* Tack on the NUL character at the end. */
    result[PHONE_NUMBER_LENGTH] = '\0';

    /* Main loop begins */
    while (1) {
        printf("%s\n", result);

        /* Start at the end and try to increment from right
         * to left.
         */
        for (i = PHONE_NUMBER_LENGTH - 1; i >= -1; i==){
            /* You're done because you
             * tried to carry the leftmost digit.
             */
            if (i == -1) return;

            /* Otherwise, we're not done and must continue. */

            /* You want to start with this condition so that you can
             * deal with the special cases, 0 and 1, right away.
             */
            if (GetCharKey(phoneNum[i], 3) == result[i] ||
                phoneNum[i] == 0 || phoneNum[i] == 1) {
                result[i] = GetCharKey(phoneNum[i], 1);
                /* No break, so loop continues to next digit */
            } else if (GetCharKey(phoneNum[i], 1) == result[i]){
                result[i] = GetCharKey(phoneNum[i], 2);
                break;
            } else if (GetCharKey(phoneNum[i], 2) == result[i]){
                result[i] = GetCharKey(phoneNum[i], 3);
                break;
```

[5]You could cut down on the calls to GetCharKey by storing each letter's three values in variables rather than making repeated calls to see whether a value is low, middle, or high. This would make the code a little more difficult, and this sort of optimization is probably unnecessary in the context of this solution.

```
                        }
                    }
                }
            }
```

What's the running time on this algorithm?

Again, there must be at least 3^n solutions, so the algorithm can be no better than $O(3^n)$ if it is correct. There is slight constant overhead in finding each word, but you can ignore it. Therefore, this is also an $O(3^n)$ solution.

CHAPTER 7

Other Programming Topics

A number of interview topics are less common than those we've seen so far. These topics do appear frequently enough in interviews, though, to merit discussion. Because the topics in this chapter are so disparate, this introduction has a separate section for each topic.

Graphics

A computer screen consists of pixels arranged in a Cartesian coordinate system. This is commonly called a raster pixel display. Computer graphics algorithms change the colors of sets of pixels. Often, the algorithm for generating a raster pixel image is based on a geometric equation. Because a computer screen has a finite number of pixels, translating from a geometric equation to a pixel display can be quite complex. Geometric equations usually have real-number (floating-point) solutions, but pixels are found only at fixed, regularly spaced locations. Therefore, every point that is calculated must be adjusted to pixel coordinates. This requires some kind of rounding, but rounding to the nearest pixel coordinate is not always the correct approach. It is often necessary to round numbers in unusual ways or add error-correcting terms. If rounding is done care-lessly, it often leads to gaps in what should be continuous lines. Take care to check your graphics algorithms for distortion or gaps due to poor rounding or error correction.

Consider something as simple as drawing a line segment, for example. Suppose you were trying to implement a function that takes two end-points and draws a line between them. After doing a little algebra, you could easily get an equation in the form of $y = mx + b$. Then, you could calculate y for a range of x values and draw the points making up the line. This function seems trivial.

The devil, though, is in the details of this problem. First, you must account for vertical lines. In this case, m is infinity, so the simple proce-dure can't draw the line. Similarly, imagine that the line is not vertical, but close to vertical. For example, imagine that the horizontal distance spanned by the line is 2 pixels, but the vertical distance is 20 pixels. In this case, only 2 pixels would be drawn—not much of a line. To correct for this problem, you would have to rework your equation to $x = (y - b) / m$. Then, if the line is closer to vertical you vary y and use this equation; if it is closer to horizontal, you use the original procedure.

Even this won't solve all your problems. Suppose you need to draw a line with a slope of 1, for example, $y = x$. In this case, using either proce-dure, you would draw the pixels $(0, 0)$, $(1, 1)$, $(2, 2)$ . . . This is mathemati-cally correct, but the line looks too thin on the screen because the pixels are much more spread out than in other lines. A diagonal line of length 100 has fewer pixels in it than a horizontal line of length 80. An ideal line-drawing algorithm would have some mechanism to guarantee that all lines have nearly equal pixel density. Another problem has to do with rounding. If you calculate a point at $(.99, .99)$ and use a type cast to con-vert this to integers, the floating-point values will be truncated and the pixel will be drawn at $(0, 0)$. You need to explicitly round the values so that the point is drawn at $(1, 1)$.

If graphics problems seem like never-ending series of special cases, you understand the issues involved. As a concluding thought on this issue, you should note that even if you were to work out all the problems with the line-drawing algorithm we've described, it still wouldn't be very good. Although this algorithm effectively illustrates the problems encountered in graphics programming, its reliance on floating-point calculations makes it very slow. High-performance algorithms that use only integer math are far more complicated than what we've discussed here.

LESSON   Computer graphics involves drawing with pixels. Always check for rounding errors, gaps, and special cases.

Bit Operators

Many computer languages have facilities to allow programmers access to the individual bits of a variable. Bit operators may appear more frequently in interviews than in day-to-day programming, so they merit a review.

Bit operators vary across languages, but bitwise operations are most often seen in C because C is the lowest-level programming language in common use. Therefore, this review will concentrate on the bit operators in C. These operators are identical to those of C++ and almost identical to Java's bit operators.[1]

To work with bit operators, you have to start thinking on the levels of bits. Numbers are usually internally represented in a computer in *binary two's complement notation*. If you're already familiar with binary numbers, you almost understand binary two's complement notation. Binary two's complement notation is almost the same as binary notation. In fact, it's identical for positive numbers. The only difference comes with negative numbers. An integer usually consists of 32 bits, but to avoid excessive length, we'll look at some examples with 8-bit integers. In binary two's complement notation, a positive integer like 13 is `00001101`, exactly the same as in regular binary notation. Negative numbers are a little trickier. Two's complement notation makes a number negative by applying the rule "Flip each bit and add 1" to the number's positive binary representation. For example, to get the number −1, you start with 1, which is `00000001` in binary. Flipping each bit results in `11111110`. Adding 1 gives you `11111111`, which is the two's complement notation for −1. If you're not familiar with this, it may seem sort of weird, but it has lots of advantages, especially when subtracting numbers. Notice that the first bit is a sign bit: If it is 0, the number is positive; if it is 1, the number is negative.

Bit operators operate directly on the bits of variables. One common bit operator is the unary operator ~, called *NOT*. This operator negates or reverses all the bits that it operates on. Thus, every 1 becomes a 0, and

---

[1]The only difference is that in Java, >> always sign extends and there is an additional operator, >>>, that shifts right with 0 extension. In C, the behavior of >> depends on whether the type is signed.

every 0 becomes a 1. For example, if ~ is applied to `00001101` the result is `11110010`.

Three other bitwise operators are | (*OR*), & (*AND*), and ^ (*XOR*). They are all binary operators applied in a bitwise fashion. This means that i th bit of one number is combined with the i th bit of the other number to produce the i th bit of the resulting value. The rules for these operators are as follows:

&: If both bits are 1, the result is a 1. Otherwise, the result is 0. For example:

```
  01100110
& 11110100
  01100100
```

|: If either bit is a 1, the result is 1. If both bits are 0, the result is 0. For example:

```
  01100110
| 11110100
  11110110
```

^: If the bits are the same, the result is 0. If the bits are different, the result is 1.

```
  01100110
^ 11110100
  10010010
```

The two remaining bit operators are >> (*SHIFT RIGHT*) and << (*SHIFT LEFT*). They shift the value the indicated number of positions to the left or the right, respectively. The new spaces created are always filled with 0's when using the << operator. The >> operator also fills with 0's when operating on an unsigned value. When operating on a signed value, the >> operator sign extends. This means that if the number is positive, the new spaces are filled with 0's. If the number is negative, the new spaces are filled with 1's. For example: `01100110 << 5` results in `11000000`. Similarly, `01100110 >> 5` gives `00000011`. Yet, a negative number like `10100110 >> 5` yields `11111101` because the operator sign extends.

The shift operators allow you to multiply and divide by powers of 2 very quickly. Shifting to the right one bit is equivalent to dividing by 2 and shifting to the left one bit is equivalent to multiplying by 2. The equivalence of shifting and multiplying or dividing by a power of the base also occurs in the more familiar base 10 number system. Consider the number 17. 17 << 1 results in the value 170, which is exactly the same as multiplying 17 by 10. Similarly, 17 >> 1 gives 1, which is the same as integer dividing 17 by 10.

Structured Query Language (SQL)

SQL is the lingua franca of relational database manipulation. It provides mechanisms for most kinds of database manipulations. Understandably, SQL is a big topic, and lots of books are devoted just to learning SQL. Nevertheless, the basic tasks of storing and retrieving data are relatively simple with SQL.

If you don't mention that you know SQL on your resume or during the interview, it's highly unlikely that you'll be asked any SQL questions. Therefore, this introduction will not try to teach you SQL. Instead, it will review the high points of SQL, placing emphasis on common interview topics and favoring example over formal syntax definition.

LESSON If you don't indicate that you know SQL, you probably won't be asked anything about it.

Most interview database questions involve writing queries for a database with a given schema, so you won't usually need to design a schema yourself. For this introduction, we will work with the following schema:

```
Player(name CHAR(20), number INT(4));
Stats(number INT(4), totalPoints INT(4), year CHAR(20));
```

Some sample data for `Player` are shown in Table 7.1, and a sample `Stats` table is shown in Table 7.2.

One fundamental SQL statement is `INSERT`, which is used to add values to a table. For example, to insert a player named Bill Henry with the number 50 into the `Player` table, you would use the statement:

```
INSERT INTO Player VALUES('Bill Henry', 50);
```

`SELECT` is the SQL statement most commonly seen in interviews. A `SELECT` statement retrieves data from a table. For example, the statement

Table 7.1 Player Sample Data

NAME	NUMBER
Larry Smith	23
David Gonzalez	12
George Rogers	7
Mike Lee	14
Rajiv Williams	55

Table 7.2 Stats Sample Data

NUMBER	TOTALPOINTS	YEAR
7	59	Freshman
55	90	Senior
22	15	Senior
86	221	Junior
36	84	Sophomore

```
SELECT * FROM Player;
```

will return all of the values in the table `Player`:

```
+------------------------+
| name           | number |
+------------------------+
| Larry Smith    |    23 |
| David Gonzalez |    12 |
| George Rogers  |     7 |
| Mike Lee       |    14 |
| Rajiv Williams |    55 |
| Bill Henry     |    50 |
+------------------------+
```

You can specify which columns you want to return like this:

```
SELECT name FROM Player;
```

returns:

```
+----------------+
| name           |
+----------------+
| Larry Smith    |
| David Gonzalez |
| George Rogers  |
| Mike Lee       |
| Rajiv Williams |
| Bill Henry     |
+----------------+
```

You may want to be more restrictive about which values you return. For example, if you want to return only the names of the players with numbers less than 10 or greater than 40, you would use the following statement:

```
SELECT name FROM Player WHERE number < 10 OR number > 40;
```

It returns:

```
+----------------+
| name           |
+----------------+
| George Rogers  |
| Rajiv Williams |
| Bill Henry     |
+----------------+
```

Often, you will want to use data from two tables. For example, you may want to print out the names of all players along with the number of points that each player has scored. To do this, you will have to join the two tables on the number field. The number field is called a *common key* because it represents the same unique value in both tables. The query is:

```
SELECT name, totalPoints FROM Player, Stats WHERE
Player.number = Stats.number;
```

It returns:

```
+----------------------------+
| name           | totalPoints |
+----------------------------+
| George Rogers  |          59 |
| Rajiv Williams |          90 |
+----------------------------+
```

The *aggregates*, MAX, MIN, SUM, and AVG, are another commonly used SQL feature. These aggregates allow you to get the maximum, minimum, sum, and average, respectively, for a particular column. For example, you may want print out the average number of points each player has scored. To do this, you would use the query:

```
SELECT AVG(totalPoints) FROM Stats;
```

It yields:

```
+------------------+
| AVG(totalPoints) |
+------------------+
|          93.8000 |
+------------------+
```

Other times, you may want to use the aggregates over a subset of the data. For example, you may want to print out the year along with the average number of points that each year's players have scored. You will need to use the GROUP BY clause to do this, as in the following query:

```
SELECT year, AVG(totalPoints) FROM Stats GROUP BY year;
```

It gives this result:

```
+-----------------------------+
| year          | AVG(totalPoints) |
+-----------------------------+
| Freshman      |         59.0000 |
| Junior        |        221.0000 |
| Senior        |         52.5000 |
| Sophomore     |         84.0000 |
+-----------------------------+
```

Most interview questions focus on using these sorts of insert and select statements. You're less likely to encounter SQL questions having to do with other features like UPDATE statements, DELETE statements, permissions, security, database design, concurrency, or optimization.

Concurrency

Concurrency is another topic that you will probably be asked about only if you indicate that you have experience. It is also a large and difficult topic, so we will just hit the major points of concurrency and provide a quick brush-up appropriate for someone familiar with the topic.

LESSON   **If you don't indicate that you know about concurrency, you probably won't be asked about it.**

Concurrency is a useful technology because it allows multiple threads of control to share processor resources and variables. For example, suppose that a computer is trying to accomplish two tasks. Task A involves waiting for user input while Task B is very processor intensive and involves no user input. If the computer executes the tasks serially, meaning one task and then the other, the processor's time is wasted in Task A while the computer waits for input. Threads allow the computer to use the waiting time in Task A to execute Task B. Thus, threaded tasks share computer resources more efficiently than serially executing tasks.

Consider the following example of a banking system to illustrate this concept. The system will consist of a program running on a single central computer, controlling multiple teller consoles at multiple branches. Each console will have its own thread, so the tellers can use their consoles simultaneously and easily share the bank's account data.

Many problems can result from poor thread control in this scenario. For example, imagine that the bank teller program has the following function that deducts money from a user's account whose account balance is in a global variable, userBalance.

```
int Deduct(double amount)
{
    double newBalance;
    if (amount < userBalance) {
        return 0; /* Insufficient funds */
    } else {
        newBalance = userBalance - amount;
        userBalance = newBalance;
        return 1;
    }
}
```

Suppose a husband and wife, Ron and Sue, know that this is a function that their bank's computer system uses. Here is one possible scenario that they could exploit. Initially, Ron and Sue have $500 in their bank account. Ron and Sue go to different bank branches and each withdraws $100. Ron goes up to a teller and indicates that he wants to withdraw $100. The teller deducts $100 from the couple's account, but the thread gets switched out after executing this line:

```
newBalance = userBalance - amount;
```

Processor control then switches to Sue's teller, who is also deducting $100. When her teller deducts $100, the account balance is still $500 because the variable, userBalance, has not been updated. Sue's thread executes until completing this function and updates that value of user-Balance to $400. Then, control switches back to Ron's transaction. Ron's thread has the value $400 in newBalance. So, it simply assigns this value to userBalance and returns. Thus, Ron and Sue have deducted $200 total from their account, but their balance still indicates $400, or a net $100 withdrawal. This is a great feature for Ron and Sue, but a big problem for the bank.

To get around this problem, you have to introduce the ability to protect access to sections of code that use shared resources. The most common way to do this in C is to use a thread package that presents a semaphore-based API. Most of these packages have three main methods associated with them. They are a function that tells the thread to wait on a semaphore, usually called wait, a function that signals the semaphore, often called signal, and a function that creates a new semaphore, often called newSemaphore.

The newSemapore function must initialize a semaphore to a given value. This value indicates how many threads to allow through the semaphore initially.

When a thread calls wait on a semaphore, it sleeps until the semaphore becomes greater than 0. Once the value is greater than 0, a thread waiting at the semaphore will decrement the semaphore and enter the protected section of code.

The signal function is the opposite of the wait function. When a thread signals a semaphore, the semaphore is incremented. Signaling a semaphore allows another waiting thread to pass through the semaphore.

In this banking semaphore example, you'll want to use a binary semaphore (a semaphore with an initial value of 1) because you want only one thread at a time to be able to access the global variable userBalance. Using semaphores makes the function look like this:

```
static Semaphore balanceLock;

void init()
{
    balanceLock = newSemaphore(1);
}

int Deduct(double amount)
{
    double newBalance;
    wait(balanceLock);
    if (amount < userBalance) {
        signal(balanceLock);
        return 0; /* Insufficient funds */
    } else {
        newBalance = userBalance - amount;
        userBalance = newBalance;
        signal(balanceLock);
        return 1;
    }
}
```

Another major problem common in thread programming is *deadlock*. Deadlock occurs when all threads are waiting on a semaphore and no thread can run. For example, if the balanceLock semaphore were incorrectly initialized to 0 instead of 1, there would be deadlock because all threads would be waiting on the semaphore and none would be able to signal it.

Other languages implement concurrency differently. Java uses the synchronized keyword. Usually, this keyword is added to the method definition. This ensures that any thread that calls this method will run to completion through the method before any other thread enters a synchronized method on the object (if it's an instance method) or class (if it's a class method). Essentially, using synchronized puts a binary lock on the object or class. There are times in Java when you may want a thread to wait for a certain condition to become true. In these cases, you use the `wait` method. This method tells the thread to sleep and wake up at a future time. At the appropriate time, you can use either the `notify` or `notifyAll` methods to wake sleeping threads.

Problem: Eighth of a Circle

■ Write a function that draws the upper eighth of a circle centered at (0, 0) with a given radius, where the upper eighth is defined as the portion starting at 12 and going to 1:30 on a clock face. Use the following prototype:

```
void DrawEighthOfCircle(int radius);
```

The coordinate system and an example of what you are to draw are shown in Figure 7.1. You will use a function with the following prototype to draw pixels:

```
void SetPixel(int xCoord, int yCoord);
```

This problem is not as contrived as it seems. If you were trying to implement a full-circle drawing routine, you would want to do as little calculation as possible to maintain optimum performance. Given the pixels for one-eighth of a circle, you can easily determine the pixels for the remainder of the circle from symmetry.[2] This problem is an example of a *scan conversion*, or converting a geometric drawing to a pixel-based raster image.

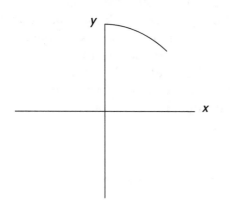

Figure 7.1   Output of DrawEighthOfCircle.

---

[2]If a point (x, y) is on a circle, so are the points $(-x, y)$, $(x, -y)$, $(-x, -y)$, (y, x), $(-y, x)$, $(y, -x)$, $(-y, -x)$.

You will need an equation for a circle before you can calculate anything. The common mathematical function that produces a circle is this:

$$x^2 + y^2 = r^2$$

The definition is nice because it contains x's, y's, and r's, just like your problem and your coordinate system. You have to figure out how to determine pairs of coordinates (x, y) on the circle using the equation, $x^2 + y^2 = r^2$. The easiest way to find a pair of coordinates is to set a value for one and then calculate the other. It's more difficult to set y and calculate x because after the scan conversion there will be several x values for certain y values. Therefore, you should set x and calculate y. Doing some algebra, you can calculate y with the equation:

$$y = \pm\sqrt{r^2 - x^2}$$

In this problem you are dealing with only positive values of y, so you can ignore the negative root. This gives:

$$y = \sqrt{r^2 - x^2}$$

For example, given an x coordinate of 3 and a radius of 5, $y = \sqrt{5^2 - 3^2} = 4$. You now know how to calculate y, given x. Next you need to determine the range of x values. x clearly starts at 0, but where does it end? Look again at the picture, and try to figure out how you visually know that you are at the end of the one-eighth of the circle. In visual terms, this happens when you are farther out then you are up. In mathematical terms, this means that the x value becomes greater than the y value. Thus, you can use the x range from 0 until $x > y$. If you put these pieces together, you have an algorithm for drawing a circle. In outline form, it is as follows:

Start with $x = 0$ and $y = r$.

While $(y > x)$

   Determine the y coordinate using the equation: $y = +\sqrt{r^2 - x^2}$

   Set the pixel (x, y)

   Increment x

This algorithm looks correct, but there is a subtle bug in it. The problem arises from treating the y coordinate as an integer, when often y will be a decimal value. For example, if y had the value 9.99, SetPixel would truncate it to 9, rather than rounding to the y pixel of 10 as you probably want. One way to solve this problem is to round all values to the nearest whole integer by adding 0.5 to the y value before calling `SetPixel`.

This change results in a much better-looking circle. The code for this algorithm is as follows:

```
void DrawEighthOfCircle(int radius)
{
    int x, y;
    x = 0;
    y = radius;
    while (y <= x) {
        y = sqrt((radius * radius) - (x * x)) + 0.5;
        SetPixel(x, y);
        x++;
    }
}
```

What's the efficiency of this algorithm? Its running time is O(n) where n is the number of pixels that you need to set. This is the best possible running time because any algorithm would have to call `SetPixel` at least n times to draw the circle correctly. The function also uses the `sqrt` function and multiplies during each iteration of the while loop. The `sqrt` function and the multiplications are likely to be slow operations. Therefore, this function probably isn't practical for most graphical applications where speed is critical. There are faster circle-drawing algorithms that don't make repeated calls to slow functions like `sqrt` or have repeated multiplications, but you wouldn't be expected to implement them in an interview.

Problem: Rectangle Overlap

■ **You are given two rectangles, each defined by an upper left (UL) corner and a lower right (LR) corner. Both rectangles' edges will always be parallel to the x or y axis as shown in Figure 7.2. Write a function that determines whether the two rectangles overlap. The function should return 1 if the rectangles overlap and 0 if they do not. For convenience, you may use the following structs:**

```
struct point {
    int x;
    int y;
};
struct rect {
    struct point UL;
    struct point LR;
};
```

The function prototype is as follows:

```
int Overlap(struct rect A, struct rect B);
```

Before you jump into the problem, it's important to work out a few properties about rectangles and their vertices. First, given the upper left (UL) point and lower right (LR) corners, it is not difficult to get the upper right (UR) and lower left (LL) corners. The coordinates of the upper right corner are the upper left's y and the lower right's x. The lower left corner is at the upper left's x and the lower right's y.

It is also useful to be able to determine whether a point falls inside a rectangle. A point is inside a rectangle if the point's x is greater than the rectangle's UL's x and less than the rectangle's LR's x and the point's y is greater than the rectangle's LR's y and less than the rectangle's UL's y. You can see an illustration of this in Figure 7.2, where point 1 is inside rectangle A. Now we can move on to the problem.

This problem seems pretty straightforward. Start by considering the ways two rectangles can overlap. Try to break the different ways that rectangles overlap into various cases. A good place to begin is by examining where the corners of a rectangle end up when it overlaps another. Perhaps you could enumerate the ways two rectangles can overlap by counting the number of corners of one rectangle that are inside the other rectangle. The cases that you must consider are when one of the rectangles will have 0, 1, 2, 3, or 4 corners inside the other. Take these cases one at a time. Begin by considering a case where no corners of either rectangle are inside the other. This is illustrated in Figure 7.3.

Consider what conditions have to be true for two rectangles to overlap without having any corners inside each other. First, the wider rectangle must be shorter than the narrower rectangle. Next the two rectangles must be positioned so the overlap occurs. This means that the narrower rectangle's x coordinates must be between the wider rectangle's x coordi-

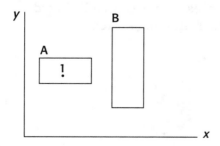

Figure 7.2   Picture of coordinate system and rectangles.

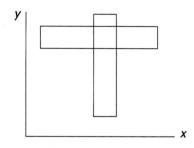

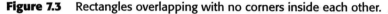

Figure 7.3 Rectangles overlapping with no corners inside each other.

nates and the shorter rectangle's y coordinates must be between the taller rectangle's y coordinates. If all of these conditions are true, you have two rectangles that overlap without having any corners inside of one another.

Now consider the second case where rectangles may overlap with one corner inside the other. This is illustrated in Figure 7.4. This case is relatively easy. You can simply check if any of the four corners of one rectangle are inside the other rectangle.

In the third case, the rectangles may overlap if two points of one rectangle are inside the other. This occurs when one rectangle is half in and half out of the other rectangle, as illustrated in Figure 7.5. Here, one rectangle has no corners inside the other, and one rectangle has two corners inside the other. If you check the corners of the rectangle with no corners inside the other, you will not find overlap. If you check the rectangle with two corners overlapping, you must check at least three corners to determine overlap. However, you can't determine ahead of time which rectangle will have no corners inside the other. Therefore, you must check three corners of each rectangle to test for overlap properly.

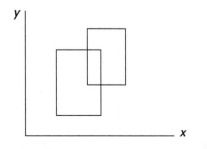

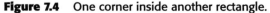

Figure 7.4 One corner inside another rectangle.

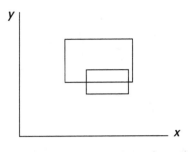

Figure 7.5 Two corners of a rectangle inside the other.

The three-point case is very simple. It's just not possible. No matter how you draw the rectangles, you can't make it so that one rectangle has exactly three corners inside the other.

The four-corner case is possible. This happens if one rectangle completely subsumes the other, as shown in Figure 7.6. If you check one corner of both rectangles, you can correctly determine overlap in this case.

Now, put your tests for determining overlap in the zero-corner, one-corner, two-corner, and four-corner cases together to encompass all of these cases. These tests are checking the widths, heights, and positions of both rectangles, the four corners of one rectangle, the three corners of each rectangle, and the one corner of each rectangle, respectively. You could test each of these cases individually, but that's very repetitive. Instead, try to develop a single test that encompasses all of these cases. Start by checking the widths, heights, and positions of both rectangles to cover the zero-corner case. Next, check the four corners of one rectangle to cover the one-corner case. Then, to include the two-corner case, you'll also have to check three corners of the other rectangle. Luckily, the four-corner case is already covered if you check four corners of one rectangle

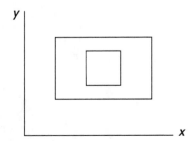

Figure 7.6 Four corners of a rectangle inside the other.

and three of the other because you're clearly checking one corner of each. The composite test to determine rectangle overlap is to check the following:

The heights, widths and positions of both rectangles

If any of four corners of one rectangle are inside the other

If any of three corners from the second rectangle are inside the first

This solution to test for overlap is correct, but it seems inefficient. It checks the heights, widths, and positions of both rectangles as well as seven of eight possible corners—and each corner check requires four comparisons. This results in 34 comparisons to calculate the answer.

Perhaps there is a better solution. Another way to think about the problem is to consider when the rectangles don't overlap, as opposed to when they do overlap. If you know when the rectangles don't overlap, you know when they do overlap. The conditions for not overlapping are much more straightforward. Call the two rectangles A and B. A and B do not overlap when A is above B, or A is below B, or A is to the left of B, or A is to the right of B. It is possible for more than one of these conditions to be true at the same time. For example, A could be above and to the right of B. If any one of these conditions is true, the two rectangles do not overlap. The specifics of these conditions are summarized in the following.

The two rectangles do not overlap when:

A's UL's x value is greater than B's LR's x value or

A's UL's y value is less than B's LR's y value or

A's LR's x value is less than B's UL's x value or

A's LR's y value is greater than B's UL's y value

This solution is much simpler, requiring only four comparisons and one negation. You can implement the function as follows:

```
int Overlap(struct rect A, struct rect B)
{
    return(!((A.UL.x > B.LR.x) ||
             (A.UL.y < B.LR.y) ||
             (A.LR.x < B.UL.x) ||
             (A.LR.y > B.UL.y)));
}
```

This function works, but you can do even better. It's possible to get rid of the logical *NOT*. A bit of logic theory called DeMorgan's law may be helpful in this. This law states that:

$$\neg(A \text{ OR } B) = \neg A \text{ AND } \neg B^3$$

$$\neg (A \text{ AND } B) = \neg A \text{ OR } \neg B$$

Also, you should recognize that:

$\neg(A > B)$ is equivalent to $(B \leq A)$

Working through these rules, you'll get the following function:

```
int Overlap(struct rect A, struct rect B)
{
    return((A.UL.x <= B.LR.x) &&
           (A.UL.y >= B.LR.y) &&
           (A.LR.x >= B.UL.x) &&
           (A.LR.y <= B.UL.y));
}
```

To make sure that you didn't make a mistake, it's a good idea to check that these conditions make sense. This function determines that two rectangles overlap if:

A's left edge is to the left of B's right edge and

A's upper edge is above B's bottom edge and

A's right edge is to the right of B's left edge and

A's bottom edge is below B's upper edge.

These conditions mean that rectangle B cannot be outside of rectangle A, so there must be some overlap. This makes sense.

Problem: Big-endian or Little-endian

■ **Write a function that determines whether a computer is big-endian or little-endian.**

This question tests your knowledge of computer architectures as much as it tests your ability to program. The interviewer wants to know if you are familiar with the term *endian*. If you are familiar with it, you should define it or at least try to point out the differences between big-endian and little-endian, even if you forget which is which. If you are not familiar with the term, you'll have to ask the interviewer to explain it.

Endianness refers to the order in which a computer stores the bytes of a multibyte value. Almost all modern computers use multibyte sequences to represent certain primitive data types. For example, an integer is usu-

---

[3] $\neg$ means NOT in the logic world.

ally 4 bytes. The bytes within an integer can be arranged in any order, but they are almost always either least-significant byte (LSB) to most-significant byte (MSB) or MSB to LSB. Significance refers to the place values a byte represents in a word. If a byte represents the lowest place values in a word the byte is the LSB. For example, in the number 5A6C, 6C is the LSB. Conversely, if a byte represents the highest place values in the word, it is the MSB. In the 5A6C example, 5A is the MSB.

In a big-endian machine the MSB has the lowest address; in a little-endian machine the LSB has the lowest address. For example, a big-endian machine stores the 2-byte hexadecimal value A45C by placing A4 in the first byte and 5C in the second. In contrast, a little-endian machine would store 5C in the first byte and A4 in the second.

You will have to choose some multibyte data type to work with. It's not important which one you choose, just that the type is more than one byte. An integer is a good choice. You'll need to determine how you can test this integer to figure out which byte is LSB and which is MSB. If you set the value of the integer to 1, you will be able to distinguish between the MSB and the LSB because in an integer with the value 1, the LSB has the value 1 and the MSB has the value 0.

Unfortunately, it's not immediately clear how to access the bytes of an integer. You might try using the bit operators because they allow access to individual bits in a variable. However, they are not particularly useful because the bit operators act as if the bits are arranged in order from least-significant bit to most-significant bit. For example, if you use the shift left operator to shift the integer 8 bits, the operator works on the integer as if it were 32 consecutive bits regardless of the true internal byte order. This property prevents you from using the bit operators to determine the byte order.

How might you be able to examine the individual bytes of an integer? A character is a single-byte data type. It could be useful to view an integer as four consecutive characters. To do this, you create a pointer to the integer. Then, you can cast the integer pointer to a character pointer. This allows you to access the integer like an array of 1-byte data types. Using the character pointer, you can examine the bytes and determine the format.

Specifically, to determine the computer's endianness, get a pointer to an integer with the value of 1. Then, cast the pointer to a char *. This changes the size of the data that the pointer points to. When you dereference this pointer you access a 1-byte character instead of a 4-byte integer. Thus, you can test the first byte and see if it is 1. If the byte's value is 1, the machine is little-endian because the LSB is at the lowest memory address. If the byte's value is 0, the machine is big-endian because the MSB is at the lowest memory address. In outline form, the procedure is this:

Set an integer to 1

Cast a pointer to the integer as a `char *`

If the dereferenced pointer is 1, the machine is little-endian

If the dereferenced pointer is 0, the machine is big-endian

The code for this test is as follows:

```
/* Returns 1 if the machine is little-endian, 0 if the
 * machine is big-endian
 */
int Endianness(void)
{
    int testNum;
    char *ptr;

    testNum = 1;
    ptr = (char *) &testNum;
    return (*ptr); /* Returns the byte at the lowest address */
}
```

This solution is sufficient for an interview. As the goal of an interview is not just to solve problems, but also to impress your interviewer, you may want to consider a slightly more elegant way to solve this problem. It involves using a feature of C called `union` types. A union is like a `struct`, except that all of the members are allocated starting at the same location in memory. This allows you to access the same data with different variable types. The syntax is almost identical to a `struct`. Using a `union`, the code is the following:

```
/* Returns 1 if the machine is little-endian, 0 if the
 * machine is big-endian
 */
int Endianness(void)
{
    union {
        int theInteger;
        char singleByte;
    } endianTest;

    endianTest.theInteger = 1;
    return endianTest.singleByte;
}
```

Problem: Number of Ones

- Write a function that determines the number of 1 bits in the computer's internal representation of a given integer.

This problem may at first sound like a base conversion problem in which you have to design an algorithm to convert a base 10 number to a two's complement binary number. That approach is circuitous because the computer already internally stores its numbers in two's complement binary. Instead of doing a base conversion, try counting the 1's directly.

You can count the number of 1's by checking the value of each bit. Ideally, you'd like to use an operator that would tell you the value of a specified bit. That way, you could iterate over all of the bits and count how many of them were 1's. Unfortunately, this ideal operator doesn't exist.

You can begin by trying to create a procedure that determines the value of each bit using the existing bit operators. Focus on figuring out a way to get the value of the lowest bit. One way to do this is to AND the given integer with the value 1. 1 is stored as 00000001 in a computer with 8-bit integers.[4] The result would be either 00000000 if the given integer's lowest bit had the value 0 or 00000001 if the given integer's lowest bit had the value 1. In general, you can get the value of any bit if you create the correct *mask*. In this case, the mask is an integer with all the bits set to 0 except the bit you're checking, which is set to 1. When you AND a mask with the value you're checking, the result is either a 0, indicating that the bit you are checking has the value 0, or a non-zero result, indicating that the bit you are checking has the value 1.

You could create a mask for each of the bits and count the number of 1 bits. For example, the first mask would be 00000001, followed by masks of 00000010, 00000100, 00001000. . . . This would work, but your interviewer probably doesn't want to watch you write out that many masks. Consider the differences between each mask. Each mask is the same as the previous mask, but the 1 bit is moved one place to the left. Instead of predefining your masks, you can construct them using the shift left operator. Simply start with a mask of 00000001 and repeatedly shift the integer one bit to the left to generate all the necessary masks. This is a good technique, and if you work it out to its conclusion, it yields an acceptable answer. However, there's a prettier and slightly faster solution that uses only one mask.

---

[4]Most modern architectures have at least 32-bit integers, but 32-digit numbers are a little hard to fit on a page, so we've chosen to illustrate our examples with 8-bit integers.

Think about what you can do with a single mask. You are trying to examine each bit of the integer, so you need to mask a different bit on each iteration. So far, you've been accomplishing this by shifting the mask and keeping the integer still, but if you shifted the integer, you could examine all of its bits using the same mask. The most natural mask to use is 00000001, which yields the least-significant bit. If you keep shifting the integer right, each bit will eventually become the rightmost bit. Try working through 00000101 as an example. The rightmost bit is 1 so you would add 1 to your count and shift the integer right, yielding 00000010. This time the rightmost bit is 0. Shifting right again gives 00000001. The least significant bit in this integer is 1, so you would increment your count to 2. When you shift right a third time, the integer becomes 00000000. When the integer's value reaches zero there are no 1 bits remaining, so you can stop counting. As in this example, you may not have to iterate through all the bits to count all the 1's, so in many cases, this algorithm is more efficient than the multiple mask algorithm. In outline, the single mask algorithm is as follows:

Start with count = 0

While the integer is not 0

    If the integer AND 1 equals 1, increment count

    Shift the integer one bit to the right

Return count

Finally, check for any error cases in this code; you'll want to look for problems with positive numbers, negative numbers, and zero. If the integer has the value of 0, the algorithm immediately and correctly returns that there are zero 1's in the binary representation. Now, consider the case where you are passed a negative number. The number will be shifted to the right, but the new bit added on the left will be a 1 and not a 0 because the shift right operator sign extends. This means that the integer value will eventually become all 1's and not all 0's as desired. To correct this, you will want to read the value as an unsigned integer. This way, the shift operator will not sign extend and the new bits that are added during the right shifting will be 0's. The result is that the number will eventually become all 0's. Finally, consider the case where you are given a positive integer. This is the sample case that you worked with, and the algorithm works correctly here.

The code for this algorithm is this:

```
int NumOnesInBinary(unsigned int number)
{
    int numOnes = 0;
```

```
        while (number) {
            if (number & 1)
                numOnes++;
            number = number >> 1;
        }
        return numOnes;
    }
```

What's the running time of this function? The function will iterate through the `while` loop until all the 1's have been counted. In the best case, the given integer is 0, and the function never executes the while loop. In the worst case, this is $O(n)$ where n is the size in bits of an integer.

Unless you're incredibly good at bitwise operations, this is the best solution you're likely to come up with in an interview. There are better solutions, though. Look at what happens at the bit level when you subtract 1 from a number. Subtracting 1 produces a value that has all the same bits as the original integer except that all the low bits up to and including the lowest 1 are flipped. For example, subtracting 1 from the value 01110000 results in the value 01101111.

If you apply the AND operation to the integer and the result of the subtraction, the result is a new number that is the same as the original integer except the rightmost 1 is now a 0. For example, 01110000 AND (01110000 – 1) = 01110000 AND 01101111 = 01100000.

You can count the number of times that you can perform this process before the integer's value reaches 0. This is the number of 1's in the computer's representation of the number. In outline form this algorithm is as follows:

Start with count = 0

While the integer is not zero

    AND the integer with the integer – 1

    Increment count

Return count

The code for this is the following:

```
int NumOnesInBinary(int number)
{
    int numOnes = 0;
    while (number) {
        number = number & (number - 1);
        numOnes++;
    }
    return numOnes;
}
```

This solution has a running time of $O(m)$ where m is the number of 1's in the solution. There may be even better solutions. Keep in mind that this solution was presented for interest, and the first solution is all that would be expected in an interview.

Problem: Simple SQL

- **Given a database with the table**

```
Olympics(city CHAR(16), year INT(4));
```

> **write a SQL statement to insert Montreal and 1976 into the database.**

This is an extremely easy question that an interviewer might use to determine whether you have ever used SQL before or whether you were padding your resume when you mentioned it. If you know SQL, you're all set. It's a straightforward SQL INSERT statement; no tricks at all. If you don't really know SQL, you're in trouble. The correct answer is:

```
INSERT INTO Olympics VALUES('Montreal', 1976);
```

Problem: Company and Employee Database

- **You are given a database with the following tables:**

```
Company(companyName CHAR(30), id INT(4));
EmployeesHired(id INT(4), numHired INT(4),
    fiscalQuarter INT(4));
```

> **You may make the assumption that the only possible fiscal quarters are 1 through 4. Sample data for this schema are presented in Table 7.3.**

> **Write a SQL statement that returns the names of all the companies that hired employees in fiscal quarter 4.**

This question involves retrieving data from two tables. You will have to join the two tables to get all of the needed information. id is the only key common to both tables so you will want to join on the value id. Once you have joined the two tables, you can select the company name where the fiscal quarter is 4. This SQL statement looks like this:

```
SELECT companyName FROM Company, EmployeesHired
WHERE Company.id = EmployeesHired.id AND fiscalQuarter = 4;
```

Table 7.3 Company and Employees Sample Data

COMPANYNAME	ID
Hillary Plumbing	6
John Lawn Company	9
Dave Cookie Company	19
Jane Electricity	3

ID	NUMHIRED	FISCALQUARTER
3	3	3
9	2	4
19	4	1
6	2	1

There is a small problem with this SQL statement. Think of what might happen if a company did not hire anyone in Q4. There could still be a tuple like EmployeesHired(6, 0, 4). The company with id 6 would be returned by the preceding query even though they hired no one during fiscal quarter 4. To fix this bug, you need to make sure that numHired is greater than 0. The revised SQL statement looks like this:

```
SELECT companyName FROM Company, EmployeesHired
WHERE Company.id = EmployeesHired.id AND fiscalQuarter = 4 AND numHired
> 0;
```

■ **Now, using the same schema, write a SQL statement that returns the names of all companies that did not hire anyone in fiscal quarters 1 through 4.**

The best way to start this problem is by looking at the previous answer. You know how to get the names of all of the companies that hired an employee in quarter 4. If you remove the WHERE condition that fiscalQuarter = 4, you will have a query that returns the names of all companies that hired employees during all fiscal quarters. If you use this query as a subquery and select all of the companies that are not in the result, you will get all of the companies that did not hire anyone in fiscal quarters 1 through 4. As a slight optimization, you can select just the id from the EmployeesHired table and print out the companies that do not have an id returned. The query looks like this:

```
SELECT companyName FROM Company WHERE id NOT IN
(SELECT id from EmployeesHired WHERE numHired > 0);
```

- **Finally, return the names of all companies and the total number of employees that each company hired during fiscal quarters 1 through 4.**

You're asked to retrieve the totals of some sets of values, which indicates that you will have to use the SUM aggregate. In this problem, you don't want the sum of the entire column, you want only a sum of the values that have the same id. To accomplish this task, you will need to use the GROUP BY feature. This feature allows you to apply SUM over grouped values of data. Other than the GROUP BY feature, this query is very similar to the first query except you leave out the fiscalQuarter = 4 in the WHERE clause. The query looks like this:

```
SELECT companyName, SUM(numHired)
FROM Company, EmployeesHired
WHERE Company.id = EmployeesHired.id
GROUP BY companyName;
```

Problem: Max, No Aggregates

- **Given the SQL database schema**

```
Test(num INT(4));
```

write a SQL statement that returns the maximum value from num without using an aggregate (MAX, MIN, etc.).

In this problem, your hands are tied behind your back—you have to find a maximum without using the feature designed for finding the maximum. A good way to start is by drawing a table with some sample data as in Table 7.4.

Table 7.4 Sample Values for num

NUM
5
23
-6
7

In this sample data, you want to print out the value 23. 23 has the property that all other numbers are less than it. Though true, this way of looking at things doesn't offer much help with constructing the SQL statement. A similar but more useful way to say the same thing is that 23 is the *only* number that does not have a number that is greater than it. If you could return every value that does not have a number greater than it, you would return only 23, and you would have solved the problem. Try designing a SQL statement to print out every number that does not have a number greater than it.

First, you will want to figure out which numbers do have numbers greater than themselves. This is a more manageable query. Begin by joining the table with itself to create all possible pairs where each value in one column is greater than the corresponding value in the other column, as in the following query:

```
SELECT Lesser.num, Greater.num
FROM Test AS Greater, Test AS Lesser
WHERE Lesser.num < Greater.num;
```

Using the sample data, this yields the results in Table 7.5.

As desired, every value is in the lesser column except the maximum value of 23. Thus, if you use the previous query as a subquery and select every value not in it, you will get the maximum value. This query would look like this:

```
SELECT num from Test WHERE num NOT IN
(SELECT Lesser.num FROM Test AS Greater, Test AS Lesser
WHERE Lesser.num < Greater.num);
```

There is one minor bug in this query. If the maximum value is repeated in the Test table, it will be returned twice. To prevent this, use the DISTINCT keyword. This changes the query to the following:

Table 7.5 Temporary Table Formed after Join

LESSER	GREATER
-6	23
5	23
7	23
-6	7
5	7
-6	5

```
SELECT DISTINCT num from Test WHERE num NOT IN
(SELECT Lesser.num FROM Test AS Greater, Test AS Lesser
WHERE Lesser.num < Greater.num);
```

Problem: Producer/Consumer

- Write a Producer thread and a Consumer thread that share a fixed size buffer and an index to access the buffer. The Producer should place random numbers into the buffer while the Consumer should remove the numbers. Implement this problem both in C using semaphores and in Java using the Java thread methods.

If you've worked with multithreaded programs before, this is a problem that you may have seen. It's one of the canonical concurrency problems. If you've never worked with multithreaded programs, you probably won't be able to solve this problem.

First, try implementing the problem without any concurrency control, and then comment on what the problems are. The algorithm isn't very difficult without concurrency control. The producer and consumer look like this:

```
static int index = 0;
static int buffer[8];
void Producer()
{
    while (1) {
        if (index < 7) {
            buffer[index] = rand();
            index++;
        }
    }
}

void Consumer()
{
    while (1) {
        if (index > 0) {
            printf("%d\n", buffer[index]);
            index--;
        }
    }
}
```

The major bug in this implementation is that the buffer is not protected. One problem that could result is that the producer may write to the buffer and get swapped out before the index is updated. Then, the consumer may consume the wrong element. Additionally, the index could be improperly updated and get out of synch with the last buffer element.

The critical area of code is the portion containing the array access and index updates. You need to protect the critical section of code with a binary semaphore that limits access to this section of code to only one thread at a time. You will initialize the semaphore to 1 because it is a binary semaphore. This change results in the code:

```
static int index = 0;
static int buffer[8];
static Semaphore bufferWrite;

void init()
{
    bufferWrite = newSemaphore(1);
}

void Producer()
{
    while (1) {
        wait(BufferWrite);
        if (index < 7) {
            buffer[index] = rand();
            index++;
        }
        signal(BufferWrite);
    }
}

void Consumer()
{
    while (1) {
        wait(BufferWrite);
        if (index > 0) {
            printf("%d\n", buffer[index]);
            index--;
        }
        signal(BufferWrite);
    }
}
```

This solution corrects the previous bug. It locks access to all shared variables and the threads will now function correctly. However, correctness is not the only concern. There is another problem that can affect efficiency. Imagine what would happen if the producer were much slower than the consumer. The consumer would often wake up, grab the lock, see that the buffer was empty, and then go back to sleep. This constant waking up, doing nothing, and then going back to sleep is called busy waiting and wastes resources. Generally, the consumer should be awake only if there is something to consume. Similarly, the producer should be awake only if there are empty slots in the buffer.

This efficiency bug can also be fixed with semaphores. One semaphore will indicate whether the buffer is full. The producer thread will wait on this semaphore. The consumer thread will signal this semaphore each time that it removes an element from the buffer. Initially, the buffer is empty. Thus, this semaphore should be initialized to the number of buffer slots so the semaphore starts to block when there are no more spaces in the buffer.

Similarly, a different semaphore indicates whether the buffer is empty. The consumer should wait on this semaphore, and the producer should signal it each time that it writes to the buffer. This semaphore should start out preventing the consumer from consuming from the buffer because the buffer is initially empty so it should be initialized to 0.

Finally, it's important to order the semaphores correctly. Consider the case where the binary semaphore protecting the critical section comes before the efficiency semaphores. This could cause deadlock if the consumer grabs the semaphore for the critical section but has to wait on the semaphore indicating that the buffer is not empty. Similarly, if the producer grabs the semaphore protecting the critical section and has to wait on the semaphore indicating the buffer is not full, deadlock could also occur. Therefore, the semaphore protecting the critical section should come after the other semaphores.

Keeping these concerns in mind, the code for this is the following:

```
static int index = 0;
static int buffer[8];
static Semaphore bufferWrite;
static Semaphore bufferNotFull;
static Semaphore bufferNotEmpty;

void init(void)
{
    bufferWrite = newSemaphore(1);
    bufferNotFull = newSemaphore(8);
    bufferNotEmpty = newSemaphore(0);
}

void Producer(void)
{
    while (1) {
        wait(bufferNotFull);
```

```
            wait(bufferWrite);
            buffer[index] = rand();
            index++;
            signal(bufferWrite);
            signal(bufferNotEmpty);
        }
    }

    void Consumer()
    {
        while (1) {
            wait(bufferNotEmpty);
            wait(bufferWrite);
            printf("%d\n", buffer[index]);
            index--;
            signal(bufferWrite);
            signal(bufferNotFull);
        }
    }
```

In Java, concurrency is dealt with a little differently. All Java threads must extend the `Thread` class. They then implement the `run` method, which is called when the thread is started. The following example also uses the Java `synchronized` keyword, the `wait` method, and the `notifyAll` method. The main function in the following example is included to illustrate how you would call these threads.

```java
import java.util.Random;

class Producer extends Thread {
    private static final int MAX_CAPACITY = 8;
    private static final int RANDOM_RANGE = 128;
    private int[] buffer;
    private int index;
    private Random generator;

    public Producer()
    {
        buffer = new int [MAX_CAPACITY];
        generator = new Random(23);
        index = 0;  // initally empty
    }

    public void run()
    {
        while (true) {
            try {
                putInt();
            }
```

```
                    catch(InterruptedException e) {}
            }
        }

        private synchronized void putInt() throws InterruptedException
        {
            while (index == MAX_CAPACITY) { // Buffer is full.
                wait();
            }
            buffer[index] = generator.nextInt(RANDOM_RANGE);
            index++;
            notifyAll();  // Let other threads know that something
                          // has happened.
        }

        // Called by the consumer.
        public synchronized int getInt() throws InterruptedException
        {
            notifyAll(); // Need to make sure that we're
                         // not stuck with this thread.
            while (index <= 0) {
                wait();
            }

            index--;
            return buffer[index];
        }
    }


    class Consumer extends Thread {
        private Producer producer;

        public Consumer(Producer theProducer)
        {
            producer = theProducer;
        }

        public void run()
        {
            try {
                while (true) {
                    System.out.println("Int is " + producer.getInt());
                }
            }
            catch (InterruptedException e) {}
        }
```

```
public static void main(String args[]) {
    Producer producer = new Producer();
    producer.start();
    new Consumer(producer).start();
}
}
```

CHAPTER 8

Counting, Measuring, and Ordering Puzzles

In addition to technical and programming questions, you will often encounter brainteasers in your interviews. Brainteasers are mathematics and logic puzzles that have no direct relation to computers. Some interviewers feel these questions are silly because they have no direct bearing on the job at hand and won't ask any of them. Many interviewers, though, think brainteasers are useful in assessing problem-solving ability—perhaps the most important job skill. Interviewers may also be influenced by the knowledge that industry leaders like Microsoft use brainteasers in their interviews. Whatever the motivation, in some interviews as many as a third of the questions you are asked may be brainteasers.

In the authors' opinion, performance on brainteasers says a lot about your experience with working mathematical puzzles and very little about whether you will be a valuable employee. The discussion and examples in this and the next chapter aim to give you this experience so you can be successful with brainteasers. These questions draw from a much broader and more diverse body of knowledge than programming and technical questions, so a topical review is not really possible. However, brainteasers do have a number of common themes. Familiarity with these commonalities and experience with brainteasers in general can be a great help in solving these puzzles.

One of the most important themes to keep in mind is that the solutions to brainteasers are almost never straightforward or obvious. Unlike the programming or technical parts of the interview, where you will sometimes be asked simple questions just to see whether you know something, brainteasers always require thought and effort. This means that any solution that seems immediately obvious is probably incorrect or not the best solution. For instance, suppose you're asked, "From the time you get on a ski lift to the time you get off, what proportion of the chairs do you pass?" Most people's immediate gut-level response is that you pass half of the chairs. This response is obvious and makes some sense. At any given time, half of the chairs are on each side of the lift, and you pass chairs only on the other side. It's also wrong—because both sides of the lift are moving, you pass all the other chairs.[1]

This property works most strongly to your advantage when you are faced with a problem that has only two possible answers (for example, any yes or no question). Whichever answer seems at first to be correct is probably wrong. It's probably not a good idea to say, "The answer must be yes because if it were no this would be a very simple problem and you wouldn't have bothered to ask it." You can, however, use this knowledge to guide your thinking.

LESSON   The obvious answer is almost never the right answer.

Although the correct solutions to brainteasers are usually complex, they rarely require time-consuming computations or mathematics beyond trigonometry. Just as writing pages of code is a warning sign that you're headed in the wrong direction, using calculus or spending a long time number-crunching is a strong indicator that you're not headed toward the best solution to one of these puzzles.

Many of these problems are difficult because they suggest an incorrect assumption that leads you to the wrong answer. Based on this knowledge, you might conclude that the best approach is to avoid making any assumptions. Unfortunately, that's not really practical—even understanding a problem is very difficult without making a whole series of assumptions. For instance, suppose you are given the problem of finding an

[1] Assuming you get on and off at the extreme ends of the lift. On most real ski lifts, you pass almost all the other chairs.

arrangement that maximizes the number of oranges you can fit in the bottom of a square box. You would probably automatically assume that the oranges are small spherical fruit, that they are all about the same size, that "in the bottom" means in contact with the bottom surface of the box, and that the oranges must remain intact (you can't puree them and pour them in). These assumptions may seem ridiculous—they are all rather obvious, and they are all correct. The point is that assumptions are inherent in all communication or thought; you can't begin to work on a problem without assumptions.

Carrying this example further, you might assume you could model this problem in 2D using circles in a square, and that the solution would involve some sort of orderly, repeating pattern. Based on these assumptions and the knowledge that a honeycomb-like hexagonal array provides the tightest pack of circles covering a plane, you might conclude that the best solution is to place the oranges in a regular hexagonal array. Depending on the relative sizes of the oranges and the box, this conclusion would be incorrect.

Although you can't eliminate assumptions, it can be useful to try to identify and analyze them. As you identify your assumptions, categorize them as almost certainly correct, probably correct, or possibly incorrect. Starting with the assumption you feel is least likely to be correct, try reworking the problem without each assumption. Keep in mind that these puzzles are rarely trick questions, so your definitional assumptions are usually correct.

For instance, in the preceding example, it would be reasonable to classify the assumptions that oranges are spherical fruit and that they must remain intact and in contact with the bottom of the box as almost certainly correct. How would you categorize the assumption that you can reduce this puzzle to a 2D problem of circles in a square? If you think about it, you can see that the oranges make contact with each other in a single plane, and that in this plane you're essentially dealing with circles inside a square. This isn't exactly a proof, but it's solid enough to decide that this assumption is probably correct. On the other hand, you'll find you have more trouble supporting the assumption that the oranges should be in an orderly repeating pattern. It seems reasonable, and it is true for an infinite plane, but it's not clear that the similarities between a plane and the box bottom are sufficient for this assumption to be true. In general, beware of any assumption that you feel is true but can't quite explain why—this is often the incorrect assumption. You would therefore conclude that the assumption that the oranges must form an ordered array is possibly incorrect. In fact, this assumption *is* incorrect. In many cases the best packing involves putting most of the oranges in an ordered array and the remaining few in unordered positions. Analyzing your assumptions is a particularly good strategy when you think you've come up with the only logically possible solution, but you're told it's incorrect. It's often the case that your logic was good, but that it was based on a flawed assumption.

LESSON   If the solution that seems logical is wrong, you made a false assumption. Categorize your assumptions, and try to identify those that are false.

Some questions are intimidating because they are so complex or difficult that you can't see a path to the solution. You may not even know where to start. Don't let this lock you up. You don't have to have a plan for getting all the way to the solution before you start—things will come to you as you work. If you can identify a subproblem, try solving that, even if you're not sure it's critical to solving the main problem. Try solving a simplified version of the problem—you may gain insights that will be useful in solving the full problem. If the problem involves some sort of process, try working through some specific examples. You may notice a pattern you can generalize to other cases. Above all, keep talking, keep thinking, and keep working. The pieces of the puzzle are much more likely to fall into place when your mind is in motion than when you are sitting at the starting line praying for a revelation. Even if you don't make much progress, it looks much better to the interviewer when you actively attack a problem than when you sit back stumped, looking clueless and overwhelmed. Remember, you came to the interview to demonstrate that you will be a valuable employee. Analyzing the problems and patiently trying a variety of approaches shows this almost as well as solving problems does.

LESSON   Don't be intimidated by complexity. Try a subproblem, a simplified version, or some examples. Be patient, keep working, and keep talking.

Other questions are tricky for the opposite reason: They are so simple or restricted that it seems that there's no way to solve the problem within the given constraints. In these circumstances brainstorming can be useful. Try to enumerate all the possible actions that are legal within the constraints of the problem, even those that seem counterproductive. If the problem involves physical objects, consider every object, the properties of every object, what you might do to or with each object, and how the objects might interact. When you're stuck on a problem like this, there may be something allowed by the problem that you're missing. If you make a list of everything allowed by the constraints of the problem, it will include the key to the solution that hadn't occurred to you. It's often easier to enumerate all the possibilities than it is to specifically come up with the one thing you haven't been thinking of. When you do this enumeration, don't do it silently; speak it aloud or write it down. This shows the interviewer what you're doing and helps you be more methodical and thorough.

> **LESSON** When you're stuck on a simple, restricted problem, brainstorm about all the possibilities to identify the one you're missing.

There's one more type of problem worth discussing. This is the estimation problem, where you're asked to use a rational process to estimate the size of some statistic you don't know. These questions are relatively rare in interviews for pure development positions, but they may be more common in interviews for jobs that include a significant management or business aspect. One estimation problem is "How many gas stations are there in the United States?" It has been so widely reported that this question is asked by Microsoft that it seems almost certain to be apocryphal; nevertheless, it is a good example.

These questions are usually not difficult compared with the more common brainteasers. You're not expected to have any idea what the actual statistic or fact is. Instead, you are expected to do a rough order of magnitude calculation based on facts you do know. Because everything is an estimate anyway, try to adjust or round your figures so that any large numbers you use are powers (or at least multiples) of ten. This will significantly simplify your arithmetic.

Taking the gas station problem as an example, your calculation might go like this: "It takes me about 6 minutes to fill up my car. I go to the gas station about once a week, and there are usually two other cars there. If I assume this is average for Americans, each gas station services about 30 cars an hour. Suppose a gas station were open 12 hours a day, 7 days a week. That would be 84 hours a week. In reality, a gas station is probably open more than 12 hours a day, so I'll say the average gas station is open 100 hours a week. That means it services 3,000 cars a week. There's somewhere upwards of 250 million people in the United States. Not everyone has a car, so say there are 100 million cars on the road. If every car goes to the gas station once a week, like mine does, and each station sees 3,000 cars a week, there would have to be about 33,000 gas stations in the United States." This figure is probably off by a lot, but it's probably within an order of magnitude (that is, there are more than 3,300 gas stations and fewer than 330,000). It's much more important that you are able to form a framework for the estimation and rapidly work through the calculations than that you accurately estimate the statistic. For more practice, try estimating the number of kindergarten teachers in your state, the circumference of the earth, and the weight of a ferry boat.

Problem: Count Open Lockers

- Suppose you are in a hallway lined with 100 closed lockers. You begin by opening all 100 lockers. Next, you close every second locker. Then you go to every third locker and close it if it is open or open it if it is closed (call this *toggling* the locker). You continue toggling every *n*th locker on pass number *n*. After your hundredth pass of the hallway, in which you toggle only locker number 100, how many lockers are open?

  In a hall with *k* lockers, how many lockers remain open after pass *k*?

This problem is designed to seem overwhelming. You don't have time to draw a diagram of 100 lockers and count 100 passes through them. Even if you did, solving the problem that way wouldn't illustrate any skill or intuition, so there must be some trick that can be used to determine how many doors will be open. You just have to figure out what that trick is.

It's unlikely that you're going to be able to intuit the solution to this problem by just staring at it. What can you do? Although it's not practical to solve the entire problem by brute force, solving a few lockers in this manner is reasonable. Perhaps you'll notice some patterns you can apply to the larger problem.

Start by choosing an arbitrary locker, say 12, and determining whether it will end open or closed. On which passes will you toggle locker 12? Obviously on the first pass, when you toggle every locker, and on the twelfth pass when you start with 12. You don't need to consider any pass after 12 because those will all start farther down the hall. This leaves passes 2 through 11. You can count these out: 2, 4, 6, 8, 10, **12** (you toggle on pass 2); 3, 6, 9, **12** (on 3); 4, 8, **12** (on 4); 5, 10, 15 (not on 5); 6, **12** (on 6); 7, 14 (not on 7), and so on. Somewhere in the middle of this process, you will probably notice that you toggle locker 12 only when the number of the pass you're on is a factor of 12. If you think about this, it makes sense: When counting by n, you hit 12 only when some integer number of n's add to 12, which is another way of saying that n is a factor of 12. Though it seems simple in retrospect, this probably wasn't obvious before you worked out an example.

The factors of 12 are 1, 2, 3, 4, 6, and 12. Correspondingly, the operations on the locker door are open, close, open, close, open, close. So locker 12 will end closed. The solution seems to have something to do with factors. Primes are numbers with unique factor properties. Perhaps it would be instructive to investigate a prime numbered locker. You might select 17 as a representative prime. The factors are 1 and 17, so the operations are open, close. It ends closed just like 12. Apparently primes are not necessarily different from non-primes for the purposes of this problem.

What generalizations can you make about whether a locker ends open or closed? All lockers start closed and alternate between being open and closed. So lockers are closed after the second, fourth, sixth, etc., times they are toggled—in other words, if a locker is toggled an even number of times it ends closed, otherwise it ends open. You know that a locker is toggled once for every factor of the locker number, so you can say that a locker ends open only if it has an odd number of factors.

The task has now been reduced to finding how many numbers between 1 and 100 have an odd number of factors. The two you've examined (and most others, if you try a few more examples) have even numbers of factors. Why is that? If a number i is a factor of n, what does that mean? It means that i times some other number j is equal to n. Of course, because multiplication is commutative ($i \times j = j \times i$), that means that j is a factor of n, too. So the number of factors is usually even because factors tend to come in pairs. If you can find the numbers that have unpaired factors, you will know which lockers will be open. Multiplication is a binary operation, so there will always be two numbers involved, but what if they are both the same number (that is, $i = j$)? Then a single number would effectively form both halves of the pair and there would be an odd number of factors. When this is the case, $i \times i = n$. So n would have to be a perfect square. Try a perfect square, say 16, to check this solution: factors are 1, 2, 4, 8, 16; operations are open, close, open, close, open—as expected it ends open.

Based on this reasoning, you can conclude that only lockers with numbers that are perfect squares end open. The perfect squares between 1 and 100 (inclusive) are 1, 2, 4, 9, 16, 25, 36, 49, 64, 81, and 100. So 10 lockers would remain open.

Similarly, for the general case of k lockers, the number of open lockers is the number of perfect squares between 1 and k, inclusive. How can you best count these? The perfect squares themselves are inconvenient to count because they're unevenly spaced. However, the square roots of the perfect squares greater than zero are the positive integers. These are very easy to count: the last number in the list of square roots gives the number of items in each list. For example, the square roots of 1, 4, 9, 16, 25 are 1, 2, 3, 4, 5; the last number in the list of square roots is the square root of the largest perfect square and is equal to the number of perfect squares. You need to find the square root of the largest perfect square less than or equal to k.

This task is trivial when k is a perfect square, but most of the time it won't be. In these cases the square root of k will be a non-integer. If you round this square root down to the nearest integer, then its square is the largest perfect square less than k—just what you were looking for. The operation of rounding to the largest integer less than or equal to a given number is often called "floor." Thus, in the general case of k lockers, there will be floor(sqrt(k)) lockers remaining open.

The key to solving this problem is trying strategies to solve parts of the problem even when it isn't clear how these parts will contribute to the overall solution. Although some attempts, like the investigation of prime numbered lockers, may not be fruitful, others are likely to lead to greater insight about how to attack the problem, as with the strategy of calculating the result for a single locker. Even in the worst case where none of the things you try lead you closer to the final solution, you show the interviewer that you aren't intimidated by difficult problems with no clear solution and that you are willing to keep trying different approaches until you find one that works.

Problem: Three Switches

- **You are standing in a hallway next to three light switches, all of which are off. Each switch operates a different incandescent lightbulb in the room at the end of the hall. You cannot see the lights from where the switches are. Determine which light corresponds to each switch. You may go into the room with the lights only once.**

The crux of this problem comes quickly to the fore: There are only two possible positions for each switch (on or off), but there are three lights to identify. You can easily identify one light, by setting one switch differently than the other two, but this leaves you no way to distinguish the two left in the same position.

When confronted with a seemingly impossible task, you should go back to basics. The two key objects in this problem seem to be the switches and the lights. What do you know about switches and lightbulbs? Switches make or break an electrical connection. When a switch is on, current flows through it. A lightbulb consists of a resistive filament inside an evacuated glass bulb. When current flows through the filament, it consumes power, producing light and heat.

How can these properties help you solve the problem? Which of them can you detect or measure? The properties of a switch don't seem too useful. It's much easier to look at the switch to see whether it's off or on than to measure current. The lightbulbs sound a little more promising. You can detect light by looking at the bulbs, and you can detect heat by touching them. Whether there is light coming from a bulb is determined entirely by its switch—when the switch is on, there is light; when it's off, there isn't. What about heat? It takes some time for a light to heat up after it's been switched on, and some time for it to cool after it's switched off. So, you could use heat to determine if a bulb had *been* on, even if it were off when you walked into the room.

You can determine which switch goes with each bulb by turning the first switch on, and the second and third off. After ten minutes, turn the first switch off, leave the second off, and turn the third on. When you go into the room, the hot dark bulb corresponds to the first switch, the cold dark bulb to the second, and the lit bulb to the third.

Although there's nothing truly outlandish about this question—it's not just a stupid play on words, for instance—it is arguably a trick question. The solution involves coming up with something somewhat outside the definition of the problem. Some interviewers believe that questions like this will help them identify people who can "think outside the box" and develop non-traditional, innovative solutions to difficult problems. In the authors' opinion, these questions are cheap shots that don't prove much of anything. Nevertheless, these questions do appear in interviews, and you should be prepared for them.

Problem: Bridge Crossing

- A party of four travelers comes to a rickety bridge at night. The bridge can hold the weight of at most two of the travelers at a time, and it cannot be crossed without using a flashlight. The travelers have one flashlight among them. Each traveler walks at a different speed: The first can cross the bridge in 1 minute, the second in 2 minutes, the third in 5 minutes, and the fourth takes 10 minutes to cross the bridge. If two travelers cross together, they walk at the speed of the slower traveler.

What is the least amount of time in which all the travelers can cross from one side of the bridge to the other?

Because there is only one flashlight, each trip to the far side of the bridge (except the last trip) must be followed by a trip coming back. Each of these trips consists of either one or two travelers crossing the bridge. To get a net movement of travelers to the far side of the bridge, you probably want to have two travelers on each outbound trip and one on each inbound trip. This strategy gives you a total of five trips, three outbound and two inbound. Your task is to assign travelers to the trips so that you minimize the total time for the five trips. For clarity, you can refer to each traveler by the number of minutes it takes him to cross the bridge.

Traveler 1 can cross the bridge at least twice as fast as any of the other travelers, so you can minimize the time of the return trips by always having 1 bring the flashlight back. This suggests a strategy where 1 escorts each of the other travelers across the bridge one by one.

One possible arrangement of trips using this strategy is illustrated in Figure 8.1. The order in which 1 escorts the other travelers doesn't change the total time: The three outbound trips have times of 2, 5, and 10 minutes, and the two inbound trips are 1 minute each, for a total of 19 minutes.

This solution is logical, obvious, and doesn't take long to discover. In short, it can't possibly be the best solution to an interview problem. Your interviewer would tell you that you can do better than 19 minutes, but even without that hint you should feel you arrived at the preceding solution too easily.

This puts you in an uncomfortable, but unfortunately not unusual, position. You know your answer is wrong, yet based on the assumptions you made, it's the only reasonable answer. It's easy to get frustrated at this point. You may wonder if this is a trick question: Perhaps you're supposed to throw the flashlight back or have the second pair use a lantern. No such tricks are necessary here. A more efficient arrangement of trips exists. Because the only solution that seems logical is wrong, you must have made a false assumption.

Consider your assumptions, checking each one to see if it might be false. First among your assumptions was that outbound and inbound trips must alternate. This seems correct—there's no way to have an outbound trip

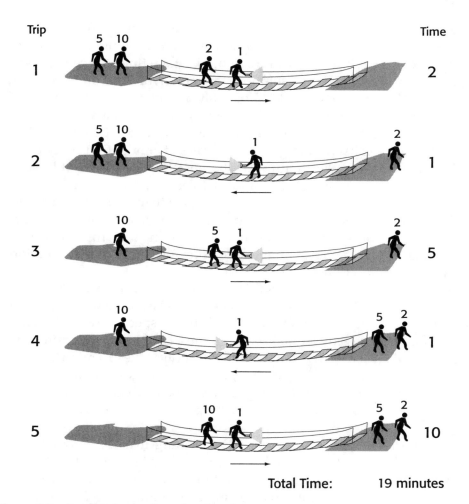

Trip   Time

Figure 8.1   Traveler 1 escorting other travelers.

followed by another outbound trip because the flashlight would be on the wrong side of the bridge. Next, you assumed that there would be two travelers on each outbound trip and one on each return trip. This seems logical, but it's harder to prove. Putting two travelers on an inbound trip seems terribly counter-productive; after all, you're trying to get them to the far side of the bridge. An outbound trip with only one traveler is potentially more worthwhile, but coupled with the requisite return trip all it really accomplishes is exchanging the positions of two travelers. Exchanging two travelers might be useful, but it will probably waste too much time to be worth it. Because this possibility doesn't look promising, try looking for a false assumption elsewhere and reconsider this one if necessary. You also assumed that 1 should always bring the flashlight back. What basis do you have for this assumption? It minimizes the time for the return trips, but the goal is to minimize total time, not return trip time. Perhaps the best overall solution does not involve minimized return trip times. The assumption that 1 should always return the flashlight seems hard to support, so it probably merits further examination.

If you're not going to have 1 make all the return trips, then how will you arrange the trips? You might try a process of elimination. You obviously can't have 10 make a return trip, because then he'd have at least three trips, which would take 30 minutes. Even without getting the remaining travelers across, this is already worse than your previous solution. Similarly, if 5 makes a return trip then you have two trips that are at least 5 minutes, plus one that takes 10 minutes (when 10 crosses). Just those three trips give you 20 minutes, so you won't find a better solution by having 5 make a return trip.

You might also try analyzing some of the individual trips from your previous solution. Because 1 escorted everyone else, there was a trip with 1 and 10. In a sense, when you send 1 with 10, 1's speed is wasted on that trip because the crossing still takes 10 minutes. Looking at that from a different perspective, any trip that includes 10 *always* takes 10 minutes, no matter which other traveler goes along. So, if you're going to have to spend 10 minutes on a trip, you might as well take advantage of it and get another slow traveler across. This reasoning indicates that 10 should cross with 5, rather than with 1.

Using this strategy, you might begin by sending 10 and 5 across. But then one of them has to bring the flashlight back, which you already know isn't the right solution. You'll want to already have someone faster than 5 waiting on the far side. Try starting by sending 1 and 2 across. Then have 1 bring the flashlight back. Now that there's someone reasonably fast (2) on the far side, you can send 5 and 10 across together. Then 2 returns the flashlight. Finally, 1 and 2 cross the bridge again. This scheme is illustrated in the Figure 8.2.

The times for the respective trips under this strategy are 2, 1, 10, 2, and 2, for a total of 17 minutes. Identifying the false assumption improved your solution by 2 minutes.

This problem is a slightly unusual example of a class of problems involving optimizing the process of moving a group of items a few at a time from one place to another. More commonly, the goal is to minimize the total number of trips, and there are often restrictions on which items can be left together. This particular problem is difficult because it suggests a false assumption (that 1 should escort each of the other travel-

Trip

Time

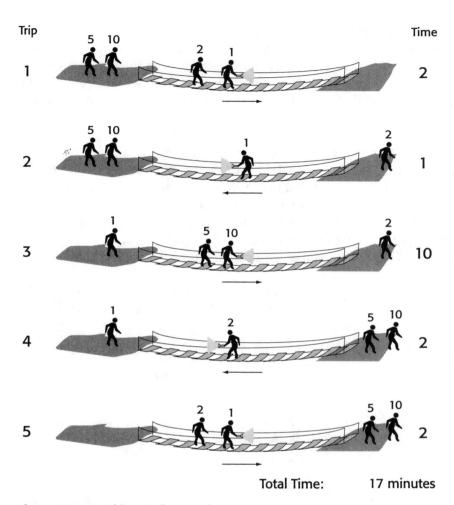

Total Time: 17 minutes

Figure 8.2   Matching similar speeds.

ers) that seems so obvious you may not even realize you're making an assumption.

Problem: Heavy Marble

■ You have eight marbles and a two-pan balance. All the marbles weigh the same, except for one, which is heavier than all the others. The marbles are otherwise indistinguishable. You may make no assumptions about how much heavier the heavy marble is. What is the minimum number of weighings needed to be certain of identifying the heavy marble?

The first step in solving this problem is to realize that you can put more than one marble in each pan of the balance. If you have equal numbers of marbles in each pan, then the heavy marble must be in the group on the heavy side of the balance. This saves you from having to weigh each marble individually, and it allows you to eliminate many marbles in a single weighing.

Once you realize this, you are likely to devise a binary search-based strategy for finding the heavy marble. In this method, you begin by putting half of the marbles on each side of the balance. Then you eliminate the marbles from the light side of the balance and divide the marbles from the heavy side of the balance between the two pans. As shown in Figure 8.3, you continue this process until each pan holds only one marble, at which point the heavy marble is the only marble on the heavy side of the balance. Using this process you can always identify the heavy marble in three weighings.

This may seem to be the correct answer. The solution wasn't completely obvious, and it's an improvement over weighing the marbles one by one.

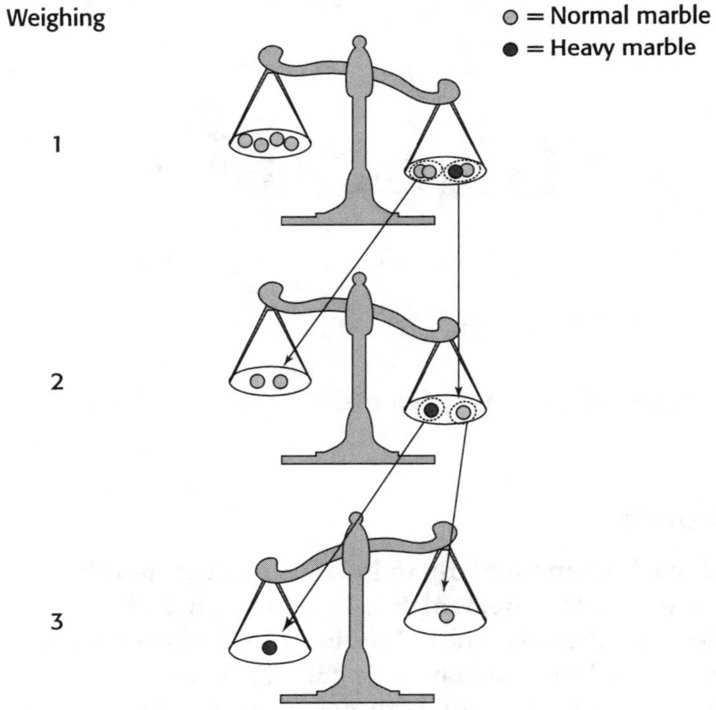

Weighing

○ = Normal marble
● = Heavy marble

1

2

3

Figure 8.3 Binary search for the heavy marble.

If you're telling yourself that this seemed too easy, you're right. The method described so far is a good start, but it's not the best you can do.

How can you find the heavy marble in fewer than three weighings? Obviously, you'll have to eliminate more than half the marbles at each weighing, but how can you do that?

Try looking at this problem from an information flow perspective. Information about the marbles comes from the balance, and you use this information to identify the heavy marble. The more information you derive from each weighing, the more efficient your search for the marble will be. Think about how you get information from the balance: You place marbles on it and then look at the result. What are all the possible results? The left pan side could be heavier, the right side could be heavier, or both sides could weigh exactly the same. So there are three possible results, but so far you've been using only two of them. In effect, you're only using ⅔ of the information that each weighing provides. Perhaps if you alter your method so that you use all of the information from each weighing you will be able to find the heavy marble in fewer weighings.

Using the binary search strategy, the heavy marble is always in one of the two pans, so there will always be a heavy side of the balance. In other words, you can't take advantage of all the information the balance can provide if the heavy marble is always on the balance. What if you divided the marbles into three equal-sized groups, and weighed two of the groups on the balance? Just as before, if either side of the balance is heavier, you know that the heavy marble is in the group on that side. But now it's also possible that the two groups of marbles on the balance will weigh the same—in this case, the heavy marble must be in the third group that's not on the balance. Because you divided the marbles into three groups, keeping just the group with the heavy marble eliminates ⅔ of the marbles instead of half of them. This seems promising.

There's still a minor wrinkle to work out before you can apply this process to the problem at hand. Eight isn't divisible by three, so you can't divide the eight marbles into three equal groups. Why do you need the same number of marbles in each group? You need the same number of marbles so that when you put the groups on the balance the result doesn't have anything to do with differing numbers of marbles on each side. Really, you need only two of the groups to be the same size. You'll still want all three groups to be approximately the same size so you can eliminate approximately ⅔ of the marbles after each weighing no matter which pile has the heavy marble.

Now you can apply the three-group technique to the problem you were given. Begin by dividing the marbles into two groups of three, which you put on the balance, and one group of two, which you leave off. If the two sides weigh the same, the heavy marble is in the group of two, and you can find it with one more weighing, for a total of two weighings. On the other hand, if either side of the balance is heavier, the heavy marble must be in that group of three. You can eliminate all the other marbles, and place one marble from this group on either side of the balance. If one side is heavier, it contains the heavy marble; if neither side is heavier, the heavy marble is the one you didn't place on the balance. This is also a total of two weighings, so you can always find the heavy marble in a group of eight using three weighings. An example of this process is illustrated in Figure 8.4.

▪ **Generalize your solution. What is the minimum number of weighings to find a heavy marble among *n* marbles?**

This is the part in which the interviewer determines whether you hit on the preceding solution by luck or because you really understand it. Think about what happens after each weighing. You eliminate ⅔ of the marbles and keep ⅓. After each weighing you have ⅓ as many marbles as you did before. When you get down to one marble, you've found the heavy marble.

Based on this thinking, you can reformulate the question as: "How many times do you have to divide the number of marbles by 3 before you

Weighing

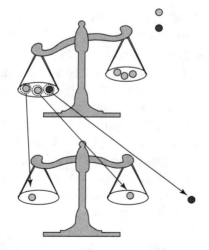

Figure 8.4 Optimum search for the heavy marble.

end up with 1?" If you start with 3 marbles, you divide by 3 once to get 1, so it takes one weighing. If you start with 9 marbles you divide by 3 twice, so it takes two weighings. Similarly, 27 marbles require three weighings. What mathematical operation can you use to represent this "how many times do you divide by 3 to get to 1" process?

Because multiplication and division are inverse operations, the number of times you have to divide the number of marbles by 3 before you end up with 1 is the same as the number of times you have to multiply by 3 (starting at 1) before you get to the number of marbles. Repeated multiplication is expressed using exponents. If you want to express multiplying by 3 twice, you can write 3^2, which is equal to 9. When you multiply twice by 3 you get 9—it takes two weighings to find the heavy marble among 9 marbles. In more general terms, it takes i weighings to find the heavy marble from among n marbles, where $3^i = n$. You know the value of n and want to calculate i, so you need to solve this for i. You can solve for i using logarithms, the inverse operation of exponentiation. If you take $\log_3$ of both sides of the preceding equation you get $i = \log_3 n$.

This works fine as long as n is a power of 3. However, if n isn't a power of 3, then this equation calculates a non-integer value for i, which doesn't make much sense, given that it's extremely difficult to perform a fractional weighing. For example, if $n = 8$, as in the previous part of the problem, $\log_3 8$ is some number between 1 and 2 (1.893... to be a little more precise). From your previous experience, you know it actually takes two weighings when you have eight marbles. This seems to indicate that if you calculate a fractional number of weighings you should round it up to the nearest integer.

Does this make sense? Try applying it to $n = 10$ and see whether you can justify always rounding up. $\log_3 9$ is 2, so $\log_3 10$ will be a little more than two, or three if you round up to the nearest integer. Is that the correct number of weighings for 10 marbles? For 10 marbles, you would start out with two groups of 3 and one group of 4. If the heavy marble were in either of the groups of 3, you could find it with just one more weighing, but if it turned out to be in the group of 4 you might need as many as two more weighings[2] for a total of 3, just as you calculated. In this case the fractional weighing seems to represent a weighing that you might need to make under some circumstances (if the heavy marble happens to be in the

---

[2]You would divide the 4 marbles into two groups of 1 and one group of 2. If the heavy marble happened to be in the group of 2, you would need one more weighing (the third weighing) to determine which was the heavy marble.

larger group) but not others.[3] Because you're trying to calculate the number of weighings needed to guarantee you'll find the heavy marble, you have to count that fractional weighing as a full weighing even though you won't always perform it, so it makes sense to always round up to the nearest integer. In programming, the function that rounds up to the nearest integer is often called ceiling, so you might express the minimum number of weighings needed to guarantee you'll find the heavy marble among n marbles as ceiling($\log_3(n)$).

This is another example of a problem designed such that the wrong solution occurs first to most intelligent, logically thinking people. Most people find it quite difficult to come up with the idea of using three groups, but relatively easy to solve the problem after that leap. It's not an accident that this problem begins by asking you to solve the case of eight marbles. As a power of 2, it works very cleanly for the incorrect solution, but because it's not a power (or multiple, for that matter) of 3 it's a little messy for the correct solution. People generally get the correct answer more quickly when asked to solve the problem for nine marbles. Look out for details like this that may steer your thinking in a particular (and often incorrect) direction.

This problem is a relatively easy example of a whole class of tricky problems involving weighing items with a two-pan balance. For more practice with these, you might want to try working out the solution to the preceding problem for a group of marbles where one marble has a different weight, but you don't know whether it's heavier or lighter.

---

[3]A fractional weighing may also represent a weighing that will always be performed but won't eliminate a full ⅔ of the remaining marbles. For instance, when $n = 8$, the fractional weighing represents the weighing needed to determine which marble is heavier in the case where the heavy marble is known to be in the group of two after the first weighing. In any case, it must be counted as a full weighing, so rounding up is appropriate.

Graphical and Spatial Puzzles

Many brainteasers are graphical or involve spatial thinking. All the techniques you've used on non-graphical puzzles are still applicable, but with these problems you have another very powerful technique available to you: diagrams. The importance of drawing diagrams cannot be overstated. Consider that while humans have only been using written language and mathematics for a few thousand years, we've been evolving to analyze visual problems (for example, can that rhinoceros catch me before I get to that tree?) for millions of years. We are generally much better suited to solving problems presented in pictures than those presented in text or numbers.

LESSON   **Whenever possible, draw a picture.**

In some cases, the actors in these brainteasers are static, but more often they are changing or in motion. When this is the case, don't draw just one picture, draw many. Make a diagram for each moment in time for which you have information. You can often gain insight by observing how the situation changes between each of your diagrams.

LESSON If the problem involves motion or change, draw multiple pictures of different points in time.

Most problems are two-dimensional. Even when a problem involves three-dimensional objects, the objects are often constrained to the same plane, allowing you to simplify the problem to two dimensions. It's much easier to diagram two dimensions than three, so don't work in three dimensions unless you have to. If the problem is fundamentally a three-dimensional problem, you should assess your relative abilities with drawing and visualization before proceeding. If you're not very good at drawing, your diagram of a three-dimensional problem may do more to confuse than elucidate. On the other hand, if you're a good artist or drafter but have trouble with visualization, you may be better off with a diagram. Whatever approach you take, try to attack spatial problems spatially, not with computation or symbolic mathematics.

LESSON Visualization may be more appropriate than diagramming for three-dimensional problems, but in either case, attack the problem spatially.

Problem: Boat and Dock

- You are sitting in a small boat, holding the end of a rope. The other end of the rope is tied to the top of a nearby pier, such that it is higher above the water than your end of the rope. You pull on the rope, causing your boat to move toward the pier, stopping directly underneath the pier. As you pull on the rope, which is faster, the speed the boat moves across the water or the speed the rope moves through your hands?

You should begin this problem by drawing a diagram, both to make sure you understand the scenario and to get you started on the solution. The edge of the pier, the water, and the rope form the legs of a right triangle, as shown in Figure 9.1. To facilitate further discussion, these segments are labeled A, B, and C, respectively.

Here you have something familiar, but with an unusual twist. You've probably worked with right triangles ad nauseum in your math classes, but those are static figures—this triangle is collapsing. Be wary of this difference. Although it seems minor, it may be enough to make the wrong answer seem intuitively correct.

Given your experience with right triangles, you may decide to attack this problem mathematically. You need to determine whether side B or

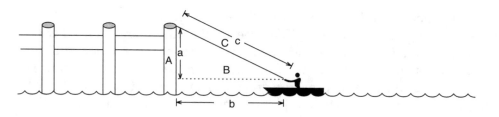

Figure 9.1 The boat on the water.

side C is shortened more quickly as the boat moves. Put another way, for a given change in length of B, what is the change in length of C? How might you calculate this? A derivative gives you the ratio of rates of change between two variables. If you calculated the derivative of C with respect to B and it were greater than 1, you would know that the rope was moving faster; conversely, if it were less than 1 the boat must have moved faster.

This is a good point to stop and consider where you've been and where you're going. You can set up an equation relating B and C using the Pythagorean theorem. It looks as if this method will eventually lead you to the correct answer. If you're good at math and comfortable with calculus, this may even be the best way to proceed. The apparent need for calculus, however, should serve as a warning that you may be missing an easier way to solve the problem.

Try going back to the original diagram and taking a more graphical approach. What other diagrams might you draw? Because you don't know the boat's initial distance from the pier or how high the pier is, all diagrams of the boat in motion are effectively equivalent. What about when the boat stops under the pier? That would be different; for one thing you would no longer have a triangle because the rope would be hanging down the side of the pier (see Figure 9.2).

How far does the boat travel, and how much rope is hauled in between the times shown in two figures? Because you aren't given any numbers, call the initial lengths of sides A, B, and C little *a*, *b*, and *c*, respectively.

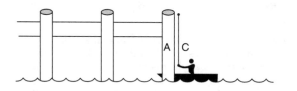

Figure 9.2 The boat under the pier.

When the boat is under the pier, side B has a length of 0, so the boat has moved through a distance of b. The rope, on the other hand, started with a length of c. In the second diagram, a length of rope equal to a is still out of the boat, so the total amount hauled in is $c - a$. Because these distances were covered in the same time, the greater distance must have been covered at a higher speed. Which is greater, then, $c - a$, or b? You will recall from geometry that the sum of the lengths of two sides of a triangle must always be greater than the length of the third.[1] So, for instance, $a + b > c$. Subtracting a, $b > c - a$. The boat traveled a greater distance, so it was moving faster across the water than the speed of the rope through your hands.

For the computationally curious, we'll pick up the calculus where we left it, to show that the solution can be determined using that method. From the Pythagorean theorem, $C^2 = A^2 + B^2$. This can be used to calculate the derivative of C with respect to B:

$$C = \sqrt{A^2 + B^2}$$
$$\frac{dC}{dB} = \frac{1}{2}(A^2 + B^2)^{-\frac{1}{2}}(2B)$$
$$= \frac{B}{\sqrt{A^2 + B^2}}$$

B is positive, so when A = 0, the final expression is equal to 1. When A is greater than 0, as in this problem, the denominator is greater than the numerator[2] and the expression is less than 1. This means that for a given infinitesimal change in B, there is a smaller change in C, so the boat is moving faster.

This problem belongs to a curious class of puzzles that seem to be more difficult when you know more math. They are particularly devilish in interviews. Because you expect difficult questions and you may be a little nervous, you're unlikely to stop and ask yourself whether there's an easier way.

One of the nastiest examples of this type of problem involves two locomotives, heading toward each other at 10 mph. When they are exactly 30

---

[1] If you think about this, it makes intuitive sense. Suppose one side were longer than the other two put together. There would be no way to arrange the sides such that they met at three vertices because the shorter two sides would be too short to span the distance from one end of the long side to the other.
[2] In case you've been out of a math class for too long, the numerator is the expression above the fraction bar and the denominator is the expression below.

miles apart, a bird sitting on the front of one locomotive flies off toward the other, traveling at 60 mph. When it reaches the other locomotive, it immediately turns around and flies back to the first. The bird continues like this until, sadly, it is smashed between the two locomotives as they collide. When asked how far the bird traveled, many calculus students will spend hours trying to set up and sum impossibly difficult infinite series. Most younger students who have never heard of an infinite series will instead determine that it took the locomotives 1.5 hours to close the 30 mile gap, and that in that time a bird traveling 60 mph would have traveled 90 miles.

Problem: Counting Cubes

■   **Imagine a cubic array made up of a 3 × 3 × 3 arrangement of smaller cubes: the cubic array is three cubes wide, three cubes high, and three cubes deep (see Figure 9.3). It may help to picture a Rubik's Cube.**

How many of the cubes are on the surface of the cubic array?

This is a spatial visualization problem. Different people find different techniques useful in visualization, so we will present a variety of approaches in our discussion. We hope you will find at least one of them useful. You can try to draw a diagram, but because the problem is in three dimensions, you may find your diagram more confusing than helpful.

One way you might try to solve this problem is by counting the cubes on each face of the array. A cube has six faces. Each face of the cubic array has nine cubes (3 × 3), so you might conclude that there are 6 × 9 = 54 cubes on the surface. There are only 3 × 3 × 3 = 27 cubes total, so it's obviously not possible for twice that many to be on the surface. The fallacy in this method is that some cubes are on more than one face—for instance, the corner cubes are on three faces. Rather than try to make complicated

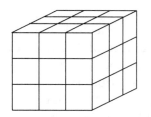

Figure 9.3   A 3 × 3 × 3 cubic array of cubes.

adjustments for cubes that are on more than one face, you should look for an easier solution.

A better way to attack this problem is to count the cubes in layers. The array is three cubes high, so there are three layers. All the cubes on the top layer are on the surface (nine cubes). All the cubes of the middle layer except for the center cube are on the surface (eight cubes). Finally, all the cubes on the bottom layer are on the surface (nine cubes). This gives a total of $9 + 8 + 9 = 26$ cubes on the surface.

The preceding method works, but perhaps a better way to find the solution is to count the cubes that are not on the surface and then subtract this number from the total number of cubes. Vivid, specific objects are often easier to visualize than vague concepts—you may want to imagine the cubes on the surface to be translucent red and the non-surface cubes to be bright blue. We hope you will be able to see that there is only one bright blue cube surrounded by a shell of red cubes. Because this is the only cube that isn't on the surface there must be $27 - 1 = 26$ cubes on the surface.

■ **Now imagine that you have a $4 \times 4 \times 4$ cubic array of cubes. How many cubes are on the surface of this array?**

As the number of cubes increases, the accounting necessary for the layer approach becomes more complicated, so try to solve this by visualizing and counting the cubes that are not on the surface. The non-surface cubes form a smaller cubic array within the larger array. How many cubes are in this smaller array? Your initial impulse may be that there are four cubes in the array; if so, consider whether it's possible to arrange four cubes into a cubic array (it isn't). The correct answer is that the non-surface cubes form a $2 \times 2 \times 2$ array of eight cubes. There are a total of $4 \times 4 \times 4 = 64$ cubes, so there are $64 - 8 = 56$ cubes on the surface.

■ **Generalize your solution to an $n \times n \times n$ cubic array of cubes. In terms of n, how many cubes are on the surface?**

Now that you can't explicitly count the cubes, the problem starts to get a little more interesting. You know that there are n^3 cubes total. If you can calculate the number of cubes that aren't on the surface, you'll also be able to calculate the number that are. Try to visualize the situation, mentally coloring the surface cubes red and the interior cubes blue. What does it look like? You should be able to see a cubic array of blue cubes surrounded by a one cube–thick shell of red cubes. If you can determine the size of the smaller array, you can calculate the number of cubes it contains. Because the smaller array fits entirely within the larger one, it must be fewer than n cubes across, but how many fewer?

Visualize a single line of cubes running all the way through the array. The line would be n cubes long. Because the shell of red surface cubes is one cube thick, both the first and last cubes would be red, and all the other cubes would be blue. This means there would be $n - 2$ blue cubes in the row, so the array of interior cubes is $n - 2$ cubes across. It's a cubic array, so its height and depth are the same as its width. Therefore, you can calculate that there are $(n - 2)^3$ cubes that are not on the surface. Subtracting this from the total number of cubes gives you $n^3 - (n - 2)^3$ cubes on the surface. Test this formula using the cases you've already worked out by hand: $3^3 - (3 - 2)^3 = 26$; $4^3 - (4 - 2)^3 = 56$. It looks as if you've got the answer for this part, but you're not done yet.

- **A cube is an object that measures the same distance across in three perpendicular directions in a three-dimensional space. A four-dimensional hypercube is an object that measures the same distance across in four perpendicular directions in a four-dimensional space. Calculate the number of 4D hypercubes on the surface of an $n \times n \times n \times n$ hypercubic array of 4D hypercubes.**

The fun really starts here. This started out as a visualization problem, but taking it to four dimensions makes it very difficult for most people to visualize. Visualization can still be helpful, though. You might (or might not) find the following device useful.

People often represent time as a fourth dimension. The easiest way to visualize time in a concrete fashion is to imagine a strip of film from a movie. Each frame in the filmstrip represents a different time, or a different location along the fourth dimension. In order to fully represent four dimensions, you have to imagine that each frame consists of a full three-dimensional space, not two-dimensional pictures as in a real filmstrip. If you can visualize this, you can visualize four dimensions.

Because a hypercube measures the same distance in each direction, the filmstrip representing the hypercubic array in this problem is n frames long. In each of the frames you see an $n \times n \times n$ array of cubes,[3] just as in the previous part of the problem. This means there are $n \times n^3 = n^4$ hypercubes total. In terms of color, the arrays you see in the middle frames of

---

[3] They're actually hypercubes because their existence in the frame gives them a duration of one frame, or a width of one unit in the time (fourth) dimension. However, it may be easier to think of them as normal 3D cubes when trying to visualize a single frame.

the filmstrip look just like the array from the previous part of the problem—a red shell surrounding a blue core. All the cubes in the first and last frames are on the surface in the fourth dimension because they are at the ends of the filmstrip. All the cubes in these frames are red. In other words, there are $n - 2$ frames that have blue cubes, and each of these frames looks like the array from the previous part of the problem. Multiplying the number of frames with blue cubes by the number of blue cubes in each frame gives $(n - 2)(n - 2)^3 = (n - 2)^4$, the total number of blue hypercubes. Subtracting from the previous result yields $n^4 - (n - 2)^4$ hypercubes on the surface of the hypercubic array.

  ■ **Generalize your solution to i dimensions. How many hypercubes are there on the surface of an $n \times n \times n \times \ldots \times n$ (i dimensions) hypercubic array of i dimensional hypercubes?**

You're almost there. At this point you may find it helpful to extend the device you've been using for visualization into many dimensions, or you may find it easier to dispense with visualization and solve the problem using patterns and mathematics. We'll examine both methods.

Visualizing a filmstrip gave you four dimensions, but there's no reason to limit yourself to a single filmstrip. If you imagine lining up n filmstrips side by side, you have five dimensions: three in each frame, one given by the frame number, and one more given by the filmstrip that holds the frame. Each of these filmstrips would look just like the filmstrip from the four-dimensional case, except for the rightmost and leftmost filmstrips. These two filmstrips would be surface filmstrips in the fifth dimension, so all of the cubes in each of their frames would be red. You can further extend this to six dimensions by imagining a stack of multiple layers of filmstrips. Beyond six dimensions, it again becomes difficult to visualize the situation (you might try thinking of different tables, each holding stacks of layers of filmstrips), but the device has served its purpose in illustrating that dimensions are an arbitrary construction—there is nothing special about objects with more than three dimensions. Each dimension you add gives you n copies of what you were visualizing before. Of these, two of the copies are always entirely on the surface, leaving $n - 2$ copies in which there are blue interior cubes. This means that with each additional dimension, the total number of hypercubes increases by a factor of n and the number of non-surface hypercubes increases by a factor of $n - 2$. You have one of each of these factors for each dimension, giving you a final result of $n^i - (n - 2)^i$ hypercubes on the surface of the array.

Alternatively, you might take a pattern-based approach and note that you raised both parts of the expression to the power of 3 in the three-dimensional case and to the power of 4 in the four-dimensional case. From this you might deduce that the exponent represents the number of dimensions in the problem. You might check this by trying the one- and two-dimensional cases (a line and a square), where you would find that your proposed solution appears to work. Thinking about it mathematically, when you have n hypercubes in each of i directions, it seems reasonable that you would have a total of n^i hypercubes; for the same reason, raising $(n-2)$ to the ith power also seems to make sense. This isn't a proof, but it should be enough to make you confident that $n^i - (n-2)^i$ is the right answer.

It's interesting to look at the progression of the parts of this problem. The first part of the problem is quite easy. Taken by itself, the last part of the problem would seem almost impossible. Each part of the problem is only a little more difficult than the preceding, and each part helps you gain new insight, so by the time you reach the final part it doesn't seem so insurmountable. It's good to remember this technique. Solving simpler, easier, more specific cases can give you insight into the solution of a more difficult, general problem, even if you aren't led through the process explicitly as you were here.

Problem: The Fox and Duck

- A duck, pursued by a fox, escapes to the center of a perfectly circular pond. The fox cannot swim, and the duck cannot take flight from the water (it's a deficient duck). The fox is four times faster than the duck. Assuming the fox and duck pursue optimum strategies, is it possible for the duck to reach the edge of the pond and fly away without being eaten? If so, how?

The most obvious strategy for the duck is to swim directly away from where the fox is standing. The duck has to swim a distance of r to the edge of the pond. The fox, meanwhile, has to run around half the circumference of the pond, a distance of πr. Because the fox moves four times faster than the duck, and $\pi r < 4r$, it's apparent that any duck pursuing this strategy would soon be fox food.

Think about what this result tells you. Does it prove that the duck can't escape? No; it just shows that the duck can't escape using this strategy. If there weren't anything else to this problem, it would be a trivial geometry exercise—not worth asking in an interview. So, this result suggests the duck can escape, you just don't know how.

Instead of focusing on the duck, try thinking about the fox's strategy. The fox will run around the perimeter of the pond to stay as close to the duck as possible. Because the shortest distance from any point in the circle to the edge lies along a radius, the fox will try to stay on the same radius as the duck.

How can the duck make life most difficult for the fox? If the duck swims back and forth along a radius, the fox can just sit on that radius. The duck could try swimming back and forth across the center point of the pond, which would keep the fox running as the duck's radius repeatedly switched from one side of the pond to the other. However, consider that each time the duck crosses the center point, he returns to the problem's initial configuration: He is in the center and the fox is at the edge. The duck won't make much progress that way.

Another possibility would involve the duck swimming in a circle concentric with the pond, so the fox would have to keep running around the pond to stay on the duck's radius. When the duck is near the edge of the pond, the fox has no trouble staying on the same radius as the duck because they are covering approximately equal distances and the fox is four times faster. However, as the duck moves closer to the center of the pond, the circumference of its circle becomes smaller and smaller. At a distance of $\frac{1}{4}r$ from the center of the pond, the duck's circle is exactly four times smaller than the circumference of the pond, so the fox is just barely able to stay on the same radius as the duck. At any distance less than $\frac{1}{4}r$ from the center, the fox has to cover more than four times the distance that the duck does to move between two radii. That means that as the duck circles, the fox will start to lag behind.

This strategy seems to give the duck a way to put some distance between it and the fox. If the duck swims long enough, eventually the fox will lag so far behind that the radius the duck is on will be 180° from the fox; in other words, the point on the shore closest to the duck will be farthest from the fox. Perhaps this head start would be enough that the duck could make a radial beeline for the shore and get there ahead of the fox. How can the head start be maximized? When the duck's circle has a radius of $\frac{1}{4}r$ the fox just keeps pace with it, so at a radius of $\frac{1}{4}r$ minus some infinitesimal amount ε the duck would just barely pull ahead. Eventually, when it got 180° ahead of the fox, it would be $\frac{3}{4}r + \varepsilon$ from the nearest point on the shore. The fox, however, would be half the circumference of the pond from that point: πr. In this case, the fox would have to cover

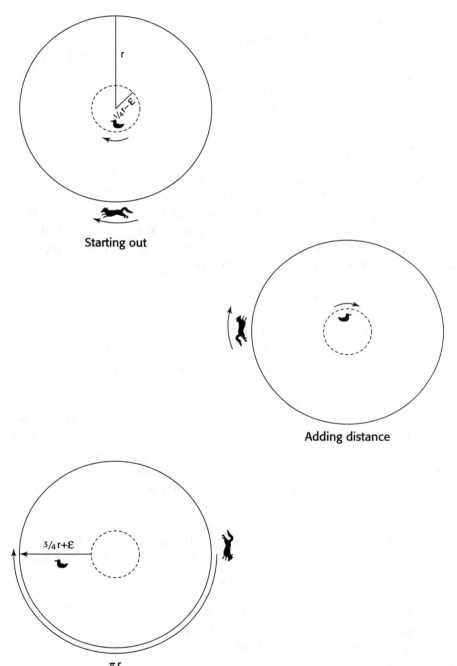

$\frac{1}{4}r-\varepsilon$

Starting out

Adding distance

$\frac{3}{4}r+\varepsilon$

πr
Making the escape

Figure 9.4 The duck's escape plan.

more than four times the distance that the duck does ($3r < \pi r$), so the duck would be able to make it to land and fly away.

You might want to try to work out the solution to a similar problem on your own: This time, the fox is chasing a rabbit. They are inside a circular pen from which they cannot escape. If the rabbit can run at the same speed as the fox, is it possible for the fox to catch the rabbit?

Problem: Burning Fuses

■ **You are given two fuses and a lighter. When lit, each fuse takes exactly one hour to burn from one end to the other. The fuses do not burn at a constant rate, though, and they are not identical. In other words, you may make no assumptions about the relationship between the length of a section of fuse and the time it has taken or will take to burn. Two equal lengths of fuse will not necessarily take the same time to burn. Using only the fuses and the lighter, measure a period of exactly 45 minutes.**

One of the difficult parts of this problem is keeping firmly in mind that the length of a piece of fuse has nothing to do with the time it will take to burn. Although this is stated explicitly in the problem, constant rates and relationships between time and distance are so familiar that it can be easy to fall into the trap of trying to somehow measure a physical length of fuse. In fact, because the burn rate is unknown and variable, the only useful measure is time. Mindful of this, you can begin to solve the problem.

The materials and actions available to you are fairly circumscribed in this problem. In such a case, it can be useful to begin by considering all possible actions, and then identify which of these possible actions might be useful.

There are two locations where you can light the fuses: at an end or somewhere that is not an end (in the middle). If you light one of the fuses at an end, it will burn through in 60 minutes. That's longer than the total length of time you need to measure, so it probably isn't directly useful. If you light a fuse in the middle, you will end up with two flames, each burning toward a different end of the fuse. If you were extremely lucky, you might light the exact center (in burn time; it might not be the physical center) of the fuse, in which case both flames would extinguish simultaneously after 30 minutes. It's much more likely that you would miss the center of the fuse, giving you one flame that went out sometime before 30 minutes and a second that continued burning for some time after. This doesn't seem like a very reliable way to make a measurement.

When you lit the fuse in the middle, you got a different burn time than when you lit the end. Why is this? Lighting the middle of the fuse created two flames, so you were burning in two places at once. How else might you use two flames? You've seen that lighting the middle of the fuse is problematic because you don't really know where (in time) you're lighting. That leaves the ends of the fuse. If you light both ends of the fuse, the flames will burn toward each other until they meet and extinguish each other after exactly 30 minutes. This could be useful.

So far, you can measure exactly 30 minutes using one fuse. If you could figure out how to measure 15 minutes with the other fuse, you could add the two times to solve the problem. What would you need to measure 15 minutes? Either a 15-minute length of fuse, burning at one end; or a 30-minute length of fuse, burning at both ends, would do the trick. Because you're starting with a 60-minute length of fuse, this means you need to remove either 45 or 30 minutes from the fuse. Again, this must be done by burning because cutting the fuse would involve making a physical (distance) measurement, which would be meaningless. Forty-five minutes could be removed by burning from both ends for 22.5 minutes or one end for 45 minutes. Measuring 22.5 minutes seems an even harder problem than the one you were given; if you knew how to measure 45 minutes you'd have solved the problem, so this possibility doesn't look particularly fruitful. The other option is removing 30 minutes of fuse, which could be done by burning from both ends for 15 minutes or one end for 30 minutes. The need to measure 15 minutes returns you to the task at hand, but you do know how to measure 30 minutes: Exactly 30 minutes elapse from lighting both ends of the first fuse until the flames go out. If you light one end of the second fuse at the same moment you light both ends of the first, then you'll be left with 30 minutes of fuse on the second fuse when the first fuse is gone. You can light the other end (the one that isn't already burning) of this second fuse as soon as the first goes out. The two flames burning on the 30-minute length of fuse will extinguish each other after exactly 15 minutes, giving you a total of 30 + 15 = 45 minutes.

Problem: Escaping the Train

- Two boys walking in the woods decided to take a shortcut through a railroad tunnel. When they had walked ⅔ of the way through the tunnel, their worst fears were realized. A train was coming in the opposite direction, nearing the tunnel entrance. The boys panicked and each ran for a different end of the tunnel. Both boys ran at the same speed, 10 miles per hour. Each boy escaped

from the tunnel just at the instant that the train would have squashed him into the rails. Assuming the train's speed was constant, and both boys were capable of instantaneous reaction and acceleration, how fast was the train going?

At first, this seems like a classic algebra word problem, straight out of a high school homework set (or middle school, if you were an overachiever). When you go to set up your x's and y's, however, you'll realize you're missing a lot of the information you would expect to have in a standard algebra rate problem. Specifically, although you know the boys' speeds, you don't have any information about distances or times. Perhaps this will be more challenging than it first appeared.

A good way to get started is by drawing a diagram using the information you've been given. Call the boys Abner and Brent (A and B to their friends). At the moment the problem begins, when the boys have just noticed the train, the train is an unknown distance from the tunnel, heading toward the boys. A and B are both in the same place, ⅓ of the tunnel length from the entrance closest to the train. A is running toward the train and B away from it, as shown in Figure 9.5.

The only additional information you have is that both boys just barely escape. Try drawing diagrams of the moments of their escapes. A is running toward the train and has only ⅓ of the tunnel to cover, so he'll escape before B. Because he reaches the end of the tunnel at the last possible instant, he and the train must be at the end of the tunnel at the same time. Where would B be at this time? A and B run at the same speed; A moves ⅓ of the length of the tunnel before escaping, so B must also have run ⅓ of the length of the tunnel. That would put him ⅓ of the way from the end of the tunnel he's headed for, as seen in Figure 9.6.

Now diagram B's escape. The train has come all the way through the tunnel, and both it and B are right at the end of the tunnel. (A is somewhere outside the other end of the tunnel, counting his blessings.) This situation is illustrated in Figure 9.7.

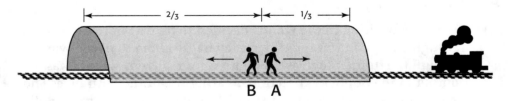

Figure 9.5 Abner and Brent notice the train.

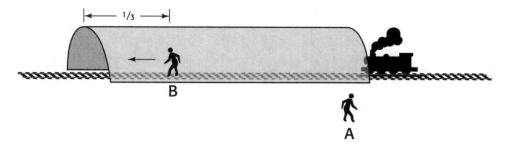

Figure 9.6 Abner escapes; Brent keeps running.

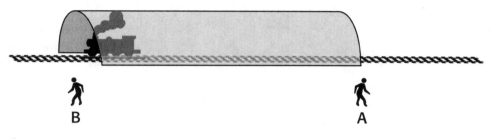

Figure 9.7 Brent escapes.

None of these diagrams seem particularly illuminating on their own. Because you're trying to determine the speed of the train, you should look at how it moves; how its position changes between your three diagrams. Between the first and second diagrams, A and B each run ⅓ of the length of the tunnel, while the train moves an unknown distance. No help there. Between the second and third diagrams, B again runs ⅓ of the tunnel length, while the train runs through the whole tunnel. So the train covers three times more distance than B in the same amount of time. This means the train must be three times as fast as B. B goes 10 miles per hour, so the train moves at 30 miles per hour.

Don't underestimate the power of diagrams.

Knowledge-Based Questions

Knowledge-based questions vary greatly in frequency from interview to interview. Some interviewers will not ask knowledge-based questions while others will focus solely on them. Interviewers often ask these questions when there is no whiteboard or paper available, such as at lunch, or when they are satisfied with your coding ability and want to test your general computer knowledge. These questions allow an interviewer to assess your background and determine your computer proficiency.

Resumes

Often, these questions focus on your resume. In fact, it's a very good idea to review your resume prior to your interview and make sure you're prepared to answer questions about every item on it. Some interviewers will even go through your resume and ask you about each item—"What is it?" and "What have you done with it?" For example, if you put "ActiveX Objects" on your resume, be prepared for the questions "What are ActiveX objects?" and "What have you done with ActiveX objects?" If your best response is something along the lines of "ActiveX objects let you do neat things with Web pages and I haven't done anything with them, but I read about them once," you should remove ActiveX objects from your resume.

LESSON   Be prepared to answer questions about everything on your resume.

The Questions

It would be impossible for us to cover every conceivable area of computer knowledge that could appear on a resume or in an interview. Instead, this chapter provides a representative sample of knowledge-based questions. These questions focus on system-level issues, trade-offs between various ways of programming, and advanced features of languages. All these topic areas make sense from the interviewer's perspective. A candidate who claims to know a lot about computers but who isn't aware of basic system-level issues such as virtual memory and disk cache certainly doesn't seem very knowledgeable. Furthermore, many job assignments are not "Solve this problem by implementing this algorithm in this language," but may be more along the lines of "We have this problem that we need solved." A candidate who understands the trade-offs between various solutions and when to use each one is always preferred to a candidate who does not understand these differences. Finally, these questions allow an interviewer to assess experience and filter out resume padding. It's unlikely that an experienced developer would have problems answering questions about advanced features in a language that he had used in development for some time. However, an inexperienced programmer or a resume padder might stumble. These questions can help interviewers separate the wheat from the chaff.

Interviewers prefer specific answers to general answers. For example, suppose you are asked, "What is a CD-ROM?" One general answer is, "It's something that can store data." While this answer is technically correct, it doesn't demonstrate that you really understand why it's such a popular medium and what its uses are. Alternatively, you could respond, "A CD-ROM is a removable, optical, random-access data storage device. It allows much faster data access than floppy drives and can store much more data. True CD-ROMs can be read from, but not written to. It's a relatively inexpensive storage medium that's the preferred choice for software in a box. There are also recordable and rewritable CDs that are becoming increasingly popular... " It seems pretty clear which answer is better.

LESSON Offer specific and thorough responses.

One final note: The answers presented here are researched answers that result from many people thinking about a question and coming up with the best answer. As a candidate hearing a question for the first time, you are not expected to replicate such detailed solutions. Consider these answers to be the goal, and try to get as close to these solutions as possible.

Problem: C++ and Java

■ **What are the differences between C++ and Java?**

C++ and Java are syntactically very similar. Java's designers intended this to make it easy for C++ developers to learn Java. Apart from this area of similarity, Java and C++ differ in a variety of ways, largely because of their different design goals. Security, portability, and rapid development were of paramount importance in the design of Java, while C++ is more concerned with performance and backward compatibility with C. Java is compiled to virtual machine byte-code and requires a virtual machine to run; C++ is compiled to native machine code. This usually makes C++ faster, but it gives Java greater potential for portability and security.

C++ is a superset of C and maintains features such as programmer-controlled memory management, pointers, and a preprocessor for full backward compatibility with C. In contrast, Java eliminates these and other bug-prone features. Java replaces programmer memory deallocations with garbage collection. Java further dispenses with C++ features such as operator overloading, templates, and multiple inheritance.[1] These choices make Java a better choice for rapid development and for projects where portability and security are more important than performance.

In Java, all objects are passed by reference, whereas in C++, the default behavior is to pass objects by value. Java does not perform automatic type casting as C++ does. In Java, all methods are virtual, meaning the implementation for a method is selected according to the type of the object as opposed to the type of the reference. In C++, methods must be explicitly

---

[1]A limited form of multiple inheritance can be simulated in Java using interfaces.

declared virtual. Java has defined sizes for primitive data types while type sizes are implementation dependent in C++.

In situations where there is legacy C code and a great need for performance, C++ has certain benefits. In situations where portability, security, and speed of development are emphasized, Java may be a better choice.

Problem: Including Files

- **What's the difference between the preprocessor directive `#include "file.h"` and `#include <file.h>`?**

The difference has to do with where the compiler goes to look for the requested file. When angle brackets are used, the compiler looks in a series of standard include directories. In the quoted case, the compiler first looks in the local directory and then checks the standard include directories only if the file is not found in the local directory. Angle brackets are generally used for standard files like `stdio.h`, whereas quotes are used for modules that the programmer writes.

Problem: Storage Classes

- **Explain the different storage classes in C.**

Storage classes determine how long a variable is kept in memory, specify the scope of the variable, and can even hint at possible compiler optimizations. There are four storage classes in C: `auto`, `register`, `static`, and `extern`.

The most common storage class is `auto`. The `auto` keyword can be used only inside a function. It tells the compiler that the variable is needed only while the function is executing and that its value need not be retained between calls to the function. Memory for `auto` variables is usually allocated on the stack. All local variables are `auto` by default, so although `auto` variables are used very frequently, most programmers omit the `auto` keyword.

The `register` keyword does the same thing as `auto`, except it also hints to the compiler that the variable will be used frequently, and therefore it may be a good optimization to keep the variable in a register to reduce loads and stores. Most modern compilers ignore the `register` keyword because compiler tests show that most application programmers are not very good at determining optimal register assignments.

static has two different meanings, depending on context. At the external level, outside any functions, it specifies that the scope of the variable is limited to the file it is defined in. It cannot be referenced from another file. Inside a function definition, it means the variable should be allocated at a fixed location in memory (instead of on the stack) so it retains its value between function calls.

The extern storage class is used when you need to reference a variable before it is defined or when you want to access a variable defined in a different file. Thus, the extern keyword allows you to declare what the variables are, but it does not create variables or allocate memory for them.

Problem: Friend Class

■ **Discuss friend classes in C++ and give an example of when you would use one.**

The friend keyword is applied to either a function or a class. It gives the friend function or friend class access to the private members of the class in which the declaration occurs. Some programmers feel this feature violates the principles of object-oriented programming because it allows a class to operate on another class's private members. This violation can, in turn, lead to unexpected bugs when a change in the internal implementation of a class causes problems with the friend class that accesses it.

In some cases, however, the benefits of a friend class outweigh its drawbacks. For example, suppose you implemented a sophisticated dynamic array class. Imagine that you wanted a separate class to iterate through your array. The iterator class would probably need access to the dynamic array class's private members to function correctly. It would make sense to declare the iterator as a friend to the array class. The workings of the two classes are inextricably tied together already, so it probably doesn't make sense to enforce a meaningless separation between the two.

Problem: Class and Struct

■ **What is the difference between a class and a struct in C++?**

To a casual programmer, this may seem like a silly question. A class allows you to have member variables, methods, and inheritance, while a struct seems much less sophisticated. In fact, a C++ struct can do everything that a class can do. The difference between a class and a struct has to do with permissions. All members default to public in a struct whereas they default to private in a class.

You may wonder why there are two virtually identical constructs in C++. There are three possible explanations: backward compatibility, design freedom, and portability.

First, C++ has to include a struct to maintain backward compatibility with C. A C struct already groups data, so it's natural to add methods and inheritance. Secondly, the C++ struct definition must always maintain full backward compatibility with a C struct. By making the fundamental object unit the class and not the struct, the C++ designers had the freedom to set appropriate default permissions on classes without being constrained by compatibility requirements. Finally, expansion of the struct definition may make it easier to port code from C to C++.

Problem: Parent Class and Child Class

- **Discuss the relationship between parent and child classes in C++.**

There are three important aspects of the parent-child class relationship in C++: inheritance, virtual methods, and pure virtual methods in abstract classes.

A child class inherits all of the parent class's non-private methods and member variables. It can override inherited members or create new ones. A child class can be passed as an instance of its parent class because it has implementations for all of its parent class's public methods and member variables. A parent class may not be passed as an instance of a child class because the child class may implement methods and member variables that the parent class does not.

When a child class overrides a method from a parent class, it is usually desirable to declare the method virtual. When an overridden method is virtual, the implementation to be executed is selected according to the type of the object on which the method is called. Otherwise, the implementation is selected based on the type of reference or pointer used to call the method.

For example, consider the following definitions:

```
public class Lion {
    public void Roar() {
        PlaySound(EARTH_SHAKING_ROAR);
    }
}

// subclass of Lion
public class BabyLion : Lion {
```

```
        public void Roar() {
            PlaySound(LITTLE_MEOW);
        }
}

// Function that calls Roar
void MakeMovieStudioSound(Lion *leo) {
    leo->Roar();
}
```

Clearly, a `BabyLion` is a `Lion` so either can be passed to `MakeMovie StudioSound`. Consider the case where a pointer to a `BabyLion` is passed to the function. If `Roar` is *not* a virtual method (as in the preceding code), the computer will use the `Roar` implementation defined in `Lion` and *not* the `Roar` method defined in `BabyLion`. No run-time checking is done to see which implementation of `Roar` should be used.

If `Roar` *is* a virtual method, the computer will check the object's type at run time, see that the object is actually a `BabyLion`, and call the `BabyLion` implementation of `Roar`.

This is an interesting situation because there are very few cases where a programmer would want the behavior exhibited by a non-virtual method. It takes longer to call a virtual method than it does to call a non-virtual method, however, so non-virtual was left as the default in C++.

A third aspect of the relationship between parent and child classes involves pure virtual methods and abstract classes. A pure virtual method is a method that is not defined but is inherited by subclasses. Any class with a pure virtual method is an abstract class and cannot be instantiated. If the parent class is an abstract class, the child class either overrides all pure virtual functions or is an abstract class itself. For example, assume that you have a parent class `Clown` that has one pure virtual method called `Juggle`. You then create another class, `SadClown`, which inherits from `Clown`. If `SadClown` does not override `Juggle` with a definition, then `SadClown` will also be an abstract class.

Problem: Argument Passing

- Consider the following C++ function prototypes for a function, `foo`, which takes an object of class `Fruit` as an argument.

```
void foo(Fruit bar);          // Prototype 1
void foo(Fruit* bar);         // Prototype 2
void foo(Fruit& bar);         // Prototype 3
void foo(const Fruit* bar);   // Prototype 4
void foo(Fruit*& bar);        // Prototype 5
```

For each prototype, discuss how the argument will be passed and what the implications would be for a function implemented using that method of argument passing.

In the first prototype, the object argument is passed by value. This means that Fruit's copy constructor would be called to duplicate the object on the stack. Within the function, bar is an object of class Fruit. Because bar is a copy of the object that was passed to the function, any changes made to bar will not be reflected in the original object. This is the least efficient way to pass an object because every data member of the object must be copied.

bar would be a pointer to a Fruit object in a function implemented for the second prototype. This is more efficient than passing by value because only the address of the object is copied onto the stack, not the object itself. Because bar points at the object that was passed to foo, any changes made through bar are reflected in the original object.

The third prototype shows bar being passed by reference. This case is very similar to the second: It involves no copying of the object and allows foo to operate directly on the calling function's object. The most obvious difference between a function using a reference and one using a pointer is syntactic. A pointer must be explicitly dereferenced before member variables and functions can be accessed, but members can be accessed directly using a reference. Therefore, the arrow operator (->) is usually used to access members when working with pointers,[2] while the dot operator (.) is used for references. A subtler but more important difference is that the pointer need not point at a valid Fruit; the pointer version of foo could be passed a NULL pointer. In the implementation using references, however, bar is guaranteed to be a reference to a valid Fruit.

In the fourth prototype, bar is passed as a constant pointer to the object. This has the performance advantages of passing pointers, but foo is prevented from modifying bar. Only methods declared as const can be called on bar from within foo. This prevents foo from modifying bar indirectly.

In the final case, bar is a reference to a pointer to a Fruit object. As in the second case, this means that changes made to the object will be seen by the calling function. In addition, because bar is a reference to a pointer, not merely a pointer, if bar is modified to point to a different

---

[2]If you're a masochist, you can also dereference the pointer using * and then use . to access the members. Because . binds more tightly than *, this requires parentheses: (*bar).property = 1;.

Fruit object, the pointer passed from the calling function will be modified as well.

Problem: Macros and Inline Functions

■ **Compare and contrast macros and inline functions in C++.**

Macros are implemented with simple text replacement in the preprocessor. For example, you could define the macro:

```
#define AVERAGE(a, b) ((a + b) / 2)
```

Then, the preprocessor replaces any occurrences of AVERAGE(foo, bar) in your code with ((foo + bar) / 2). Macros are commonly used in places where the thing that you're substituting is ugly and common enough that it warrants abstraction behind a pretty name, but too simple to be worth the overhead of a function call.

Inline functions are declared and defined much like regular functions. Unlike macros, they are handled by the compiler directly. An inline function implementation of the AVERAGE macro would look like:[3]

```
inline int Average(int a, int b)
{
    return (a + b)/2;
}
```

From the programmer's perspective, calling an inline function is like calling a regular function. However, when the compiler encounters a call to an inline function, instead of generating a function call, it writes a copy of the compiled function definition.

Both inline functions and macros provide a way to eliminate function call overhead at the expense of program size. While inline functions have the semantics of a function call, macros have the semantics of text replacement. This can create bugs due to the unexpected behavior of macros.

For example, suppose you had the following macro and code:

```
#define CUBE(x) x * x * x

int foo, bar = 2;
foo = CUBE(++bar);
```

---

[3]Member functions (methods) can be implicitly declared inline by including their definition in the class definition. Note that the argument and return types must be specified for an inline function, which is not necessary for the macro. Some degree of type flexibility can be regained using templates, but that goes significantly beyond the scope of this problem.

You would probably expect this code to set `bar` to 3 and `foo` to 27, but look at how it expands:

```
foo = ++bar * ++bar * ++bar;
```

So instead, `bar` is set to 5 and `foo` is set to 60. If cube were implemented as an inline function, this problem wouldn't occur. Inline functions (like normal functions) evaluate their arguments only once, so any side effects of evaluation happen only once.

Here's another problem that stems from using macros. Suppose you have a macro with two statements in it like this:

```
#define INCREMENT_BOTH(x, y) x++; y++
```

If you favor leaving off the curly brackets when there's only one statement in the body of an `if` statement, you might write something like this:

```
if (flag)
    INCREMENT_BOTH(foo, bar);
```

You would probably expect this to be equivalent to:

```
if (flag) {
    foo++;
    bar++;
}
```

Instead, when the macro is expanded, the `if` binds to just the first statement in the macro definition, leaving you with code equivalent to:

```
if (flag) {
    foo++;
}
bar++;
```

An inline function call is a single statement, regardless of how many statements there are in the body, so this problem would not occur.

A final reason to avoid macros is that when you use them, the code that is compiled is not visible in the source. This makes debugging macro-related problems particularly difficult. In general it's a good idea to avoid macros and opt for inline functions.

Problem: Inheritance

▪ **Assume you have the class hierarchy shown in Figure 10.1.**

You are given a method that takes a B* as an argument. Which of the classes can you pass to the method?

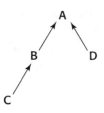

Figure 10.1 Sample class hierarchy.

Clearly, you can pass B because that's exactly what the method takes. Also, you can't possibly pass D because it may have totally different characteristics than B. A is the parent class of B. Consider that a child class is required to implement all of the methods of the parent, but the parent does not necessarily have all of the methods of a child. Thus, the parent class, A, cannot be passed to the method. C is the child class of B and is guaranteed to have all of the methods of B, so you can pass C to the method.

Problem: Object-Oriented Programming

- **What are the advantages of object-oriented programming over non-object-oriented programming?**

Object-oriented programming's (OOP) most obvious advantage is that it provides an excellent way to model the real world by associating data to the methods operating on them. This is accomplished by preventing direct access to member variables from outside the class and retaining the values of the member variable throughout the life of the object. Parts of the program outside the class may work with the member variables only through methods that allow the caller to retrieve and modify the data. This makes it easy to segregate various parts of a program, and it can make large projects more manageable by hiding disparate parts of a project from one another.

These benefits, however, can be achieved in non-object-oriented programming using modules or a similar construct. For example, in C, it is common to use constructs known as abstract data types (ADTs). These are modules associating data to the functions operating on them and allowing a caller to retrieve and modify the data. This association is accomplished by defining an ADT that is a pointer to a `struct` of values. These values are equivalent to the member variables in OOP. All functions that access the data require this ADT as an argument. In this manner, it is possible to bind data and functions. While this is less elegant than using the class construct in C++ or Java, it can be used to obtain the same advantages.

The truly unique benefit of OOP is inheritance. It is generally not possible to use inheritance in non-object-oriented languages. Inheritance is extremely important because it makes large libraries more manageable and encourages code reuse. While large, useful libraries have been around since the dawn of programming, inheritance makes them easier to use. Inheritance gives programmers an easy way to modify or tailor a library to their needs without having to modify the library code. Finally, inheritance allows programmers doing similar or repetitive tasks to inherit common functionality from a base class. This code reuse leads to faster development. Inheritance makes OOP a better way to program.

Problem: Thread Programming Issues

- **Discuss some problems that can result from incorrect thread programming.**

Some problems resulting from incorrect thread programming are race conditions, deadlock, livelock, busy waiting, and over-locking.

A race condition happens when threads are not correctly synchronized. Race conditions often occur when two threads are accessing and updating a global variable at the same time. For example, consider the case where two threads simply increment a global variable that initially has the value 5.

Incrementing often requires three operations in machine code: a load, an addition, and a store. If the first thread does a load, obtains the value 5, and then gets swapped out, the second thread might also do the load, obtain the value 5, add 1, and then store the value as 6. Then, the control would return to the first thread that obtained the value 5; the first thread would do the addition and also store the value as 6. Thus, even though the global variable was incremented twice, the result is incorrectly 6 and not 7 because of poor thread synchronization.

Deadlock means two (or more) threads cannot move because each one is waiting on a lock the other one is holding. For example, thread A is holding one lock and waiting on another lock held by thread B. At the same time, thread B is waiting on the lock thread A is holding. Thus, neither thread will be able to run and the threads are in a state of deadlock. This is a very serious issue because it causes the program to halt.

Livelock results from deadlock. Some machines have mechanisms to detect deadlock. Often, to resolve deadlock, all the threads drop all their locks and try to move forward. It is possible, though, that after the locks are dropped, the threads may run through the same code that produced the initial deadlock and end up in deadlock again. This process of reaching deadlock, dropping locks, and returning to deadlock is called livelock. Even though the threads are not in deadlock, they have stopped accomplishing their tasks.

Busy waiting is a thread problem that doesn't stop the program from working correctly but affects performance. It occurs when a thread wakes up, realizes it needs to wait on a resource, and continues to check the resource until it is swapped out. This is a problem because nothing useful happens while a thread is continually checking the same thing. The efficiency a program gains by using threads can be lost in busy waiting. Threads waiting on a resource should sleep until the resource becomes available. This avoids busy waiting.

Over-locking is another problem that affects performance. Consider the following code:

```
wait(semaphore);
/* value is a global variable that needs to have its access
 * synchronized.
 */
value++;

/* lots of time consuming stuff that doesn't have to be
 * synchronized
 */

/* ... */

signal(semaphore);
```

While this code will run correctly, it unnecessarily locks resources. It forces time-consuming code to be run serially when it doesn't need to be. This can create severe performance problems that eliminate the advantages usually gained by using threads.

Problem: Garbage Collection

- **Discuss garbage collection and explain the different ways that it is implemented in Perl and Java.**

Garbage collection is the process by which a program automatically deallocates memory. This reclamation occurs without programmer assistance. Java, Lisp, and Perl are examples of languages with garbage collection facilities.

There are several major advantages of garbage collection over the lower-level method of having programmers deallocate memory. First, garbage collection eliminates bugs resulting from the common problems of dangling pointers and memory leaks. Garbage collection also promotes greater simplicity in program and interface design because the complicated mechanisms traditionally used to ensure that memory is properly freed are unnecessary. Because the task of memory deallocation is removed from the programmer, development in garbage-collected languages is often more rapid than in languages with traditional memory management schemes.

Garbage collection suffers from the major problem of efficiency. Garbage-collected programs often run more slowly because of the overhead needed for the system to determine when to deallocate and reclaim memory no longer needed. Additionally, the system will occasionally over-allocate memory and may not free memory at the earliest possible time. Therefore, in applications where speed is important and memory is at a minimum, garbage-collected languages are rarely used.

Perl and Java have very different garbage collection implementations. Perl uses a scheme called reference counting. This involves allocating memory for every object as necessary and keeping track of how many variables reference that object. Initially, there will be one reference to a piece of memory. The reference count will increase if the variable referencing it is copied. When a variable referencing an object changes value or goes out of scope, Perl decrements the object's reference count. If a reference count ever goes to 0, Perl frees the memory associated with the object. Because it is not possible to access the memory anymore, the memory is no longer needed.

Reference counting is simple and relatively fast. However, it misses the case of a circular reference. Consider what happens in the case of a circular linked list with nothing external pointing to it. Every element has a reference count of 1, yet the memory can never be referenced. Thus, the memory should be deallocated, but Perl's garbage collection will not deallocate it. A Perl programmer has to be careful to break circular references before losing the last external reference to a circular data structure.

Java's garbage collection scheme is in a sense more complete than Perl's. There are no special cases a programmer has to be aware of. Java uses a mark and sweep process. This means that occasionally the memory manager will mark all memory that can be accessed at that moment. Then, a second pass sweeps up, or deallocates, everything that is not marked.

This implementation has the advantage that the programmer doesn't have to watch out for circularly linked structures as in Perl, but it is often less efficient. It can also lead to an unpredictable memory deallocation because the mark and sweep may not occur at the same point in each program execution.

Problem: 32-Bit Operating System

■ **Windows NT is a 32-bit operating system (OS). What does it mean to be a 32-bit OS?**

A 32-bit OS runs on at least a 32-bit processor and generally makes a flat, 32-bit virtual address space available to programs. Programs running on a 32-bit OS will generally use 32 bits as their fundamental word size. For instance, an integer will be a 32-bit value rather than a 16-bit value. The term "32-bit OS" has also come to imply a variety of technologies, such as preemptive multitasking and process isolation, that are common to most 32-bit operating systems but not necessarily inherent to a 32-bit operating system.

Problem: Network Performance

■ **What are the two major issues in networking performance?**

Any network can be measured by two major characteristics: latency and bandwidth. Latency refers to how long it takes a given bit of information to get through the network. Bandwidth refers to the rate at which data moves through the network once communication is established. The perfect network would have infinite bandwidth and no latency.

A pipe is a good analog for a network. The time it takes for a molecule of water to go through the whole pipe is determined by the length; this is analogous to the latency. The width of the pipe determines the bandwidth: how much water can pass in a given time.

Latency and bandwidth problems are often encountered when searching the Web. If you wait a long time for a page to display and then it appears quickly, this indicates good bandwidth but high latency. On the other hand, if a page starts loading right away but takes a long time to load, that is a symptom of a low-latency, low-bandwidth connection.

Problem: Faster Disk Access

■ **Assume your boss tells you that a section of your code runs too slowly and is significantly slowing down the entire product. You have to make your section of code run faster. Specifically, your** code retrieves certain information from the hard drive, and the repeated hard drive accesses are the slow part of the code. It is not possible to forgo retrieving this information. Additionally, you cannot physically speed up the time it takes to read from the hard drive by installing a faster hard drive, faster bus, or more efficient file system. What method can you use to solve this problem?

At first, this doesn't seem possible. It's like being asked to drive 80 miles per hour when your car only goes 60. It's important to realize what information the interviewer is trying to determine. Because you're not given any specifics, your answer won't have to be very specific. The interviewer is interested in your ability to take a specific problem and generalize. In this vein, try rephrasing the question as this: What is a generic technique to speed up hard drive accesses?

This question is simpler. The common technique is called disk caching. This means a certain amount of main memory stores recently accessed hard drive blocks. Before any hard drive block is accessed, the computer first checks to see if the block is in the cache. If the block is in the cache, the information is retrieved from memory, which is much faster than the disk. Otherwise, the computer fetches the block from the hard drive. Whenever a block must be read from the disk, that block and the neighboring blocks are stored in the cache. The cache can store only a small portion of the hard drive in main memory. People often repeatedly access the same blocks, so this technique can speed up hard drive accesses considerably in some cases.

The only possible answer to your boss's question is to use disk cache; this is not a perfect solution. Generally, disk caching is dealt with on a lower OS level and not on the application level because an application-level disk caching is potentially buggy. For example, if a separate user program wrote to a disk block that you had cached, it would have to notify your program of this event, or else your cache would have old information. Also, it is unclear whether disk cache would help solve this problem because you are not given the hard drive access patterns. Thus, this answer has its problems. Even so, given the constraints of the problem, it's the only possible solution.

Problem: Database Advantages

- What is the advantage of storing information in a database as opposed to implementing your own data storage system? What are the disadvantages?

If you use a database, you can more easily expand functionality, increase maintainability, and reduce bugs. Databases can do a lot in terms of analysis, backup, and queries. Databases are also generally easier to maintain than custom-coded data stores. Anyone who understands how to use the database can (in theory) easily take over your code and continue development.

On the down side, databases are often expensive (though there are some free ones) and may tie you into the product offerings of a certain vendor. There is also usually a lot of overhead to get data in and out of a database. If you don't need the extensive searching, indexing, and relational facilities of a database, you may be needlessly sacrificing performance. Additionally, databases may be overkill for small projects and may distract attention from the project's core goals.

Problem: Cryptography

- **Discuss the differences between symmetric key cryptography and public key cryptography. Give an example of when you would use each.**

Symmetric key cryptography, also called shared key cryptography, involves two people using the same key to encrypt and decrypt information. Public key cryptography makes use of two different keys: a public key for encryption and a private key for decryption. Symmetric key cryptography has the advantage that it's much faster than public key cryptography. It is also generally easier to implement, less likely to involve patented algorithms, and usually requires less processing power. On the down side, the two parties sending messages must agree on the same private key before securely transmitting information. This is often inconvenient or even impossible. If the two parties are geographically separated, a secure means of communication is needed for one to tell the other what the key will be. In a pure symmetric key scenario, secure communication is generally not available. If it were, there would be little need for encryption to create another secure channel.

Public key cryptography has the advantage that the public key, used for encryption, does not need to be kept secret for encrypted messages to remain secure. This means public keys can be transmitted over insecure channels. Often, people use public key cryptography to establish a shared session key and then communicate via symmetric key cryptography using the shared session key. This solution provides the convenience of public key cryptography with the performance of shared key cryptography.

Both public key and symmetric key cryptography are used to get secure information from the Web. First, your browser establishes a shared session key with the Web site using public key cryptography. Then you communicate with the Web site using symmetric key cryptography to actually obtain the private information.

Problem: New Cryptography Algorithms

- **If you discover a new cryptography algorithm, should you use it immediately?**

This is not a trick question, but goes to the heart of modern cryptography. Basically, no algorithm stays secret for long, and almost every algorithm has at least minor bugs in it or in its implementation. It's virtually impossible to hide an algorithm given the number of people who develop it and know about it and the advanced techniques used by today's best crackers. If your security is based on the secrecy of your algorithm, you have what is called "security by obscurity," which is effectively no security at all. It's very likely that a determined cracker could discover your algorithm. This can render your security worse than useless because you think you have security when, in fact, you have none.

Thus, it's best to make any algorithm public from the beginning and flush out the bugs rather than keep it secret and have lots of security problems when it is discovered. Only keys should be kept secret. If, after extensive public review and discussion, your algorithm is accepted as secure, then you can probably securely use the algorithm.

Problem: Hashtables and Binary Search Trees

- **Compare and contrast a hashtable and a binary search tree. If you were designing the address book data structure for a handheld personal organizer with limited memory, like a Palm Pilot, which one would you use?**

A hashtable does one thing well. It can store and retrieve data quickly (in $O(1)$ or constant time). However, it's uses beyond this are limited.

A binary search tree can insert and retrieve in $O(\log(n))$. This is fast, though not as fast as a hashtable's $O(1)$. A binary search tree, however, also maintains its data in sorted order.

In a handheld personal organizer, you want to keep as much memory as possible available for data storage. If you use an unordered data structure like a hashtable, you need additional memory to sort the values, as you undoubtedly want to display the values in alphabetical order. So, if you use a hashtable, you have to set aside memory for sorting that could otherwise be used as storage space.

If you use a binary search tree, you won't have to waste memory or processing time on sorting records for display. Although binary tree operations are slower than hashtable operations, a device like this is likely to have no more than about 10,000 entries, so a binary search tree's $O(\log(n))$ lookup will undoubtedly be fast enough. For these reasons, a binary search tree is more suited for this kind of task than a hashtable.

Non-Technical Questions

Most technical interviews include some non-technical questions. These questions are often asked early in the interview process to determine if your experience and goals make you appropriate for the available job. Many interviewers also ask non-technical questions to get to know you because you may be spending more than 40 hours a week together.

In a traditional interview, all the questions are non-technical and your interviewer decides about you based on your answers to these questions. In a technical interview, you have to do well on the technical questions to get an offer. No one will give you a job on the strength of your non-technical answers alone, but a poor performance on non-technical issues can lose you an offer you otherwise might have had.

Non-technical questions may seem like the easy questions, especially after rounds of challenging technical questions. In the big picture, however, non-technical questions are just as difficult and important as technical questions, so avoid the temptation to blow them off.

LESSON   **Non-technical questions are important! Treat them that way.**

The Questions

In spite of their simple nature, non-technical questions can be challenging because there are no right or wrong answers. Answers are unique to each person, and different interviewers may expect different answers. Much has been written on how to answer non-technical questions effectively. Many authors even provide canned answers to canned questions and discuss how to lean in toward your interviewer and nod at the appropriate times.

Rather than rehash details of what is now a tired topic, this chapter focuses on a few non-technical questions that are particularly common in technical interviews.

Non-technical questions are generally designed to assess a candidate's experience and ability to fit in with other employees. Experience includes your work history and knowledge base. For example, even if you answer all of the technical questions perfectly, you may not seem like the ideal candidate if the job isn't consistent with your previous experience. Therefore, be careful when answering questions about your experience. Experience questions often indicate that the interviewer doubts that you are capable of doing the job. It's important for you to allay any fears that your experience is lacking. For example, suppose you're asked the question, "Have you ever used Solaris?" Your interviewer has seen your resume, so he probably has a pretty good idea that you haven't. In effect, what the interviewer is really asking is "We're using Solaris—will you be able to do the job even though you've never used it?" Don't answer the question, "No." Instead, emphasize a similar strength. For example, you could respond, "I haven't used Solaris, but I have used lots of development tools on lots of different operating systems, and so I'm never concerned about using a new OS. I'm an OS-independent developer." Pay attention to the job description when it's explained to you. Emphasize any similar and relevant experience that makes you a strong candidate.

Fit is the other key theme of non-technical questions. Fit refers to how well you will adapt to the organization and become a contributing member. Most people think this just means being a nice person, but that is only half the picture. It's also important to be good at working with others. For example, suppose you say something like "At my last job, I designed and implemented a system to move our HR information gathering to the Web all by myself." This may sound like a positive comment about yourself, but it can set off alarms about whether you can and will work with other people. Therefore, it's important to emphasize the team concept. Describe how you want to be part of a great team and a contributing team player. Everyone likes hearing the word team—*everyone*.

LESSON Most non-technical questions are designed to make sure that you have relevant experience and can fit in with the existing team.

When reading the sample questions and following discussions, try to come up with a sample answer yourself. Think of how you would respond to such a question and what points you would want to emphasize in different situations. It's much easier to think of an answer now than when you're in front of an interviewer. Don't be afraid to refine your response if you find that it isn't effective. Finally, make sure that every response positions you as a valuable employee.

Question: What do you want to do?

Always pay attention to who is asking this question. If it's a human resource representative scheduling interviews, be honest and tell him what you want to do. The HR rep will generally use this information to set up interviews with appropriate groups.

If you're asked this question by a more technical interviewer, watch out! If you answer this question poorly, you won't get an offer. These interviewers ask this question partly because they want to find out about your goals and ambitions. If you want to do something different from the job that is available, your interviewer will probably decide that you should look for a different job. So if you want the job, make sure you indicate that you're interested in doing it, sound sincere, and give a reason. For example, you could say, "I've always been interested in systems-level programming and really enjoy it, so I'm looking to join a large company and do systems-level work." Or, you could say, "I want to do Web programming so I can show my work to my friends. I'm hoping to do this at a start-up where I can use my Web server experience and watch the company grow."

Sometimes, you may not be sure what specific kind of job you're interviewing for. In these cases, you can always fall back on describing the company you're applying to as the ideal company for you. Mention that you're hoping to do development that's exciting and provides lots of opportunity to contribute and learn. You can say that you see the work as just one part of the package; other important parts are the team and the company. This sort of response shows that you have your act together and prevents you from talking your way out of a job.

There is a fine line between sounding enthusiastic and seeming dateless and desperate. No one wants an employee who has been rejected by everyone else. Make sure your answer never sounds like, "I'd take any sort of job you'd be willing to offer." This sort of response virtually guarantees nothing more than a "thank you for coming in" letter.

It's also possible that you know exactly what you want to do and wouldn't accept any other kind of job. If so, don't talk yourself up for a job you'd never accept. This approach may prevent you from getting some job offers, but they aren't jobs that you want anyway. One advantage to expressing exactly what you want to do is that even if you don't begin the day interviewing with an interesting group, you may end the day interviewing with such a group.

One final note on answering this question: It is a good opportunity to mention that you want to work with a great team—don't pass it up. Make sure being a member of a great team comes across as one of your priorities.

Question: What is your favorite programming language?

This may seem like a technical question, and there are certainly technical aspects to it. You want to give specific, technical reasons why you like any language that you mention. There is also a hidden non-technical agenda in this question. Many people develop almost religious attachment to certain languages, computers, or operating systems. These people can be difficult to work with because they often insist on using their favorites even when they are ill suited to the problem at hand. You should be careful to avoid coming across as such a person. Acknowledge that there are some tasks for which your favorite language is a poor choice. Mention that you are familiar with a range of languages and believe that no one language is a universal solution. It's important to pick the best tool for the job.

This advice holds for other "favorites" questions: for instance, "What is your favorite kind of computer?" or "What is your favorite operating system?"

Question: What is your work style?

This question usually indicates that the company that you're interviewing with has an unorthodox work style. For example, it may be a start-up requiring long hours in cramped conditions or a larger company that's just beginning a new project. In any case, know what your work style is and make sure it's compatible with the company.

Question: Tell me about your experience.

This question is one everyone should practice and have an answer for it. We cannot over-emphasize this! Make sure your answer highlights specific achievements and be enthusiastic as you talk about your projects. Talk not only about the factual aspects of your previous assignments, but also about what you learned. Talk about what went right, but also what went wrong. Describe positive and negative experiences and what you learned from each of them. Keep your response to around 30–60 seconds, depending on your experience. Again, be sure to practice this ahead of time.

Question: What are your career goals?

This question gives you a chance to explain why you want this job (apart from the money) and how you see it fitting into your overall career. This is similar to the question about what you want to do. The employer is concerned that you may not want to do the job. In this case, it is because the job may not fit into your career goals. It's certainly OK to be confused about what you want to do; lots of people are. Try to have at least a general idea of where you see yourself going. Your answer might be as simple as, "I'm hoping to work in development for a while and work on some great projects. Then, I'm looking to go into project management. Beyond that, it's hard to say." This answer shows motivation and also convinces the employer that you'll succeed on the job.

Question: Why are you looking to change jobs?

Interviewers generally want to know what you don't like to do. Clearly, you don't like your last job or you would probably still be there. Also, there's a fear that you may be trying to cover a weakness that caused you to leave your last job. Therefore, try to answer this question by citing either a change in environment, a factor out of your control, or a weakness that the interviewer already knows. For example, to cite a change in environment you could say, "I've worked in a large company for five years and seen software development. I no longer want to be a number in a large company. I want to join a start-up and be a key person from the ground up and watch something grow." Or, you could answer, "I worked at a start-up that didn't have its act together. Now I want to work at a company that does."

To cite a factor out of your control, you could say, "My current company has given up on the project I've been working on and they're trying to relocate me to something that I don't find interesting." Or, you could respond, "My company was acquired, and the whole atmosphere has changed since then."

It's also generally acceptable to cite a weakness that the interviewer already knows. You could say, "My last job required extensive systems-level programming. I was way behind everyone else on that topic, and I don't find that sort of work very exciting. I'm much more interested in doing Web programming, which I do have experience in."

One final note: Even though money is often a good reason to change jobs, be careful about citing it as a prime reason. This raises the possibility that your current employer doesn't offer you more money because you're not that valuable and you're hoping someone else won't notice this fact.

Question: How much money do you want to make?

This question may appear in any context. It's most common, though, either at the initial screening or when the company has decided to make you an offer. If it's asked at the beginning, the employer may want to know if it's even worth talking to you, given your salary expectations, or the employer may genuinely have no idea what the position should pay. It is generally considered wise to put this question off as long as possible. It is not in your interest to discuss numbers until you've convinced the employer of your value. If you can't escape this question in the early stages of an interview, try to give a range of salaries with the amount that you want at the low end. This gives you good bargaining room later.

If you're asked the question near the end of the process, this can only indicate good things. If this interviewer has no interest in hiring you at this point, he won't bother asking this question. Generally, larger companies have less latitude in compensation packages than smaller companies. If you're asked this question, it probably indicates the company is willing to negotiate. It's important to realize companies are often unaware of how to make a competitive offer. This is your chance to tell them how to do exactly that.

First, it's important to do your homework ahead of time when answering this question. If you find that people with similar jobs in your area are making $40,000–$55,000 a year, you're probably not going to make $80,000 a year. Second, never undersell yourself. If you're looking for an annual salary of $70,000, don't tell an employer that you're looking for around $60,000 a year with the hope that the employer will, for some reason, offer more. This response makes it almost impossible for the employer to make a good offer. Third, you should consider what you want in a total compensation package. You may be graduating from college and want a signing bonus to offset the costs of finding an apartment, moving, and placing deposits. Or, you may be looking to join a start-up offering generous stock options and slightly lower salaries. In any case, it's important to figure out exactly what you're looking for in terms of bonuses, benefits, stock options, and salaries.

In general, try not to tip your hand too early when answering this question. The person with more information generally does better in a negotiation. Instead of answering a question about salary directly, ask what range the interviewer is expecting to offer. He will answer in one of four ways.

First, the range may be about what you expected. In this case, you can usually gain a slightly higher salary by following these rules. First, try not to act too excited—stay cool. Next, say that you had a similar but slightly higher range in mind, setting your minimum at his maximum. For example, if your employer says, "We're expecting to pay $40,000 to $45,000," you should respond, "That seems about right. I'm looking to make $45,000 to $50,000 and hoping for the high end of that range." Finally, negotiate in a professional manner until you agree on a number with him; you'll probably receive an offer between $43,000 and $48,000.

The second possibility is that the negotiator starts with a range higher than you expected. This is great!

The third case is that the negotiator may not answer your question. He may give a response like "We have a wide range of salaries depending on the applicant. What were you expecting?" This response is actually quite favorable because it indicates that he probably has the authority to pay you a competitive salary. The response shows that the negotiator is willing to negotiate, but it also indicates that you may be subject to some hardball negotiating skills. Bearing in mind that negotiation will follow, respond with one number, the high end of your range. This gives you room to negotiate and still receive a favorable offer. For example, if you're expecting between $55,000 and $60,000, say, "I'm expecting $60,000 a year." Presenting it like this leaves the other negotiator less room to low-ball you than if you give a range. Avoid weaker expressions like "I'm hoping for . . ." or "I'd really like . . ." The negotiator may accept your number, or he may try to negotiate a slightly lower salary. If you remain professional and negotiate carefully, your final salary should fall within your desired range. Alternatively, the negotiator may respond by telling you that he had a substantially lower range in mind. In this case, your response should be the same as in option four, which is described next.

The fourth option is that the offer may be less than you expected. In these cases, here are some tactics to try to increase the offer. First, reemphasize your skills and state the salary range you were expecting. For example, if you were offered a salary of $35,000 but were expecting $50,000, you may say, "I have to admit I'm a little disappointed with that offer. Given my extensive experience with Web development and the contributions I can make to this company, I'm expecting a salary of $50,000." The negotiator may need time to get back to you, which is perfectly fine. If the negotiator doesn't increase the offer after hearing your range, he will often cite one of the following three reasons:

1. That amount wasn't budgeted.
2. Similar employees at the company don't make that much.
3. Your experience doesn't warrant such a salary.

None of these is an acceptable reason. First, the budget may be a constraint on the company, but it shouldn't be a constraint on your salary. If the company really wants you, it will find the money and a way around this artificial barrier. If the company truly can't find the money, it's such a cash-strapped, close-to-death organization that you probably don't want to work there anyway.

Second, it doesn't matter what the company pays other employees. That's between the company and those employees. Other employees shouldn't determine your compensation. You can respond by saying, "I wasn't aware that my compensation would be tied to other employees' compensations. I'm looking for a package that is commensurate with my skills of X and believe that $Y is such a package."

Finally, if you've done your homework, you know your experience and skills do warrant such a salary and the company is trying to lowball you. Simply reemphasize your skills and explain that, after doing your research, you know your desired salary is indeed the competitive market salary. The company may realize it is out of touch with the market and increase its offer.

If the negotiator does not increase the offer but you still want the job, you have two last-ditch tactics. First, you can say that you're tempted to take the job, but that you'd like a salary review in six months to discuss your performance and compensation. You generally have a much stronger hand before you join a company, so you shouldn't expect miracles. Most negotiators, however, will grant this request. Make sure you get it in writing if you go this route. Second, try to negotiate other parts of the package. For example, you may be able to get additional vacation days, flex hours, or a sign-on bonus.

Here are a few final thoughts on the salary issue. Some people are embarrassed or shy about talking about salary. You should realize that you're already looking to engage in a business relationship, and salary is just one more part of the picture. No employer expects you to work for free, and there's no reason you should act as if compensation isn't important.

Many negotiators will cite factors like benefits or work style to draw you to a company. These factors may be important reasons to join a company, and you'd certainly want all of the benefits spelled out. These perks, though, are generally not negotiable. Don't bother discussing nonnegotiable factors in a negotiation, and don't get sidetracked if your negotiator mentions them.

Question: What is your salary history?

This is a different question than what are you expecting to make. In this case, the negotiator wants to know your previous salary—most likely to use this as a guide to determine your offer. If this question is raised (unless you were very happy with your previous salary), say that you expect compensation appropriate for the new job and responsibilities and that the compensation that you received for a different set of tasks isn't relevant. Also, resist any temptation to inflate your old salary because you may be asked to back up any claim with pay stubs or other proof.

Question: Why should we hire you?

This question is obnoxious, rude, and belittling. It implies that there's no obvious reason why you're qualified for this job. Clearly, you have skills and experience that make you qualified; otherwise, the interviewer wouldn't be talking to you. In these instances, avoid becoming defensive and reciting your resume to list your qualifications. Instead, keep things positive by talking about why you want to work at the company and why the job is a good match for your skills. This response shows you can handle criticism and may deflect your interviewer.

Question: Do you have any questions for me?

Conventional wisdom has always said to ask a question because it shows enthusiasm. Nothing spoils a good interview, though, like asking a stupid question right at the end. Asking a contrived question just because you feel you should won't count in your favor. A thoughtful and articulate question can tell you a lot about the company and impress your interviewer. Often, your interviewer doesn't tell you what he does. This is a good time to ask him . This lets you know more about what you would potentially be doing and shows genuine interest in the person. Also, if the interviewer mentioned anything during the interview that sounded interesting, ask him to go into more detail about it. This can yield further insight into your potential future employer. Finally, if you don't have questions, you can make a joke of it. You could say, "Gee, I know that I'm supposed to ask a question, but the people I interviewed with this morning answered all my questions. I guess you're off the hook!"

Resumes

Whether you have a contact in industry, are going through a company's recruiting process, or are using a headhunter, everyone will ask to see your resume. Your resume convinces people that you have relevant skills and talents and are worth consideration as a candidate. A person is most often rejected from consideration for a job when someone looks at his resume, doesn't find relevant information, and quickly nixes it. This is why it's so important that your resume doesn't sell you short.

Technical resumes are written differently than the non-technical resumes described in most resume books. Non-technical jobs generally have some latitude in terms of necessary skills, but technical jobs usually require a very specific skill set. Employers aren't interested in talking to candidates who don't have the necessary skills. This means that technical resumes generally require more specific information than non-technical resumes. In this appendix we examine and improve some typical developers' resumes to illustrate the techniques you can use to get your resume in shape. The example we'll start with is an extreme case of a very bad resume from a junior developer. Although we hope that no real resume would ever be this bad, the steps taken to improve it are relevant to almost anyone's resume and are made clearer by using an extreme case.

FIGURE APP.1   SAMPLE RESUME BEFORE IMPROVEMENTS

George David Lee

Current Address:
18 CandleStick Drive #234
San Mateo, CA 94403
650-914-3810
george@windblown.com

Permanent Address:
19 Juniata Dr.
Gladwyne, PA 19035
610-221-9999
george@my_isp.com

Objective: I am looking to join a growing and dynamic company. I am specifically interested in working for a company which provides interesting work and career opportunity. I am also interested in an organization which provides the opportunity for me to grow as an employee and learn new skills. Finally, I am interested in companies in the high-tech space that are looking to hire people.

Information:
- **Citizenship:** United States of America
- **Birthdate:** April 18, 1970
- **Place of Birth:** Denver, Colorado, USA
- **Hometown:** Philadelphia, Pennsylvania, USA
- **Social Security Number:** 445-626-5599
- **Marital Status:** Divorced

Work History:
June 1997-Present, Programmer
Windblown Technologies, Inc., San Francisco, California
I was part of a large group that moved old legacy applications from old computers like PDP 11s to newer computers made by Intel and used lots of new technologies and languages to do this. The advantages to our clients was that new computers are cheaper than old computers and they don't break as much. This way, it makes sense for them to have us do this. I did a portion of the programming on the new machines, but also had to work with the old machines. Our clients were able to see substantial cost savings as a result of our project. The group got quite good at moving these things and I was part of six projects in my time here. Another big project involved a lot of web stuff where I had to use a database and some other neat technologies. I am leaving because our current projects have not been very intresting and I feel like I am no longer learning anything here.
Reference: Henry Rogers
Windblown Technologies, Inc.
1818 Smith St. Suite #299
San Francisco, CA 94115

FIGURE APP.1 *(Continued)*

415-999-8845

henry@windblown.com

May 1997-June1997

BananaSoft Inc. Developer of apps., San Francisco, California

This job didn't really work out and I left really soon. All I did was work on some HTML programming which was never used.

No Reference

January 1996-May1997

F=MA computing corp. Engineer, Palo Alto, California

My role here was to work with a group of people on our main project. This project centered around developing a piece of software that allowed you to figure out dependencies between clients and servers. The advantages of this device are that you can more quickly debug and maintain legacy client/server devices. This was an exciting and interesting position. The reason that I left was because my boss left and the company brought in a different boss who didn't know what he was doing.

Reference: Angelina Diaz

1919 44th St.

Palo Alto, CA 94405

650-668-9955

Angelina.diaz@fma.com

June 1996 – December 1996

I did not have a job during this time because I spent it traveling around Europe after college. I traveled through:

- England
- France
- Germany
- Czech Republic
- Ireland
- Italy
- Spain

September 1992 – June 1996

UCLA Housing and Dining Student Food Server, Los Angeles, California

My responsibilities included preparing dinner for over 500 students in the Walker Dining Commons. I started out as a card swiper for the first year. Later, I started to cook food and spend one year as a pasta chef. After working as a Pasta chef, I spend the last two years overseeing the salad production. I left this job because I graduated from college.

Reference: Harry Wong

UCLA Housing and Dining

1818 Bruin Dr.

(Continues)

FIGURE APP.1   *(Continued)*

Los Angeles, CA 91611
310-557-9988 extension 7788
hwong@dining.ucla.edu

June 1995-September 1995 and June 1994 – September 1994
AGI Communications, Intern, Santa Ana, California
Learned how to work in a large company and be part of a dynamic organi-
zation. Worked on a project for the human resources department which
they eventually scrapped even after I had worked on it for two summers.
Reference: Rajiv Kumar
AGI Communications
1313 Mayflower St. Suite #202
Santa Ana, CA 92610
rajiv@agi.com
June 1992 – September 1992
Elm St. Ice cream shop, Senior Scooper, Bryn Mawr, Pennsylvania
   My responsibilities included serving ice cream to customers, dealing
with suppliers and locking up. After one month, I was promoted to senior
scooper meaning that I got to assign people tasks.
Education:
University of California Los Angeles, Los Angeles, CA 1992-1996.
Bachelors of Science in Computer Systems Engineering, GPA 3.1 / 4.0
Member of Kappa Delta Phi Fraternity
Abraham Lincoln High School, Rosemont, PA 1988-1992, GPA 3.4/4.0
  - Chess club president
  - 11th grade essay contest award winner
  - 3 Varsity letters in Soccer
  - 2 Varsity letters in Wrestling
Hobbies:
  - Partying
  - Hiking
  - Surfing
  - Chess
Additional References are available upon request.

   Most of this resume's problems result from a single fundamental error.
Lee wrote his resume to describe himself, not to get a job. Lee's resume is
much more an autobiography than it is a sales pitch for him and his skills.
This is a very common problem. Many people believe their resume
should simply describe everything they've ever done. This way, a potential employer can carefully read all of the information and make an
informed decision on whether to interview them. Unfortunately, it doesn't

work this way. Employers spend very little time on each resume they read. Your resume must be a marketing tool that sells you and convinces an employer that you're valuable—quickly. When you keep this idea in mind, most of the other problems become self-evident.

LESSON Write your resume to sell yourself.

Lee's resume has a number of other very common problems. One of the biggest is length. An interviewer may receive 50 resumes for an opening. From previous experience, he knows that the vast majority of the candidates are probably not appropriate for the job. The interviewer will have time to speak with only four or five of the candidates, so he must eliminate 90 percent of the applicants based on their resumes. Interviewers don't carefully read through each resume; they quickly scan the resume to see if they can find any reason to keep it. The one question going through the interviewer's mind is "What can this person do for me now?" Your resume has to look so good that the interviewer can't possibly risk passing on you. An interviewer won't wait very long to throw out a resume. If he doesn't see anything he likes after 15 or 20 seconds of looking at the first page of a resume, the resume won't make it any further.

Despite the need to make an impression, avoid the temptation to lie or add items you're unfamiliar with. Inflating your resume can create a variety of problems. First, many interviewers will ask you about every item on your resume; if you clearly aren't familiar with one, it calls your entire resume into question. Second, if you claim knowledge of a wide variety of technologies outside your experience, an interviewer may not even have to talk to you to figure out that you're lying. Finally, if you throw in a grab bag of random buzzwords that don't follow any particular theme, you may appear to be a jack-of-all-trades and master of none. The net result is that your resume becomes a hindrance to your getting a job, as opposed to a tool that helps you.

As a rule of thumb, try to keep your resume as short as possible. As absolute maximums, if you have less than 5 years' experience, keep your resume under one page. If you have less than 15 years of experience, keep your resume under two pages. Under no circumstances should any resume exceed three pages.

LESSON Keep your resume short. Make every word count.

There are lots of ways besides just deleting information to shorten Lee's resume. While much information should be deleted, there is also information that should be modified, and even a fair amount of information that should be added.

Content-wise, Lee's resume is not buzzword compliant—it doesn't mention technologies by name. This poses a big problem for him. Many companies scan resumes into their computer systems and index them by keywords. Then, when someone requests a "Java Developer with XML experience," the system prints out all resumes with the words "Java" and "XML." Other companies file resumes by skills, but the result is the same. Because Lee's resume is short on buzzwords, it is unlikely to even make it into the stack of resumes that an interviewer sees. He should list all software products, operating systems, and languages that he's used. He should also list any other relevant topics he has experience with—for instance, security algorithms or network protocols. Then, Lee should organize his skills. He can categorize his skills by topic as in Figure App.2.

When you list a specific product in your resume, you probably want to include version numbers with products to show that you're up to date with the latest and greatest. We've omitted most version numbers from our examples because they would be out of date by the time you read this, but your resume should be updated much more frequently than a book. You should always keep your resume updated with your most recent experiences. Listing an out-of-date version number on your resume is much worse than just listing the product without a version number.

FIGURE APP.2   RESUME SKILLS SECTION

COMPUTER SKILLS:

- Languages: C (Lex and Yacc); C++; Java; Perl; Visual Basic, and VBScript; JavaScript
- Internet Technology Experience: Extensive experience with Java Servlets; JSP; mod_perl; XML and XSL; client/server architecture; HTML; CGI scripts; Korn Shell scripts; ASP
- Operating Systems: UNIX (Linux, Solaris, HP-UX, FreeBSD); Macintosh; Windows 98, NT
- Databases: SQL; Oracle Products (Oracle RDMBS 8i, Oracle SQL*Plus, PL/SQL, PRO*C); MS SQL Server; IBM DB2; MySQL; Informix; JDBC; ODBC
- Security: DES; RSA; El-Gamal; MAC; Hashing; PGP; SSL; Digital Cash; Authentication
- Graphics: OpenGL; extensive knowledge of scan-conversion routines

LESSON   **Explicitly list your skills by name on your resume.**

Lee's resume needs to be formatted more cleanly. In its current form, it uses too many fonts, formats, and lines. This is generally annoying—some would say it makes his resume look like a ransom note. It can also cause problems for an automated scanning system. He should choose a standard font like Times and stick with it throughout the resume.

Lee's content is difficult to read, rambling, unfocused; it doesn't describe his contributions and doesn't sell him as a valuable employee. This is especially true regarding his work experience. First, Lee should reorganize his content into bulleted lists. These are faster to read than descriptions in paragraph form, and they make it easier for an interviewer to absorb more in less time. This increases the chances that his resume will be one of the few that the interviewer decides to call.

Lee's descriptions should be more focused. His descriptions don't clearly state exactly what he did. He describes what the team did and the general company focus, but not his role, which is the most important part of selling himself as a good candidate. He should also use action verbs like *implemented, designed, programmed, monitored, administered,* and *architechted* to describe his contributions. These should describe specific actions, such as "designed database schema for Oracle 8i database and programmed database connectivity using Java threads and JDBC." When possible, he should quantify his tasks and describe the results of his work. For example, he could write, "administered network of 20 Linux machines for Fortune 100 client, resulting in $1 million in revenues annually." This is a good sell job because it answers the question "What can you do for me right now?" One caveat is to make sure that any metrics you give are impressive. If your metrics are not impressive, omit them.

Another part of focusing the content is to decide the order in which to list responsibilities for a certain job. Generally, you want to list responsibilities from most impressive to least impressive. However, make sure that you get the main point across first. For example, if you did both sales and development at a job, you may have some very impressive sales, some impressive development work, and a few less impressive sales. Since the main point of you want to emphasize is that you were successful in sales, you should list all of your sales work first, followed by all of your development work. Finally, make sure your points follow a coherent order. This often means grouping items by topic area, even if it causes them to deviate slightly from a strict ranking by importance.

Many people have trouble selling themselves in their resumes. Often, this happens because they feel that they have to be modest and avoid boasting. As a result, they end up underselling themselves. You should never lie, but you should put the most impressive slant on whatever you have done. If you really have trouble saying nice things about yourself, it's often useful to ask a friend for help.

LESSON   **Present your experience in bulleted lists and cast it in the best possible light.**

Lee's resume also includes irrelevant items that take up valuable space. One of the first items an interviewer reads is that Lee is a citizen of the United States and born in Denver. Even though his citizenship or residence status may be important later in the game, none of this information will convince an interviewer that he's the person for the job. It is simply wasted space. Other irrelevant information includes his birth date, home town, social security number, marital status, hobbies, and travel history. None of this information makes him a more attractive candidate. Lee's use of the word "I" is unnecessary because the resume is obviously about him. Lee shouldn't bother to mention references, either. Interviewers won't check references until they're considering making an offer, so it's pointless to put them on your resume. He doesn't even need to include "References are available upon request" because that's always implicit. Similarly, a resume is not the place to mention why he left earlier jobs. This question is likely to come up in interviews, and it's a good idea to have a strong, positive response prepared, but it doesn't belong on a resume. Lee's middle name should also be omitted unless he usually goes by George David. Finally, any additional information that would make you a less attractive candidate should generally be omitted from your resume. For example, don't put something on your resume like "looking for half time position until graduation in June, then conversion to full time." Most interviewers would pass over someone like this and look for someone available full time instead. However, if the interviewer speaks with you and is impressed, it's a different story.

Lee needs to look at his resume and focus all necessary information to make it as short and useful as possible. Every word must count. For example, he can start with his address information. It's not clear whether he should be contacted at his permanent or current address. He should give only one address, phone number, and e-mail address. Lee also lists too much information about his high school accomplishments. Old awards, accomplishments, or job tasks that are not relevant to your current job search should generally be omitted. Any job that occurred more than 10 years ago or is totally different from the job that you're seeking should be mentioned only briefly. For example, Lee goes into too much detail about his work at the ice cream shop and the dining hall. It's fine to mention this employment, but he won't get the job based on his responsibilities scooping vanilla ice cream. He should give only relevant job data. Lee should omit the job that he held for two months because it will only count against him. Finally, Lee's objective statement doesn't add anything. Everyone is looking for an "interesting" job with a "dynamic" company. His objective statement should briefly state what sort of job he wants, such as "software engineer" or "database programmer."

LESSON   **Include only relevant information.**

After improving the resume's content, Lee needs to decide how to order his information most effectively. One obvious way to do this is chronologically. In this case, Lee would start out with his high school education, then his job at the ice cream shop, then college, and so forth. A reader could easily follow Lee's experience throughout his life. Even though this is a consistent ordering, it is a poor choice. Always put the most compelling reason for you to be considered for a job first, at the top of the resume. Interviewers start reading resumes from the top, so you want to put your best stuff first, where it can convince the interviewer to read the rest of the resume. After that first reason, you should continue to follow a clear and concise organization that spells out your qualifications. The end of the resume is for the least impressive information. Your most recent experiences are more relevant than your earliest experiences, so where you do use chronological ordering, put things in reverse order.

In Lee's case, his most impressive asset is undoubtedly his skills. He has a wide range of relevant skills. He should begin his resume with these skills. Next, Lee should list either his work history or education. Early in your career you should generally put your education first, especially if you went to an impressive school. Ever after, put your experience first. In Lee's case, it's a toss-up as to whether to list his education or his work experience next. He's right on the cusp of when he should switch from listing education first to work history first. Lee did graduate from an impressive school not too long ago, and he has held several jobs since then, none of them for very long. Therefore, there's probably a slight advantage to listing his education before his work history. In Lee's case, his education is a single item. If he had more than one degree, he would put the most impressive one first.

Lee also needs to proofread his resume better. For example, he spelled "interesting" as "intresting" and used "spend" when he should have used "spent." Mistakes make you look careless and unprofessional. Many people stop reading a resume as soon as they find a single mistake. At the very least, mistakes make you a weaker candidate. The only way to avoid mistakes is to proofread. Proofread over and over and over. Then, let the resume sit for a while, come back to it, and proofread some more. It's also a good idea to ask a trusted friend to proofread for mistakes. As long as you have that friend reading your resume, find out if he thinks a section is unclear, has a recommendation on how to improve your resume, or thinks you could do a better sell job. Your friend's reactions may give you a clue about how your resume will appear to an interviewer.

One final matter has to do with printing your resume. Often, you will submit your resume electronically and printing won't be an issue. If you print out your resume, there's no need to use special paper or have your resume professionally printed. Resumes are often photocopied, scanned, faxed, and written on, making fancy paper and printing a wasted expense. A laser printer and simple white paper will always suffice.

Following all of the preceding recommendations, Lee's improved resume appears in Figure App.3.

As you can see, this resume is more likely to make the cut and get Lee opportunities to speak with interviewers. The resume is based on the experiences and skills of the same person, but it looks almost entirely different.

FIGURE APP.3   LEE'S IMPROVED RESUME

George Lee
18 Candle Stick Drive #234
San Mateo, CA 94403
650-914-3810
geoge@my_isp.com

OBJECTIVE: Developer

COMPUTER SKILLS:
- Languages: C (Lex and Yacc); C++; Java; Perl; Visual Basic and VB Script; JavaScript
- Internet Technology Experience: Extensive experience with Java Servlets; JSP; mod_perl; XML and XSL; Client/server architecture; HTML; CGI scripts; Korn Shell scripts; ASP
- Systems: UNIX (Linux, Solaris, HP-UX, FreeBSD); Macintosh; Windows 98, NT
- Databases: SQL; Oracle Products (Oracle RDMBS 8i, Oracle SQL*Plus, PL/SQL, PRO*C); MS SQL Server; IBM DB2; MySQL; Informix; JDBC; ODBC

FIGURE APP.3   (*Continued*)

- Security: DES; RSA; El-Gamal; MAC; Hashing; PGP; SSL; Digital Cash; Authentication
- Graphics: OpenGL; extensive knowledge of scan-conversion routines

EDUCATION:
University of California Los Angeles, Los Angeles, CA 1992-1996.
BS, Computer Systems Engineering GPA 3.1 / 4.0

EXPERIENCE:

6/97– Present	**Developer and Consultant, Windblown Technologies, Inc., San Francisco, CA**

- Lead developer on four projects generating $1 million in revenues.
- Ported 100,000-line enterprise payroll application from PDP 11 to Sun Ultra Sparc 10.
- Designed database schema for Oracle 8i database; programmed database connectivity using Java threads and JDBC.
- Architected Web tracking application to monitor packages for shipping firm using JSP, JDBC, and an Oracle 8i database.
- Wrote front-end Java Servlet code to allow an airline to securely communicate with its suppliers via the Internet.

1/96–5/97   **F=MA Computing Corp. Server-side Engineer, Palo Alto, CA**
- Improved on Internet order procurement performance by 25 percent using Apache, Perl CGI scripts, and Oracle 7.
- Developed TCP/IP stack tracer to find client/server dependencies.
- Created Web-based reporting system using Java Servlets and IBM's DB2 database.
- Wrote Perl scripts to monitor mission-critical systems and notify administrators in case of failure.
- Ported DOS-based C client to Windows NT for automobile production monitoring.

9/92–6/96   **UCLA Housing and Dining Student Food Server**

6/95–9/95   **AGI Communications, Santa Ana, CA, Developer**
- Developed HR time tracking system

6/92–9/92   **Elm St. Ice Cream Shop, Bryn Mawr, PA, Ice Cream Scooper**

Although the same ideas that improved Lee's resume will also improve a senior person's resume, there are other issues to consider. Senior people generally have some management responsibility, and it's important that their resumes show they are capable of this task. For example, consider the following resume for a senior manager, Sam White. His initial resume is presented in Figure App.4. As you read through his resume, try to see

FIGURE APP.4 SAM WHITE'S RESUME

Samuel Thomas White
3437 Pine St.
Skokie, IL 60077
813-665-9987
sam_white@mindcurrent.com

Statement:

Over the past 3 decades my career has evolved from a lab technician to Web project manager. During that time, I spent some time away and earned my Ph.D. in physics. I have taught college computer science off and on for over 18 years and published numerous journal publications. I have spent the past four years as a project manager overseeing a large Web application development.

At the present, I am actively pursuing MSCE certification to better architect the necessary solutions. I have completed introductory hands-on courses in Networking Fundamentals; NT Server, and SQL Server. I am taking continuing education courses in management and in other advanced technology topics. Last March, I attended my company's manager seminar conference.

Brief Computer History:

1977: Completed dissertation, moved to Chicago
1977: I received my first personal computer. I wrote a program that implemented a rudimentary spreadsheet.
1979: I started to consult for a living. I was independent and worked primarily on assembly programming.
1980: Formed my company, Big Dipper Consulting. Worked on a variety of projects ranging from network debugging tools to graphics chip optimizations.
1994: My first trip on the Web with NCSA Mosaic. I knew that this would be big. I started out running simple static pages, then moved onto cgi scripting. I have been on the forefront of Web technologies and have fulfilled numerous consulting contracts and led many development efforts.

FIGURE APP.4 *(Continued)*

Work History:

CorePlus Corporation
7/1997–Present   Senior Web Manager

Responsibilities include: management and maintenance of Web development effort for both U.S. and Canadian sites, management for network redesign, establishing and implementing protocols, migrating from Windows NT to Solaris, leading security audit using cutting-edge tools and managing 12 employees, providing 24/7 access for both internal deployment and overseas operations, establishing procedures to ensure constant monitoring during non-working hours in case of failures, upgrading all software as new software is released and determined to be stable, ordering computers for both everyday (e-mail, Web), development and travel, establishing proper backup procedures, evaluating different vendors' software packages for current needs and anticipating future needs in both infrastructure and licenses.

Pile-ON Technologies
11/1995–8/1997   Senior Web Developer

Responsibilities included: designing a UNIX-based Web development environment, installing necessary software including web server, development tools and source control, integrating legacy applications on PDP 11 heirarchical database to work with cgi scripts that get and set the necessary information, selecting third-party screen scraping products to receive necessary information from legacy system, implementing security procedures to prevent denial of service, spoofing and other attacks, managing three junior developers and ensuring coordination and timeliness of efforts, verifying cross Web-browser compatibility for all Web design efforts, purchasing necessary infrastructure to ensure robustness against all possible problems, built in redundancy, hiring and building development team, reporting directly to the Senior VP of engineering, coordinating with customer support, upgrading network to include newest and fastest solutions, working with consultants to integrate new products.

Athnorn Inc.
6/1990–11/1995   Senior Engineer, MIS

Responsibilities began by working as a C++ developer working on client/server application and doing some system administration tasks such as ensuring network reliability and integration between onsite and offshore

(Continues)

FIGURE APP.4 *(Continued)*

developers. Promoted to senior engineer after two years. Additional responsibilities included designing enterprise-wide source control system and development environment spanning multiple sites, enabling dial-up and telnet connections via a VPN, managing a team of 5 developers and coordinating with marketing to ensure timeliness and quality of product, worked with contractors to implement third-party development products, evaluated and selected various vendors solutions, traveled to Europe, Japan, and the Middle East to meet with clients and assess future needs and problems, worked on moving several products to UNIX based environment, designed system to allow synchronous development across multiple time zones, attended company management philosophy seminar, attained certification in advanced use of all products, ensured compliance with corporate standards, worked with customer support to respond to common problems.

Detroit Motor Company
Corp. of Engineers
1/1990–5/1990   Contract Programmer Analyst

Four-month contract position which involved substantial modifications and enhancements to existing database program. This included custom generation of reports, additional ways to add information to database, and integration with existing products to achieve common functionality and data change. Also created files which allowed for much faster uploading and downloading of information. Also provided help with the LAN and WAN, technical support and full documentation of existing system. Worked on integration with legacy applications as well.

Tornado Development Corp.
6/1988–10/1989   Contract Programmer

Responsible for planning, development and the administration of BSD File servers. Used Oracle and SQL to do a variety of tasks mostly having to do with order tracking and HR tasks such as payroll and employee benefits. Worked to provide technical support for all users on various types of platforms. Additionally installed and maintained a variety of common applications and was responsible for troubleshooting when problems occurred.

Garson and Brown, Attorneys at Law
6/1985-5/1988   Computer Engineer

Responsibilities include troubleshooting, maintenance, repair, and support of LAN/ WAN networks, often had to use telephone and

FIGURE APP.4 *(Continued)*

troubleshoot problems with novice user, updated all company software including Novell, Windows and other third-party proprietary products, designed and installed LAN in office place, maintained LAN and was responsible for new users, provided all support and coordinated with vendors

Hummingbird Chip Designs
5/1980–6/1985   Chip Tester

Responsibilities included testing all chip designs thoroughly using a variety of third-party products that ensured reliability and yield, worked with consultants to attain knowledge using third-party testing products, wrote scripts that automated repetitive tasks, reported potential problems to developers, coordinated all yield test efforts, worked with customer service to verify customer problems, was a liaison between customer support and development

EDUCATION

Indiana University, Bloomington, IL, 1966-1970 BA in Physics
Junior Year Electronics Award Winner
Member of Lambda, Alpha, Nu Fraternity
Member of junior varsity fencing team
University of Wisconsin, Madison, Wisconsin, 1970-1977 PhD in Physics
Doctoral Thesis Work on Molecular Structure of Molybdenum compounds when exposed to intense laser bursts of varying intensity.

Skills: Attended technical courses for Microsoft Windows NT 4.0 Server & Workstation, Extensive experience with TCP/IP protocols, security protocols including SSL and PGP, HP Openview, Java, VB, VBScript, ActiveX, ASP, IIS, Apache, Netscape Enterprise Server, FoxPro, SQL Relational databases including Oracle, Informix, Sybase, DB2 and SQL server, UNIX system administration (Irix and Linux), C, C++, Network Architect, Shell Scripting, CGI scripting, HTML, DHTML, repairing printers
Hobbies:
Barbershop Quartet, Golf, Tennis, Frisbee
Horseback Riding, Walking, Swimming
Reading, Traveling, Cake Decorating
Other:
Conversant in Spanish
Citizen of the United States of America
References available upon request.

which of the techniques that benefited Lee's resume could also be helpful for White.

White's resume has the same major problem as Lee's first resume. It is an autobiography, not a marketing tool. This structural problem is evident from the beginning where he gives a brief time line of his life over the past 30 years. Writing an autobiography is a common problem for senior people with impressive credentials such as White's. Many senior people believe that if they describe their accomplishments, interviews will follow. This belief is mistaken, just as it is for junior people. Regardless of the seniority of the applicant, the only question going through an interviewer's mind is, "What can you do for me now?" In many ways, focus is even more important for a more senior job because you need to make a greater impression in just as little time.

Many of the specific problems with this resume are the same as with Lee's initial resume. This includes being too long. White should cut his resume to no more than two pages and strive for one and a half. White should also arrange his descriptions in bulleted lists so that they are easier to read. However, White's main content problem is that his resume doesn't sell him for the sort of job he's trying to get. White spends lots of time describing various job tasks that are clearly junior tasks. Senior positions generally require some management and have less emphasis on technical skills. The ability to perform junior tasks won't get you an interview for a job that requires senior tasks. When applying for a senior position, you should stress your management skills and experience more than your technical skills or achievements in junior positions.

White needs to show positive results from his past leadership. In this vein, it is necessary to both describe the experience and quantify the result. For example, White's resume says, "management and maintenance of Web development effort for both U.S. and Canadian sites." This is an impressive achievement, but the size of the undertaking is not clear; nor is it clear whether the project was a success. The description in White's resume leaves open the possibility that the project was a total failure and he is being forced to resign in disgrace or that the project was trivial and consisted of posting a few documents to a Web server. White should quantify the results of his work whenever possible. For example, he could write, "Managed team of 7 in developing and maintaining U.S. and Canadian Web sites. Sites generate 33 million hits and $15 million annually."

White is looking for a job that is heavy on project management and lighter on skills. He should deemphasize his "flavor of the month" buzzwords and emphasize his experience. He may even want to eliminate his

technology skills inventory to make sure the reader doesn't think he's trying to get a less senior position.

White's revised resume appears below in Figure App.5. Notice how the
resume explains his accomplishments much more clearly and does a
much better sell job. White becomes someone who a company couldn't
afford not to interview.

This revamped resume is a much more effective marketing tool for
White. The two resumes presented so far cover many of the cases you're
likely to encounter when you write your resume. You may want to see
more examples of good resumes for different sorts of people to get a feel

---

FIGURE APP.5   WHITE'S REVISED RESUME

Sam White
3437 Pine St.
Skokie, IL 60077
813-665-9987
sam_white@mindcurrent.com

Objective: Senior Manager in Internet Development

Experience:

7/97–present   **CorePlus Corporation, Director of Web Development,
Santa Rosa, CA**

- Managed team of seven in developing and maintaining
  U.S. and Canadian Web sites. Sites generate 33 million
  hits and $15 million annually.
- Led team of three system administrators to implement
  full network redundancy, perform a security audit,
  develop backup procedures, and upgrade hardware
  and software for an 800-computer Linux and NT
  network.
- Evaluated all major systems purchases.
- Purchased $400,000 of software and professional
  services after evaluation of seven packages and three
  firms, leading to 20 percent faster customer service
  response times.
- Hired four developers and managed staff of seven with
  100 percent retention.
- Selected contractors to migrate Web servers from
  Windows to Unix. Migration occurred one month
  ahead of schedule and 20 percent under budget.

(Continues)

FIGURE APP.5 *(Continued)*

11/95–8/97 **Pile-ON technologies, Senior Web Developer, San Jose, CA**
- Designed UNIX Web development environment and supervised team of five in implementation of Web log visualization tools. Tools have generated $5,000,000.
- Evaluated and selected over $200,000 of software and services to supplement Web logs development efforts.
- Developed feature set for $7,000,000 product based on interviews with 20 clients.
- Wrote 100,000-line C++ libraries used by three products with similar database access patterns.
- Recruited and trained two junior developers.

6/90–11/95 **Athorn Inc., Lead Engineer, Fremont, CA**
- Coordinated five developers in on-time six-month project to develop client portion of client / server application to enable department store cash registers to update central databases in real time. Product has 50,000 users.
- Met with clients to determine future feature sets for cash register client.
- Implemented Virtual Private Network between San Francisco Bay Area office and New York City office.
- Installed and supported internal enterprise-wide source control used by 30 developers on 10 projects.

6/88–10/89 **Contractor at many companies**
- Upgraded network systems at Detroit Motors, Inc.
- Installed and designed database applications for Tornado Development Corp.

6/85–5/88 **Garson and Brown, Attorneys at Law, Computer Engineer, Palo Alto, CA**

5/80–6/85 **Hummingbird Chip Designs, QA Tester, San Jose, CA**

Education:
University of Wisconsin, Madison, Wisconsin, Ph. D. in Physics, 1970–1977
- Doctoral thesis work on molecular structure of molybdenum atoms when exposed to laser bursts of varying intensity.

Indiana University, Bloomington, Indiana, B. A. in Physics, 1970

Other:
- Fluent in Spanish

for how to write an effective resume. The remaining portion of this appendix presents three resumes of people with different experience searching for different kinds of technical jobs. As you look at the resumes, notice what content stands out and how this helps sell the person as a potentially valuable employee.

FIGURE APP.6   HOT RESUME SAMPLE #1

Jenny Ramirez
jenny_ramirez23@mit.edu
MIT University
PO BOX 4558
Cambridge, MA 02238
227-867-5309

EDUCATION:

9/96–1999 **Massachusetts Institute of Technology, Cambridge, MA.**
BS, Electrical Engineering, 2000 (GPA 3.7/4.0)
- Specialist in databases and security
- National Merit Scholar, Phi Beta Kappa

EXPERIENCE:

6/98–8/98 **E-Commerce Developer, WebWorks Corporation, Huntington Beach, CA.**
Implemented search feature on Fortune 500 company's Internet storefront using ASP and SQL Server.
Designed sample projects, using Oracle, Informix, and MS SQL Server to demonstrate performance trade-offs between the products to clients.
Made initial contact with two companies that became clients and resulted in $80,000 in revenues.
Wrote three proposals that were accepted and resulted in $200,000 in revenues.

6/97–9/97 **Web Software Developer, The Aircraft Tech., Renton, WA.**
Designed, researched and implemented a database solution to improve tracking and reporting of employee accomplishments.
Designed and implemented CGI scripts to dynamically report Web server statistics.

(Continues)

FIGURE APP.6 (Continued)

9/97–12/97 **Computer Instructor, MIT Computer Science Department**

1/97–3/97 **Deans Tutor, MIT School of Engineering**

COMPUTER SKILLS:

- Languages: C, C++; Java; ADA
- Internet Technology: Java Servlets; ASP; mod_perl; XML and XSL; HTML
- Systems: UNIX (HP-UX, Solaris); Windows 98, NT
- Database: SQL; MS SQL Server; IBM DB2

LANGUAGES:

Fluent in French, proficient in German

FIGURE APP. 7   HOT RESUME SAMPLE #2

Mike Shronsky
1814 Park Dr. #244
Albuquerque, NM 98872
352-664-8811
mikey_s227@warmmail.com

Objective: Software Engineer in Web Development

Work Experience:

5/96–present **Warner Tractors Manufacturers, Albuquerque, NM, Software Engineer**
- Created Java applets using Symantec Visual Café to allow customers to compare various tractors.
- Wrote Java servlets to generate dynamic Web content from Oracle database.
- Implemented Perl CGI reporting scripts for CORBA system.
- Wrote SQL queries and designed database schema for Oracle database.
- Researched and selected development environment of Solaris, Apache, and Apache Jserv extension.

FIGURE APP. 7 (*Continued*)

7/94–4/96   **Problems Solved, Inc., Albuquerque, NM, Programmer**
- Incorporated focus group input into redesign of order tracking UI to improve workflow efficiency by 20 percent.
- Wrote 160 pages of product documentation for order tracking application.
- Analyzed product performance by writing shell scripts.
- Wrote hundreds of Perl scripts to test various Web server responses for clients. Major focus of scripts was fin_wait_2 Web server problems.

5/92–7/94   **Hernson and Walker Insurance Agents, Austin, TX, Systems Administrator**
Maintained network, ordered systems, and implemented data tracking system.

Computer Skills:
- Languages: Java, Perl
- Databases: Oracle, DB2, MySQL
- Systems: Windows 98, NT, Unix (Solaris, Linux)
- Web Skills: CGI, JSP, Apache, IIS, Netscape Enterprise Web Server

Education: Harcum College, Ardmore, PA, 1996, BA in management

Other: Fluent in Russian

FIGURE APP.8   HOT RESUME SAMPLE #3

Elaine Mackenzie
22 Mt. Rogers Rd.
Nashville, TN 37212
615-667-4491
macky52@yeehah.com

Objective: Technology Consulting

Computer Skills:
- Languages: C, C++, Visual Basic, VBScript, JavaScript
- Operating Systems: Windows NT, Windows 98
- Internet: ASP, ActiveX, IIS, ColdFusion, HTML, DHTML, XML and XSL, Resonate

(*Continues*)

<u>Experience:</u>

9/97–present   **Web Integrations Specialist, National Web Consulting, Inc., Nashville, TN**

- Lead consultant on three projects generating $900,000.
- Built Web front end in ASP to interact with legacy databases and perform all Human Resources-related functions for a Fortune 100 client.
- Wrote ASP code to interface with legacy hierarchical IBM database.
- Constructed Web user interface component on six different projects.
- Managed $300,000 project resulting in on-time and on-budget delivery.
- Landed three accounts, generating $720,000 in revenues.
- Formed partnerships with three third-party software vendors. Partnerships generated $1,500,000 through joint contracts.

8/93–9/97   **Information Systems Technology Specialist, Johnson & Warner, Systems Integration Division, Nashville, TN**

- Wrote 200,000 lines of C++ code and 150 pages of documentation and billed $1,200,000.
- Built order tracking system for Fortune 500 client, using ASP and SQL Server.
- Led design team that architected system layout for 25 Windows NT Web Servers using Resonate load balancing software.
- Landed two accounts generating $250,000 total.
- Sold $200,000 in follow-on services.
- Hired and trained two associate consultants.

<u>Additional Information:</u>
Fluent in Spanish and Czech

<u>Education:</u>
Foothill College, Los Altos Hills, CA, BA in Accounting, 1990

Index